The Monkey's Mask

identity, memory, narrative and voice

The Monkey's Mask

identity, memory, narrative and voice

Chris Kearney

Trentham Books

Stoke on Trent, UK and Sterling, USA

Trentham Books Limited

Westview House	22883 Quicksilver Drive
734 London Road	Sterling
Oakhill	VA 20166-2012
Stoke on Trent	USA
Staffordshire	
England ST4 5NP	

First published 2003

British Library Cataloguing-in-Publication Data
A catalogue record for this book is available from the British Library

ISBN 1 85856 290 2

Designed and typeset by Trentham Print Design Ltd., Chester and printed in Great Britain by Hobbs the Printers, Hampshire.

Contents

Acknowledgements • vi

Preface: An Infinity of Traces • ix

Part One: Conflicting Loyalties
Chapter One:
The Monkey's Mask: Identity and Autobiography • 1

Chapter Two:
Growing through Contradiction: The Life Stories • 11

Part Two: The Riddle of Identity
Chapter Three:
Pure is a Bore: The Riddle of Identity • 35

Chapter Four:
Honour and Authenticity: analysing life histories • 57

Part Three: Deep Excavations
Chapter Five:
The Patterns that Connect: The Content of the Narratives • 77

Chapter Six:
Orchestrating Contradictions: Identity Construction • 113

Chapter Seven:
Ghost Values: What persists across the generations? • 135

Chapter Eight:
Conclusions
Minds Wide Shut: identity and policy • 155

Appendices
Appendix 1:
Examples of grid analysis of part of Asif's narrative • 169

Appendix 2:
Shape of Conversation with Asif • 171

Bibliography • 173

Index • 185

Acknowledgements

This is the most difficult bit to write. Any list is by its nature incomplete and there is always some hint of pomposity and self-importance on the part of the author. However, there are many people to be thanked in helping me get the 'thing' into its current shape.

As most of it stems from my life as a primary teacher in Hackney and Tottenham, I'll begin there. I owe much to the many classes of primary school children, who taught me a great deal about the world we inhabit and that good learning is not necessarily painless. I am also grateful to my colleagues in those schools and on the Reading and Language Development Team in Haringey.

However the greatest contribution to this book comes from the six people who participated in the project and gave so generously of their time. I am thankful for their courage, integrity and honesty in sharing their very personal thoughts and memories in what are sensitive and difficult areas of their lives. I hope I have done justice to their faith in me.

Of my more formal education I was also fortunate to have studied for my MA at the University of London Institute of Education, when it was taught by Tony Burgess, Margaret Meek and Jane Miller, who are all inspirational teachers. Tony has been a particular influence on my thinking and really helped to set me on this course and given me the benefit of his time, friendship and erudition. I am also grateful to Richard Andrews for his unfailing encouragement and support.

I am especially grateful to have the friendship and support of a team of quite exceptional (and exceptionally modest) colleagues, who teach at Goldsmiths on the Primary and MA programmes. In particular, it has been my privilege to work with Eve Gregory, whose friendship, expertise and unstinting support has been most influential in shaping this book. The book also owes a great deal to the thorough (yet always sensitive) editing of Gillian Klein.

But I owe the biggest debt to my family, Berly and Emma, whose love, encouragement and patience have always kept everything in perspective and made it all possible.

The starting point of critical elaboration is the consciousness of what one really is, and is knowing thyself as a product of the historical processes to date which have deposited within you an infinity of traces, without leaving an inventory: therefore it is imperative at the outset to compile such an inventory
Gramsci (cited in Said, 1997:25)

...the culture has become so complex, incoherent and incomprehensible that hardly anyone tries to come up with any syntheses anymore
Marcelle Clemenys

Preface: An Infinity of Traces

Listen to this...

– *So school didn't help you at all, in any way?*

– *No. No ... I had nice advice from college lecturers ... I think the thing that really bumped up my confidence when I left drama school ... We had a student initiated thing and I did a one woman show which was all about my culture. I'll have to give it to you ... It's all about identity*

– *Tell me about it*

– *Okay ... .I'll tell you about it.*

It's set in the future, in Cyprus. And the future is ... that they've taken away the buffer zone, the green line, the separation line between north and south, between Turks and Greeks. They've taken that away and they've said to the whole country, 'Do what you want!'. And the woman ... this is the night before she has to go back to her village. Not (the one) she grew up in, because she was only a small child ... She was seven when she left. Now she's in the south, with her uncle in the south, because her parents ... . Her mother died and her father just disappeared.

And it's the night before [she is due to leave]. And the thing about Greeks is, that every single one of them will say (even the little kids, will say) 'Yeah ... One day we'll go back to our land,' And this girl has grown up with that, from her uncle ... And she's packing and, as she's packing, she's packing the things she's brought down with her from her own village, like her mother's apron. And she's remembering things about her parents. And as she's doing that she's kind of, like, realising ... Because, it's twenty years later, and she's grown up and she's established herself down in the south. She's kind of thinking, 'Well? Do I really want to go back? And if I do go back, what will be *there for me? **That's** old. **That's** past ... **That** was when I was a child. But I'm a woman **now**. And my parents are dead (or they're not there any more). And if I **do** go back, what will there be there for me? The Turks have left the area more or less derelict, so I'm going to have to start again, and do I want to start again?'*

She also has a relationship at the time with a British soldier. And they don't actually speak a language together. She doesn't understand English and he doesn't understand Greek. So their whole relationship revolves around: 'Yes' 'No' 'Yes' 'No', which is quite quirky! But they, somehow, manage to realise that they love each other. They understand those words. And the night that she leaves to go back to her village, (because it is always assumed that she will go back, one day) he says to her, 'Let me take you to England.'

So, it's either a choice between going back to her village, where her ghosts [are] (and, that is past; that is history), or going with this Englishman to another country, which is foreign to her, that is alien to her, but she still loves him ... Does she love him? Or is it just a fantasy, a dream of being something else? ... Or does she stay put, where she is; where she's grown up? [With] things that she knows; things she identifies with?

Aliki and I were talking to her about her life at college on a Community Arts degree course, when she told me this story. Her parents had fled their small village in Cyprus in the late sixties and she was born and brought up in Hackney in East London. This story struck me forcibly from the start. I have shared it many times in talks at universities and teachers professional development centres. It has never failed to make a powerful impression. There is always at least one person who comes up at the end of the talk to tell me how they recognise similar issues in their own life. I believe that its power derives from the fact that it distils the dilemmas of negotiating identities as we cross borders; geographically, politically and psychologically. It also illuminates the complexity and ambivalence of the process. Aliki is not only describing how this happens to the female character in her play, she is also making sense of her own identity. She is storying her own life too. Making an inventory of the 'infinity of traces, which history has deposited in her'.

This is a book of stories and about stories. It is about the stories we tell each other about ourselves and the stories we tell ourselves about ourselves. It is also about what happens when the two don't fully coincide. In short it is about the ways in which we maintain a coherent, yet ever changing, sense of self: an identity. It is how this connects with our cultural heritage. But it is also about how this connects with the learning process. It grew out of my conviction (Kearney: 1990.1995) that the best learning is self-motivated. In my view real learning only occurs when we have to have a personal desire or a need to know. When we have to have a real investment in it. Then learning becomes truly integrated into our consciousness at a profound level.

As a teacher in culturally diverse and economically disadvantaged parts of London, I realised that such motivation was linked intimately to children's personal histories, language(s) and social identities. As a teacher, I also learned that connecting with the children's home backgrounds was no easy task. For example, I began to realise that culture and language are not completely over-lapping concepts. Some children whose parents or grandparents came from Bangladesh or Zaire, Vietnam or Hong Kong did not actually speak their so-called home language, even at home. (Aliki speaks very little Greek.) Fewer still could read or write their 'mother tongue', even where a written form was avail-able. Often these same children were struggling with literacy in English and the largely anglo-centric curriculum on offer. To compound this, existing literature from both practitioners and official sources (see Swann:1985) provided a de-pressing catalogue of failure at school. Things were getting very messy and con-fusing. Nevertheless, I realised that this knotty problem of identity is *the* central factor in our quest to secure a meaningful education in a culturally diverse society.

It is interesting to note how the question of identity has become foregrounded as more and more people across the world have become displaced. Some as economic migrants. Others in flight from violent conflict. A direct relationship between identity and a particular geographical location is becoming ever less likely (if it ever existed). The rapid development of telecommunications, mobile phones and laptop computers exacerbates this loss of a sense of place, even for those who don't travel far.

Of course none of these phenomena are entirely new. After all, the book, the letter and the newspaper are direct ancestors of the mass media and cyberspace. What characterises these new manifestations is their power, quantity, speed, availability (for those who can afford the goods) and, above all, their ubiquity. This has been ensured through the global reach of the powerful corporations in the 'market' and their ability to permeate all communities. These commodities demand a great deal of our time and attention through their intrinsic glamour which dazzles and the sophistication of the advertising and promotion that sur-rounds them. They are truly irresistible for the majority of us; objects of synthetic desire. Although they are synthetic they are, nonetheless, very power-ful. Because they enter into the framework of our desires so cleverly and seductively, they become an integral element in our individual sense of self.

There is a common sense view that such identities have superseded older, more traditional and organic forms of community. To confound this view, some of those older forms have reasserted themselves vigorously and often violently in the last few decades. We need to understand why this happens.

A great deal has been written about repertoires of identity, hybrid identities and syncretism. Identities are now acknowledged to be very complex, but so far very few studies have attempted any structured empirical analysis of the process through which we construct our identities. For teachers (or workers in the social domain) there is a pressing need to develop a thorough and sophisticated understanding of how people negotiate such a complex world and explore their relationship to it. Where do we belong? What constitutes our identity? How does it relate to our individual and collective pasts? Are we at the end of history? We need to address these questions if we are to design relevant and stimulating curricula, which build on children's actual experience of the world. We need to avoid a return to an anglo-centric curriculum or move to a curriculum which oversimplifies children's personal and social histories and perpetuates the catalogue of failure.

When I began this journey of exploration there was little emphasis on systematic analysis. Much of what has been written in Cultural Studies and ethnography has been directly or indirectly autobiographical. Much of it is inspiring and illuminating, but there is little systematic analysis of the problem of identity. The official picture is changing. The Economic and Social Research Council has recently begun a programme entitled 'Social Identities and Social Action' in which they state:

> It is claimed that social and technological changes have led to the replacement of monolithic identities such as class and gender with multiple and fragmented identities based on the choices facing us as consumers. Correspondingly, political and communal commitments based on older loyalties have been replaced by a volatility based on a tendency to view everything as a commodity. By contrast, many have stressed the upsurge of intense solidarities based on religious, ethnic and national identities. The negative side of this is expressed through exclusion and through hostility towards those with different identities.
>
> Despite the currency of such claims in political and public debates, the evidence used to support them is largely anecdotal. Although social identity figures in a wide range of social science research, its significance is often taken for granted and there is no integrated analysis of how, when and why social identity and social action interconnect. (ESRC, 2002)

They go on to call for research, which will:

- provide systematic empirical evidence about the structure of identities in contemporary society

- analyse the processes by which social identities are produced in society and assumed by individuals

- examine how social identities relate to social action in key areas of social concern and thereby inform policy in those areas

This book attempts to begin that systematic process. It is based upon interviews with six people who had been educated in Britain (three men and three women) who had been academically successful, that is they had a first degree from a British University. Far from demonstrating that we have finished with history and are ready to become defined only by our consumption patterns, all six individuals in the study demonstrate a critical and complex view of self. They all draw on a deep sense of their own family histories, even though they may not subscribe to all the cultural values of their elders. All have been successful in an academic sense, yet all believe that their lives would have been made easier and more fulfilling if teachers had attended more closely to what they brought from home and provided a space for their own authentic voices to develop. Most feel that they had to silence their own voices to succeed. Most felt, like Aliki, that they had succeeded on their own.

Initially this was disappointing. I had hoped to find that their success was due to sensitive support from teachers. They all went to school during the 1970s when many local authorities were funding multicultural and antiracist initiatives. Most went to school in London, which was supposed to have many teachers working on such initiatives. Yet only one of them identified one teacher she considered to have actively connected with her home background. However, the stories revealed clearly what the process of crossing boundaries looks like and feels like.

Although this book is a systematic and empirical study, it is principally about the way in which we construct our identities by telling stories... I have divided it into three sections.

Part One: Conflicting Loyalties (Chapters 1 and 2) consists of an introductory chapter in which I give some relevant historical background, and declare my own interests in these matters. Following that the six characters introduce themselves. Their stories raise many questions concerning the nature of identity, which I explore in the remainder of the book.

A great deal has been written already on the question of identity and of the problem of researching identity construction. So in **Part Two: The Riddle of Identity** (Chapters 3 and 4) I examine the main theories of identity construction and discuss some of the problems involved in researching identity.

In **Part Three: Orchestrating Contradiction** (Chapters 5 to 7) I explore in detail the ways in which the six people narrate their identities. To analyse the development of their sense of identity in their narratives (i.e. the process of self-expression and self-creation) I employed three frameworks or layers of analysis.

- **The first layer**: the content of the narratives: I begin by looking at 'patterns which connect'; common factors in their stories and how this contributes to their constructions of identity. These factors are analysed thematically (Chapter 5).

- **The second layer**: how identities are structured in the narratives: In this section I analyse how they have arrived at their current conception of their own identity. Their stories are analysed according to a framework devised by Bakhtin for analysing character development in the novel. He sees this development as the complex orchestration of the internal motivations and external influences we experience (Chapter 6).

- **The third layer**: Narrative style and the question of voice: Here I examine the way that one person's narratives are patterned and make some tentative judgments or hypotheses about that slippery concept, voice (Chapter 7).

What emerges is a complex and fascinating process by which people manage diverse social and linguistic influences to produce a critical sense of self, which is dynamic, yet coherent. I believe that the findings have implications for educationalists and social policy makers. These are discussed in the final chapter. Their importance cannot be underestimated, particularly in terms of curriculum development. We need to ensure that the curriculum on offer has relevance to the day-to-day life of our students. We cannot talk about an inclusive curriculum if we leave out the identities, languages, dialects and histories of the majority of pupils. We also need to be fully aware of the depth and complexity of identities in the modern world and the considerable extent to which past joys and painful struggles of communities and individuals are part of that process. Identities cannot be merely subsumed into comfortably bland notions of 'citizenship'. We need to create more opportunities for pupils and students to explore the true reality of their lived experience. Otherwise, however worthy our policies of 'inclusion' may appear, they will remain merely empty rhetoric.

PART ONE:
CONFLICTING LOYALTIES

1

The Monkey's Mask:
Identity and Autobiography

year upon year
the monkey's mask
reveals the monkey
Basho

... the question, and the theorisation, of identity is a matter of considerable
political significance, and is only likely to be advanced when both the
necessity and the 'impossibility' of identities, and the suturing of the psychic
and the discursive in their construction are fully and unambiguously
acknowledged. Stuart Hall (1996:17)

It is documented that the children of exiles returning to Chile after the advent of democracy, suffered a strange sense of displacement (Hite: 1991). Although they had grown up in households where their parents and grandparents celebrated the virtues and the beauties of the homeland and their strong cultural traditions were evident everywhere, these children also drank from other streams: the street culture of European cities, coupled with American films and MTV. Giving these up was difficult. Hite argues that most of those who grew up in exile eventually abandoned their idealisations of Chile 'in order to redefine who they were and where they belonged. As adults today, often with bicultural families of their own, they cannot imagine more than a visit to their former home, despite the end of dictatorship' (Hite: 1991:4).

Since the end of the Second World War easier, faster and more effective communications and a proliferation of material goods have altered our sense of identity and belonging. Our social life and our own values have undergone massive changes, rifts and fragmentations. Scarcely any community or any person is untouched by the attractions of individualism, romantically purveyed by Hollywood and the music industry and more insidiously underpinned by the financial process of the market. To some extent in the modern world we are all exiles. We are all living in translation. Alongside a steady determination to get what is ours, the great majority of us need wide cultural and linguistic repertoires merely to survive.

My interest in such questions can be traced back to my own childhood and adolescence. My own confusions were real despite growing up through a period of relative affluence and being relatively successful in the state education system.

In terms of my own identity I feel I have inherited sets of paradoxes and ambivalences which are by no means rare in the modern world. My cultural heritage is predominantly Catholic Irish. From my earliest glimmerings of memory, this was apparent through the litanies of family histories, the stories and the humour. Despite this, we never participated in an active Irish culture. Although I was christened a Catholic, my parents scarcely attended mass and I was sent to non-denominational state schools. The only words of Gaelic I know are 'Pogue Mahone' and these were taught to me by a roguish uncle who had very little of the tongue himself. We never attended social gatherings or belonged to political organisations, yet I knew about the violence of the Orange parades in Liverpool and heard of the heartless exploits of 'the black and tans' and even of Cromwell's crimes at Drogheda, long before I understood their significance.

As I have grown older I have found myself increasingly drawn to Irish music and literature and am proud of that part of my heritage; proud to belong to a culture which since 1169 has been invaded and oppressed but never truly conquered. It is only relatively recently that I visited Ireland for the first time, since my sister now lives there and my mother spent the last years of her life there. Yet I still have no desire to be part of it. So many things irritate and depress me about it; parts of which I continue to find in myself, from time to time. An insincere gregariousness and forced hospitality. A maudlin sense of self-pity. Compulsory gaiety and good humour in public places. An oversensitivity to the comments of others. The list is almost endless.

This complexity is compounded by issues of class, which set up similar paradoxical reactions within me. My grandparents were Irish lower middle class. I suppose they would have had much in common with those Joyce delineates so vitally in *Dubliners*. Quite different from their English counterparts. By the time my parents were growing up during the years following the Great War, they were poor – ruined by a combination of poor financial judgment, alcohol and unremitting unemployment. Both my parents left school when they were fourteen. I grew up in what would have been described as a working class neighbourhood.

Irvine Terrace in New Ferry was a row of ten three-storey Victorian houses. They had large rooms and had once belonged to middle class people. They crouched on the edge of the Wirral bank of the Mersey, between Bromborough Docks and Cammell Laird shipyards. By the time my parents rented the top two floors of number two, the sea had already begun to reclaim the gardens. As children we played on the broken sea wall. The most derelict part served as everything from a climbing frame to a shop counter. A place for fighting and role play. It was here that I began to learn that class was not so simple and that community can be a misleading term. Some of the most affluent people in that area were fiercely working class and some of the poorest had 'ideas above their station.'

Although they were never parochial in their attitudes, both my parents had great faith in education as providing a way out of poverty. With their encouragement, both my sister and I were successful. Still, I didn't feel totally comfortable at Wirral Grammar School. Most of the children I had played with went to the secondary modern school. But gradually I made new friends and, like many of my generation, found common ground through the music of the sixties and the styles of expression which grew out of it. Reading Salinger was a profoundly liberating experience. It seemed to free me from the constraints of the past. This continued throughout my time at North Western Polytechnic, where the attractions of the counter culture focused our attention on a range of radical possibilities informed by a tradition which went back past the beat poets, to Dickenson, Pound, Yeats, Beaudelaire, Rilke and Blake. It was an era full of contradictions. Radical, egalitarian politics coexisted (often uneasily) with eastern and western mysticism. It is difficult to describe with any conviction the sense of possibility and optimism which characterised that era.

This was the personal baggage I brought to my work as a teacher in Hackney in the early 1970s and later in Tottenham. Here I encountered a range of further complexities and contradictions. Many of the children seemed alienated from the work we were trying to do. At that stage few teachers had much knowledge of the lives of the children in our classrooms. It was through this experience that many teachers began to discover other ways forward. Looking back, I see that many of our approaches were naive and often patronising. But we were learning. Throughout the 1970s, teachers began to develop and extend their knowledge. The growth of anti-sexist and antiracist perspectives were often supported financially by sympathetic Local Education Authorities. Resources were built up and authors and publishers began to address the issues and fill the gaps. The process was one of continual debate and refinement of our sensibilities. Still they were difficult areas full of dilemmas and contradictions. The more I looked at the issues, the more I was drawn to the idea that lack of motivation was connected to issues of identity, particularly as they are refracted through the sensitive medium of language. I wrestled with this idea for many years, through my own practice and through my readings of Margaret Meek, Harold Rosen, Tony Burgess, James Britton, Jane Miller, which in turn introduced me to the work of Clifford Geertz, Lev Vygotsky, Mikhail Bakhtin, Paulo Friere, Antonio Gramsci and poets and novelists from all over the world. But our greatest teachers were the pupils themselves. The children taught us a great deal, once we were prepared to listen.

For me this process helped to develop a more complex understanding of identity. I came to believe that many people develop a repertoire of various roles and linguistic styles to cope with a variety of social and cultural settings. I realised, as with my own experience, that identity is not fixed or predetermined. It also demonstrated for me that we needed to scrutinise the political perspectives which underpin the relationship between identity and education and its effect upon children with complex social identities, who lack status and power within the existing social order.

During the 1970s and early 1980s, there was a growing awareness among teachers about the need to provide support for children's home languages, cultures and identities. Many Local Education Authorities (LEAs) set up centres and ran in-service courses, which raised awareness among liberal teachers working in mainly inner-urban settings. In retrospect, it is apparent that the concepts of culture and identity were too narrowly focused and were premised on exotic and over-generalised views of culture. This was unsurprising since such views of culture came mainly from anthropologists whose views still bore the hallmarks of their 19th century colonial origins. Moreover, many of the methods and approaches used in schools implicitly built upon instrumental and behaviourist approaches to learning. Issues of stereotyping in children's books were raised, but were often dealt with in crude and rather insensitive ways. Sometimes the result was sanitised texts which ignored the messy and contradictory nature of social reality and sidestepped uncomfortable issues, for fear of appearing racist (or sexist).

In the 1980s structuralist approaches to literature seemed to offer more critical ways forward, but again the desired values were still implicit in the selection and framing of the texts. These were perhaps inevitable stages in the construction of a more sophisticated consciousness. Moreover they were developed in a hostile political climate where, in Britain, there were moves to implement a conservative and eurocentric National Curriculum. These values were backed by interlocking legislation and a diversion of funding away from support of children's community languages and home cultures and towards the learning of

English as an additional language. The effect of these policies has operated on a deep and subtle level. As Tomlinson (1997) has argued, market driven forces, justified as extending choice, operate against the children of 'ethnic minority' families.

As a counterbalance to this, research by Eve Gregory (1996) illustrated how little regard liberal educators have had for the diversity of approaches to learning which children bring from home or their community schools (often run through religious organisations). As Geertz (1995:3) points out:

> Not only have societies changed dramatically over the past three or four decades, our concept of culture and identity (ie how we intellectually frame them) has also altered so that we no longer have the cosy certainties of the past. (If, indeed, they ever really existed for everyone.)

The burgeoning of cultural studies, from its antecedents in the work of Richard Hoggart and Raymond Williams (1958), through the work of Stuart Hall and the Centre for Cultural Studies in Birmingham (1980) to the current work of bell hooks (1990, 1996), Paul Gilroy (1992), Homi Bhabba (1992, 1996) has not only helped us to understand Gramsci's notion of the organic intellectual, it has also shaken fundamental conceptions of culture and identity and problematised methods of researching culture. Its genesis is charted in Stuart Hall's largely autobiographical piece, 'Cultural Studies and its Theoretical Legacies' (1992). By dealing with the complexity of identity in the wider context of recent economic, social and technological changes, such writers developed more sophisticated frameworks by which to interpret such slippery concepts as culture and identity.

What has altered is that we can no longer think of culture as related to a 'natural way of life'. Because cultures and identities had previously been built up slowly over long periods of time, in pragmatic and largely unselfconscious ways, they had acquired an essentialist feel. In the modern, mass mediated world, this viewpoint is untenable. Movement of people, dispersal (or diaspora) has exacerbated this uncertainty, as Ien Ang (1994:16) notes:

> Since diasporas are fundamentally and inevitably transnational in their scope, always linking the local and the global, the here and there, past and present, they have the potential to unsettle essentialist and totalising conceptions of 'national culture' or 'national identity'

During the last three or four decades anthropology has come home; diluting the ethnographic distance between the 'home' and the 'field.' As Samadar Lavie and Ted Swedenburg (1996:154) put it:

> Fieldwork becomes homework as differences between ethnographer and the subject under study are broken down as the ethnographer is incorporated into the text, and as theory and text reflect and participate in the multipositioning and fluctuating realities of quotidian life

This 'self-consciousness' of the fabricated nature of culture has precipitated calls for a radical reappraisal of notions of culture and identity, which incorporates:

- the idea that new cultural webs are possible and necessary (what Homi Bhabba (1995) refers to as the third space)

- that it needs to be informed by a transnational radical political base (Chantal Mouffe, 1995; Ernesto Laclau, 1995; bell hooks, 1996)

- that it needs a more honest exploration of issues involving cultural memory particularly as it articulates with the mythologies of diaspora (Ien Ang, 1994; Paul Gilroy 1992)

This is not to play down the part played by communities in the construction of an individual's identity or their ways of coming to know the world. It is rather an attempt to contextualise and critically appraise such influences. In educational terms consideration of the above points pose profound questions, some epistemological (what's worth knowing?), others pragmatic (what approaches work best?).

What has been surprising is the exclusively Eurocentric nature of the curriculum in compulsory schooling as experienced by all six people involved in this study, particularly as five of them had experienced schooling in the London area, often viewed as the bastion of multicultural and antiracist education. The situation is unlikely to have improved since the introduction of the narrow and prescribed National Curriculum. However, it may be a romantic and inaccurate generalisation to view the 1970s as a golden age in terms of multicultural education. Certainly it was far better than earlier decades in terms of funding and governmental support. However, the concepts of culture and identity were for the most part crudely conceived based, as they were, on John Locke's notions of culture and identity as fixed and consistent (see Aronowitz, 1995). This approach gave rise to some of the cruder educational initiatives in that period, such as the black and white doll test (Milner,1975). A more complex theoretical framework is necessary to make sense of the concepts of culture and identity.

To understand the emerging patterns I have found it more useful to refer to modern cultural theory and interpretive ethnographers like Clifford Geertz (1986:15), who puts the problem this way:

> Like nostalgia, diversity is not what it used to be; and the sealing of lives in separate railway carriages to produce cultural renewal or the spacing of them out with contrast effects to free up moral energies are romantical notions, not undangerous. Moral issues that used to arise … mainly between societies … now increasingly arise within them

The stories presented here are testimony to this complex view. They also articulate Stuart Hall's (1991: 47) view that 'identities are never completed, never finished; they are always, as subjectivity, in process'.

Education is part of that process. But part of the problem has been in finding a theoretical base and conceptual frameworks which acknowledge specific heritages, whilst at the same time avoiding the pitfalls of over-generalisation. bell hooks (1995) makes the point that:

> Nationalist attachment to a narrow vision of black identity is often as rigidly conservative as racist white stereotypes. Narrowly focused black identity politics do a disservice to black liberation struggle because they seek to render invisible the complex and multiple subjectivity of black folks

This point is echoed by Paul Gilroy (1992) in his arguments against ethnic absolutism, which emphasise the historical inaccuracy of such over-generalisations, even during the colonial period. All the interviewees have come to see how concepts of culture and identity are not essentialist but socially constructed, underlining Bhabba's (1995: 49) view that:

> The transnational dimension of cultural transformation – migration, diaspora, displacement, relocations – turns the specifying or localising process of cultural translation into a complex process of signification. For the natural(ized), unifying discourse of 'nation', 'peoples', 'folk' tradition, these embedded myths of culture's particularity – cannot be readily referenced. The great, though unsettling advantage of this position is that it makes one increasingly aware of the construction of culture, the invention of tradition, the retroactive nature of social affiliation and psychic identification.

For Bhabba this allows a creative space to work through notions of culture and identity, but one which needs to avoid a saccharine vision which ignores the realities of power and struggle. As Hall (1997: 34) comments:

> Ethnicity is the only terminology we have to describe cultural specificity, so one has to go back to it, if one doesn't want to land up with an empty cosmopolitanism – 'citizens of the world' as the only identity … The diaspora has a line through it too: in the era of globalisation, we are *all* becoming diasporic.

The stories related and analysed throughout this book show people in the midst of these complex changes, making difficult and often painful decisions about their own locations and vantage points. Their stories should have particular resonance for teachers as curricula in Britain and many other parts of the world are becoming more narrowly and rigidly defined in cultural terms.

The stories themselves raise sets of questions relating to public education, particularly regarding the curriculum. In recent years the education agenda has been dominated by the corporate voice of multinational business, which articulates the utilitarian need for a skilled workforce. What have been sidelined are debates about the personal and social aspects of the educational process. In the US and Britain there have been vigorous attacks on multicultural and antiracist education. 'Political correctness', which was coined as healthy self-criticism has now become a universal term of abuse. This is underlined by the purely commercial considerations which dominate the mass media and which are, in many ways, becoming more pronounced. In his book, *Information Inequality* Herbert Schiller (1996) places this in a broader context of the lack of accountability of large corporations, the concentration of the media control in fewer hands (dominated largely by the concerns of corporate America through advertising revenue) and the destruction of public sources of information such as libraries and the public education service in the US.

Both culturally and technologically, education seems to be becoming distanced from people's daily lives. The life stories reveal the wealth of experience to be explored, which could inform our teaching. The world is in the classroom. It can only be translated into new cultural webs if we enter into dialogues and explore people's lived experience.

To understand the complex issues surrounding notions of identity we need to examine the process in systematic and empirical ways and place them in an historical context. In Part Two, I examine how current notions of self and self identity have arisen in Western scholarship. I also take a critical view of the various research tools and approaches which have been used to examine the concepts of culture, community and identity and the use of what is variously described as autobiography, life history, self narrative and self creation. In this way I explore the problems and dilemmas involved in establishing an authentic picture of the complex changes which first generation British-born people are currently experiencing. These in turn highlight the ethical dilemmas which confront anyone who undertakes such research.

In Part Three I explore patterns common across different cultural groups. Where significant differences appear, I wish to determine the reasons for this. I am seeking to understand the nature of new cultural formations and explore the role of the mass media in the transformations. Accordingly, I examine the stories to show how people of different heritages manage their different social identities. I also analyse their ways of telling, examining rhetorical devices to discover not only what changes but also what stays the same when people cross borders and increase the scope of their social networks. I try to reveal how a sense of coherence and continuity is carried and maintained across generations.

As Linde (1993:3) points out:

> In order to exist in the social world with a comfortable sense of being a good ... and stable person, an individual needs to have a coherent, acceptable and constantly revised life story

In the maelstrom of modern living, it is probably more essential than ever to 'have a firm foundation when the winds of change do shift' (Dylan: 1974). Even in this fast paced world most of us have a more coherent and continuous sense of self than those who support a strong reading of postmodern thought would suspect. The key to understanding this lies in a close examination of the inter-relationship between narrative, memory and history.

Let me introduce the six people through their fascinating stories.

2

Growing through Contradiction: The Life Stories

There is a long tradition in Jewish literature ... of bearing witness through telling stories ... In this way, history is preserved as personal history; history is given shape and meaning through the interpretation of individual lives. And just as history is made up of personal histories so too are personal identities formed in relation to a larger ethical and cultural context.
Victoria Aarons (1996:60)

Introduction

I met all six people through my work, at the university, so perhaps it's no co-incidence that they have all taught at some time in their lives. In preparation for our conversations I sent each a list of questions I was interested in exploring. I told them that we did not need to stick strictly to the questions, as I wanted them to talk freely about their lives. But I also I wanted to be as candid and open as possible about my intentions. By the second interview I realised that asking them about their parents' lives leading to the time they settled in Britain drew fruitful responses. This may account for the chronological approach most of them took.

The sessions were taped and lasted between about 40 minutes and two hours. The actual length of the sessions was dictated by time available. In one case it was cut short due to faulty recording equipment. Most of the conversations took place in the person's place of work; neutral territory. This was more by accident than design. One discussion took place in the person's own home and one in my study at the university. In the event these different venues do not appear to have in-fluenced the outcome, since they all give fluent accounts of themselves. The full tapes were returned soon after the sessions to allow them to check for accuracy and exercise editorial control. Then they were transcribed and analysed.

Their stories demonstrate vastly diverse attitudes and approaches to negotiating their various social networks. However, before I analysed them I needed to treat their stories carefully. Miller and Glasner (1997:99-111), point to the danger of representing individuals as 'subjects' who become mere 'data', so that their individual identities suffer a severe dismemberment, emerging only as theoretical patterns. This is something I try to avoid. To remain true to the spirit of their narratives I present them as the complex individuals they are. So there is a great deal of direct quotation, since I want them to represent themselves as much as possible. They appear in the order in which I interviewed them.

Aliki – Ending a period of self-doubt

Aliki is in her late twenties and was brought up in Hackney. She is currently head of a drama department in a secondary school. Her family are from a small village in Cyprus. They are Greek-Cypriot and their village was occupied by Turkish troops after the invasion in 1973. During his time in Britain her father has worked mainly in the catering trade. In later years, as the family prospered, they moved several times and her parents now live in Enfield. She grew up in a street where many of her neighbours were from the same village in Cyprus. Although her family did not seem to have strong ties with their original community, her stories indicate how they followed the everyday habits of the community and participated in larger cultural events.

Her narratives are punctuated with deep ambivalences towards Greek Cypriot culture. Early in life she sensed a definite difference from the culture of white middle class English people. This emerged at the start of our conversation when I asked her to recall her earliest memories of her own culture:

A: I think a wedding ... weddings. I really hated weddings.

C: Why?

A: There were so many Greek people and I found them so different to people at school and I used to feel embarrassed about that. About the fact that, you know, I was part of these people in this hall. And you know why couldn't we be out in a tent in the garden like English people.

C: ... what was the source of that embarrassment?

A: Because I wasn't English. I wasn't like my friends. I didn't talk like them. I didn't have the same ... I think at the time I probably categorised it as, 'I'm not posh.' But when I look back now it's, 'I'm not that culture.'

C: ... was it school that reinforced that?

A: I think so yeah, yeah ... school and television. Particularly with television, which may be why I was into drama and film and theatre. The fact that the images on television were not related to, you know, the images around me, in my home with my family. And if you think that television is the be all and end all of how a child might see it, I probably thought, you know, at the time, 'How come we're not on the television?' ... and whenever we were, we were funny ... I used to think ... oh ... 'This is unfair ... I'd rather be English so that I could be on television, and if I was English, I would be on television.' And I think that translates into school, because I thought that, 'Well, none of my family are academic. None of my family have proper jobs. They either work from home on a sewing machine or they drive an ice cream van,' as my dad did ...

This reminiscence illustrates the complex forces operating on Aliki as a small child. It is complicated further by the dimension of social class. Her parents are engaged in working class occupations. However, also contained within this reflection are the seeds of her future ambitions, and her motivation to succeed at school. In a later part of the interview she talks of a significant moment in her early schooling when a teacher projected the picture of a performer on a screen. Aliki said she wanted to be the person on the screen. She also talks frequently of her desire to become famous through her acting. She pursued this dream until she decided to train to become a teacher.

Several anecdotes illustrate some of her misunderstandings at the time, often involving aspects of English culture. For instance, she was under the impression that all English wedding receptions were held in a marquee. The reality is that most would be held in halls, the same as the Greek ones she despised. Another recurring misconception was her belief that English people had their meals at set times. This led to a deeper misconception, which demonstrates that children at school often have limited understanding of each other's home culture.

One of her greatest friends at school was called Kula. Later in her life she was shocked to learn that Kula was Greek, and that her family came from the same village as her own parents.

A: This is really funny, but I didn't realise that they were Greek. ... I used to go around her house and her parents used to speak Greek and I didn't realise they were Greek

C: How was that then?

A: I don't know ... they were different to us. They had their meals at set times, which is what I thought English people used to do ... I thought they were English or another country ... But I never knew they were Greek until I heard my mum talking about her mum. And I asked her, 'Do you know her then?' and she said, 'Of course! She's a fellow villager'

At the start of the interview, she demonstrated how other factors have become entangled with her own sense of identity. I asked her to think back to her first memory. After a pause of a full twenty seconds, she says:

> I think..er..I know what's happening here because, I'm thinking, 'Is that because of my sister? Because you know I've got a sister who has cerebral palsy and this is something I think I'm still trying to work out in my own head, years and years later. When I think of my behaviour or how I was as a child, I either put it in terms of culture – that I was because I thought of *that* culture and didn't feel that I fitted into *that* [meaning the other (ie English) culture]. Or ... that we felt..er..I felt uncomfortable about not being part of a normal family unit, because I had a sister who could not walk so we didn't do the normal family things. ... in terms of, language and ability and confidence and self image. I think that some of it relates to my sister and some of it relates exclusively to my culture, but it's just trying to identify exactly which ones do ...

This passage reveals how complex the issues of individual identity are. There are dimensions of social class and an awareness of how many people had negative views of disability. It also illustrates the strong normalising effect of the media.

Later she talked of more subtle manifestations of racism. This is not just a matter of ignorant habitual racism encountered on the street or in the school playground, but also from liberal white people she had encountered at college. She describes a project at college where students on her Community Drama degree course were left to organise themselves into groups and devise their own project. At the end of a week all the white middle class students had organised them into groups, leaving rest of the students without a group. When Aliki brought this to the group's attention one student remarked that they could form a group of their own. To which she replied, ' Just because we were from ethnic groups doesn't mean to say we get on'. They took the matter to the tutor, who apologised but suggested that they make the best of it. Aliki's solution was to write a play about sweatshop workers from different cultural backgrounds who did not get on.

The interesting point about her work in drama is that she uses her creative work to explore complex issues of identity and particularly her ambivalences towards her home culture. In her final year at college, Aliki wrote the one-woman play, cited in the preface, in which she deals explicitly with such dilemmas. Her character, as a young woman in an imaginary yet critical time in Cyprus, is faced with certain dilemmas. They appear to mirror her internal conflicts.

This illustrates with great clarity the internal dilemmas faced by many first-generation British born settlers and explains why many take what she describes as the negative choice. She is forced to decide between a difficult situation that she knows: a romantic fresh start in an unknown place and culture, or a return to a mythologised homeland. Eventually, she chose to stay. When Aliki commented that it was a negative choice, I asked her to elaborate. She reiterated the point that all Greeks, even young children, say that they will return. Her decision separates her from this popular view.

Throughout our conversation, she expresses her distaste for the behaviour of Greek men towards women. She is determined never to marry a Greek man. When I asked whether this is an extreme form of stereotyping, she replied that perhaps there may be Greek men who do not behave in sexist ways, but she has yet to be proved wrong. Although, having established her independence, she now feels more comfortable and confident, the cultural concerns of marrying a Greek man still bother her. This is where her conflict with her own heritage comes into sharpest relief. She cannot return to a state of acceptance, even if she wished. Her story illustrates the dangers of the idea of a mythologised homeland. Speaking as it does to a utopian condition there is a danger that the idea can be used as a way of silencing voices for change within communities, by representing dissent as a threat to the community. On one level this is understandable. In the face of the onslaught of the mass media, identities outside the mainstream are in a vulnerable position. While this persists, real dilemmas remain for people who have ambivalent feelings towards their heritage cultures,. How are they to reconcile the aspects of their identity, when there are conflicts of value at a fundamental level?

When we spoke, Aliki was moving out of a long period of uncertainty and appeared to have reached a sense of equilibrium between 'where she was from' and 'where she was at'. She wanted to learn to speak Greek to communicate properly with her mother, who speaks very little English. Moreover she expressed a desire to work in Cyprus for some time. She was proud of many aspects of her heritage and at ease with those aspects of her personality and her social behaviour by which others would identify her as Greek Cypriot. Yet she was challenging some of the oppressive features of that tradition. In this she is similar to Nandine, who as a child had a radically different relationship with her family and community.

Nandine – At crisis point

Nandine is thirty, and works in North London as a primary school teacher. Her parents are from Sylhet, the most north-easterly point in Bangladesh, where many British Bangladeshi families originally emigrated from. The irony is that it is the part of the country which is furthest from the sea. Although this migration started with seamen in the 1920s, it accelerated in the 1950s and 1960s, when there was a need for labour in Britain. In her MA dissertation, Nandine studied the history of migration from the region.

Following the general pattern, Nandine's father came to Britain first. Although he had been a teacher in Sylhet, he secured a clerical position in the Pakistani high commission. Her father owned several properties in the Mile End area. After a time her father returned home and married. He was thirty and Nandine's mother was sixteen. It was a traditional arranged marriage. A year later Nandine was born in East London. Nandine mentioned that her father had difficulty finding work, so for a while he worked as a bus conductor. In her early years, her family lived in Newham. Later, as the family prospered they moved to Gants Hill in Essex, an affluent suburb of London.

Her upbringing was in many ways conventional for a fairly well heeled Bangladeshi family. Her parents wanted their children to succeed at school and were very supportive. However there are contradictions here, since as the eldest daughter, Nandine always played a strong nurturing role within her family. She attended the local primary school and later the comprehensive school. As the family's fortunes improved, her brother was sent to private school and on their move to Gants Hill she was sent to a Roman Catholic girls' school to complete her sixth form education.

Her story adds to the complexity of identity the factor of social class. Whilst Aliki could recognise that 'she was not posh', Nandine's family had middle class values and her life has little in common with the academically successful Bangladeshis from lower income families who told their stories to John Eade (1995) and who lived in the Spitalfields area of London. It was not until she attended college that Nandine became aware of the living conditions of the Bangladeshi community in Spitalfields. She knew less about the effect of the class-based constraints upon their hopes of academic achievement. In her interview, she says that her family knew about them, but thought of them 'as a bit of a lost cause.'

As a young child, Nandine experienced no conflict between the values of home and school. She was an avid reader, who 'had a flair for languages.' By the age of eight she was a 'free reader'. In English schools this meant that she had finished all the reading scheme books (primers) and was deemed to be an independent reader.

Her parents encouraged her achievement at school. Contrary to common assumptions, many Asian girls are encouraged at school by their families. In common with many of John Eade's informants (1995), Nandine expresses this negatively. She was not obstructed. Later she was released from some of the duties which would have been expected of her as the eldest daughter. Nevertheless, on many other occasions she refers to her passive and dutiful behaviour. It is also interesting that as the family prospered, it was her brother who was the first to be sent to private school, which her family perceived as guaranteeing a better education. At school, like Aliki, she had support from her peer group, which consisted of Asian girls from several different cultural and religious backgrounds. At the earlier stages there was no conflict between home and school since, as she says, she had not begun formally to learn about the Qur'an. Her parents wished for her to achieve and she was a willing and enthusiastic student. One anecdote about her having to reject one set of friends is testimony of this.

> I wanted to do well at school and I was called 'a walking dictionary' and a snob because I wanted to separate myself ... In the second year of secondary school I changed my friendship group because the girls I was hanging around with started smoking and I just wasn't interested and I just changed groups and became part of another group who were more serious about their work. I suppose I wasn't a rebel in the sense that the other girls were and I had that very much drummed into my head that I was at school to learn and not to muck about and I enjoyed work you know and I enjoyed learning.

Throughout the taped conversation she talks warmly about most of her teachers, but at no stage does she mention any who acknowledged her cultural heritage. Her reading material at school is predominantly eurocentric. Her decision to take English is because teachers praised her written work. She attended a local comprehensive secondary school. In the sixth form she transferred to a Roman Catholic girls secondary school. It was only at this stage that she had difficulties with her schoolwork, and the family employed a private tutor.

But schooling and education do not take place in a vacuum. Inevitably conflicts of values arose. Whilst education can be viewed as a commodity and a passport to material advantage, as recent governmental initiatives have emphasised in Britain, Western education is imbued with liberal and individualistic values, which tend to conflict with hierarchical and collective values which often feature strongly in families from non European backgrounds. In their book, *Intercultural Communication* (1995), Ron and Suzanne Scollon analyse such distinctions in relation to the Chinese communities from Hong Kong. Following the work of the German sociologist Ferdinand Tonnies, they use the terms *Gemeinschaft* (community) and *Gesellschaft* (society) to explain such cultural distinctions.

Tonnies (see Scollon and Scollon: 1995) argued that the problems of modern industrial society had arisen because of a split with the traditional, community based social organisation (*Gemeinschaft*) of the Middle Ages based on a common history and common traditions. This he contrasted with the corporate organisation (*Geselleschaft*) of modern industrial society where relationships are more contractual, rational or instrumental. Using this as a point of departure, they make the observation that businesses in Hong Kong and Taiwan are run more along the lines of *Gemeinschaft*, being family owned and controlled. Although they see this as a useful distinction to make and perhaps this helps us to understand issues of identity relating to community, generation and gender, they add a word of warning:

> No modern culture or discourse system, of course, is purely organised as *Gemeinschaft* or *Gesellschaft* alone. In any social structure we will see a mixture of elements of both forms of organisation. What is important in understanding intercultural communication is to understand in which contexts one of these forms is preferred over the other. (Scollon and Scollon: 1995: 137)

They are useful distinctions to make in the case of Aliki and Nandine whose parents came from predominantly rural backgrounds. For these women, however, there is a further dimension: how the two forms of thinking and sets of values interact and how they manifest themselves in often painful decision making. This could be seen in the way Aliki challenged many values of her 'community'. As Nandine tells it, her role within the family as eldest daughter was clearly defined. She states that she was a dutiful daughter fulfilling her communal obligations fully and entering into an arranged marriage, which is a strong tradition within the Bangladeshi Muslim community. However, when her marriage broke down the family offered a great deal of support. She returned to the family home.

Nandine continued her formal studies, completing a BA in Education (a standard teaching qualification in Britain) and a Master's degree, in which she studied the history of Bangladeshi settlement in Britain. However, conflicts were appearing between her own aspirations and desire for independence and the demands of family life and the traditions of the community. Through her education she had begun to question certain aspects of her own tradition, particularly the business of the arranged marriage. This is a growing phenomenon in several cultures. In her book of short stories entitled *Arranged Marriage*, Chitra Bannerjee Divakaruni (1997) illustrates the complexity of such issues in the context of the United States. She herself runs a help-line for women of South East Asian origin. Similar dilemmas are reported by women from other cultures, such as Greek and Turkish Cypriot. It is here that the tension between the demands of the family and community on the one hand and the freedom of the individual on the other are brought into sharpest relief.

In Nandine's case, the decision to stick her ground has been particularly painful. She has married a man of Irish descent and has been rejected by her whole family. They feel that she has discredited the family in the eyes of the community. It is particularly painful for her as she had had an extremely close relationship with her mother.

However, although she has broken with her own cultural background in dramatic ways, she feels that people who have gone into commerce and law are in much greater danger of losing their heritage culture, because they enter into English middle class culture without reflecting upon the consequences. Although she has experienced her dissent in personally painful ways, her identity is still strongly grounded in her Bangladeshi Muslim origins. She has always maintained a fluency in Bengali and has immense knowledge of Bengali culture and history. The school she teaches in has a large Bangladeshi community who come predominantly from a poor socio-economic background. She sees herself as a role model for the children.

As with Aliki, Nandine's conflict with her community revolves mainly around what she perceives as gender issues and differences in generational attitudes. At one point she states that the Bangladeshi community needs a liberalising set of changes such as Western societies experienced in the 1960s. As the next portrait shows, this more liberal approach is often easier, in many ways, for the men within the communities.

Asif: a fluid, self-assured approach to identity

Asif was twenty nine when we spoke and had just left his teaching post in an inner urban secondary school, where he had taught media studies. He has a Master's degree in this subject. When I interviewed him he was working in a Secure Unit, dealing with young people who have broken the law. In contrast to Aliki and Nandine, his parents come from different cultural backgrounds. His mother was a midwife from Delhi who, after Partition in 1948, did the 'long walk' across to Pakistan, ending up in Karachi. His father was a pharmacist from the Punjab.. They met while working in the same hospital in Karachi. His father came to Britain first in 1963 and his mother followed three years later. Asif was born in 1968.

His father could not get a job as a pharmacist, so he worked digging 'footings' (tunnels for the pipes) for the Water Board. Within five or six years he was in charge of the site, which comprised sixty workers. In this capacity he ex-perienced a great deal of racism. As Asif states,

> Not the best time in Britain, to be doing that. You've got the 'Keep Britain White' campaign ... Enoch Powell in '68. The ethnic-racial context is quite tricky at that point. It's the first time you're really seeing Commonwealth immigrants in a position of power as he was then. With quite a heavy duty lot of people. These weren't middle class people or liberals.

Asif's father's job was to check their work. Often lodged in the pipes were little messages of racist abuse. Later the men went on strike, complaining about his work. In a surprisingly liberal move, the Water Board promoted him out of trouble. However, he couldn't settle in the office job and shortly afterwards he began his own business. Asif told me,

> There are two things you can do as an immigrant: There's the shops and there's textiles. Both of them need a little bit of capital and don't have an awful lot of labour intensitivity. Hence the proliferation of those two ...

After having moved around the country during his time with the water board, Asif's father settled in Swindon. It was here that he set up the business with his father and two of his brothers. They bought a Halal butcher's shop and began an interesting trade catering for the needs of various communities. Beansprouts, rice and peppers for the Chinese restaurants. A wide variety of pasta and even grapes from Southern Italy for the Italian community's wine making season in early autumn. Meat, spices and herbs for the various communities of the Indian sub continent. The shop was a focal point for non-white cultural exchanges, also attracting the occasional middle class white customer with an interest in international cuisine.

At home the family spoke both Urdu and English, although, especially in the children's pre-school years, English tended to predominate:

> because they were very keen that we would be able to cope with school. With my dad being away a lot, my mum would do a lot of the education. Because we moved a lot so I wasn't stable in nursery. So she did the early stuff. And when I actually got to nursery schools I remember, she was a bit distressed, because the other kids didn't know their times tables and I did ... Theirs is a very set traditional way of doing it and I could do it. And it was arithmetic, spellings and writing. And I could do a lot more than most of the other kids. So it was tricky for her to put me into this system, which she didn't know anything about, and had an awful lot of respect for. Her expectations of the system were much higher than she felt were actually delivered. We had extra tuition. It was deemed necessary even at six or seven

Although he was successful at school, he didn't seem to reach his full potential. At sixteen he achieved only four passes in his Ordinary Level, General Certificate in Education. But he had built up a wide range of social contacts. As there were only two Asian boys at his secondary school many of his friends were white. Paradoxically, some held strongly racist views. At one point during the early nineteen eighties he found himself sitting in a friend's bedroom reading his friend's brother's fascist magazines. At the time he belonged to a group who described themselves as 'mods' and listened to various types of pop music, which included Tamla Motown, the Jam and the Specials. His lived experience shows a development of wide social networks. This contrasts with the experiences of the three women, who don't refer to this social aspect, being centred much more closely around the home and family. However, like them, he has a detailed and intimate knowledge of the history and culture of his origins. When he speaks of his own identity a very complex picture emerges:

> I'm at that stage where I'm sort of ... I've never been I've never been quite able to clearly say, because there are so many other factors. As an immigrant whose dad dug footings, am I working class, am I middle class (being an educated person?) ... and then the class divisions within my own family ... So, I mean locations in terms of class, in terms of career, as I am now, also in terms of race ... there's the question of Mirapuri kids [not achieving high scores] in the league tables [of examination results] ... if you look at those ... yet dad's from a Mirapuri background.. and if you look at kids from an Indian background in the league tables, they're usually quite high. That's my mum's side. So there are inherent contradictions of me trying to locate anywhere. And then tying that in with my English identity and nationhood. And then, with that, I half reject the idea of nationhood. And I quite like the idea of being a European traveller ... So its actually quite convoluted ...

He has similar difficulties in describing his religious identity. His current position is one of atheism:

> I like the idea of religion and what it provides for people. But I also think in terms of a sociological perspective of religion, the Marxist ideas of religion and that I find a major block to it. And also this idea of faith. I don't feel it. So it's not working for me on an emotive level. But it could work on an intellectual level to counter things when people say, you know, that this is Islamic and I could say, 'Well no it isn't actually. That's why I quite like the idea of reading the Qur'an, because I can say, 'But where does it say that?'

Most of these ideas of identity and religion are referred to in relation to ongoing discussions he has with his father and his uncles. There are limits to his tolerance of dissent from this cultural heritage, which demonstrate further complexities. He is a great admirer of the works of Salman Rushdie and it surprised him that he, as an atheist, could be shocked by the irreverence of *The Satanic Verses*. But he said that, in his opinion, it was blasphemous and he fully understood how offended some people could be by the work, even though he is more outraged at the idea of *fatwa*. Later he told me that he was similarly disapproving of a Hindu friend who was willing to convert to Christianity to have a white wedding in an Anglican church. What offended him was that she was willing to do this merely to satisfy her vanity.

Like Nandine he thinks that those who opt for business careers are often more likely to lose their sense of history and heritage. He cites his brother-in law as an example. As a barrister he has taken on many of the habits of his colleagues and drinks with them regularly, but hides this from the family. What disturbs Asif is what he sees as his brother-in-law's lack of integrity and sincerity.

In common with Aliki and Nandine, his attitude towards his heritage culture is ambivalent and often contradictory. Like Aliki he has toyed with the idea of working for some time in his 'home' country, but ultimately rejected it as a romantic and nostalgic idea. He realised that the realities of daily life would not suit his current predisposition. His partner is English and his home is in Britain. He is aware of his political allegiances and the complexities of his own identity. Like Aliki he sees this as a process which he is working through and which has many sources. All three have broken from their tradition in a quite fundamental way. The next group of three demonstrate different kinds of links with their own heritage groups. Nevertheless the conversations reveal an equally complex view of identity.

My: A quiet fire

My was one of the Boat People who fled from North Vietnam in the late '70s. Her family had been Chinese settlers in the northern part of Vietnam. Her father and mother had been educated in China and had moved to Vietnam as merchants, trading mainly in silks and other rich fabrics. By 1979 the situation was becoming desperate for the Chinese-Vietnamese. The Vietnamese wanted to establish the supremacy of their own language and culture.

My remembers. In the middle of the night the children were woken and, together with other families, they boarded horse drawn carriages. The procession, led by soldiers who had been bribed, left under cover of darkness and headed silently for the mountains. They left behind most of their belongings. Not even taking food. My's father carried a suitcase containing rich fabrics, which he hoped to trade when necessary.

My recalls her bewilderment at having to cross major obstacles in the dark, often in rainstorms. On one occasion they had to cross a rope bridge spanning a deep ravine. A pebble, or anything, dropped by accident would fall through the darkness for at least a minute before it reached the bottom. Her baby sister was being carried by her older brother. Midway across the bridge the baby began to cry. The soldiers ordered the family to throw her over the edge for fear that they would all be discovered and killed by enemy soldiers. Thinking quickly, My's mother took the baby and fed her. Her brother filled the baby carriage with a heavy object and let it drop into the ravine.

After several days they reached a mountain, which My remembers having to climb in the rain and the wind. At the summit they put up tents and rested for a few days. My's father took out his suitcase and opened it. Inside, in place of the bolts of silks and rich fabrics, was a rock wrapped in rough cloth. Soldiers had robbed them.

A kindly farmer gave them food and sustenance before they headed for the port. Even here their difficulties were not over. At the port they did not have enough money to bribe the guards. Somehow My's father was able to borrow some from relatives and they secured a place on a boat. It was an old Chinese junk with scarcely enough room for them all. Cramped, and without any real knowledge of their destination, they set off. My remembers a storm so violent that they did not know whether they would survive.

Eventually they reached Hong Kong and were kept there for months while they waited to see where they could settle. Their plight was publicised sympathetically in the media. Many countries offered help. My's family chose Britain. On arrival they were kept in a centre to learn basic English. Then they were sent to different parts of Britain. Her family settled in Cornwall.

In terms of the people I have interviewed, My's case is exceptional. Unlike the initiatives for bilingual support described by the others, theirs was consistently planned and coordinated. They had a period of initiation, in immersion schools.

> **M**: And from Hong Kong ... erm ... we stayed in a refugee camp and we learned a tiny, tiny amount of English. Just the basic A,B,C,s and all that. And then I stayed in Hong Kong for about three months in the refugee camp. And then once our visas were y'know organised and that, we moved to Thorny Island..I think it's in Sussex ... and we stayed there for almost half a year were they gave us basic English and we were actually taken to primary schools and it was..er.. the local area in Sussex actually made ... started a new primary school in Sussex for the refugees, who came to England ... so we're talking about probably a thousand or so families in that area going to the same school ... and they had coaches in the morning to pick us up taking us to primary schools and ... the whole class probably twenty of us in a class were all Vietnamese and the teachers were all English. And they taught us basic ... 'Hi, how are you?' 'My name is ... '. and taught us just, like learning to read ABCs and that depending on what level we were at and after a year ... my family moved to a place called Launceton. So we went to the primary school ... they thought it was good if we could stay together ... we can still have our culture. We can still talk our own language, yet we were immersed into a class full of English speakers as well.

My added that her teacher had really worked to connect with their culture, preparing work which was relevant to her background and showing an interest and curiosity about their lives and culture. But more than this she had encouraged them to share their experiences as refugees, so that the Cornish children would understand their courage. She is full of praise for this approach and recalls learning English in a very short time; three months after arriving in Cornwall, about a year after arriving in Britain. By way of contrast the other five people tell of having to struggle, if not with the language then to have their own heritage valued or even recognised by the school.

But it was not just at school that My received a great deal of support. Her parents, particularly her father, were also anxious that she should succeed and guided them firmly to this end. This is a phenomenon of cultural transmission, which Michael Coles (1996) calls 'prolepsis'. That is, the parents shape the children's futures by offering strategies and priorities, which they think will serve them well in adult life. In terms of My's story it is characterised by its lack of conflict – she seems to have gone along with everything those in authority expected of her. She does not even voice any complaint about her father's authoritarian approach to them as children. There is no mention of racism. Perhaps she did not experience discomforts and dissatisfactions. Perhaps the real reason for the silence is cultural. Perhaps it is a question of etiquette in her narrative style. Even when she is describing moments of great danger, she relates it in careful measured tones. Perhaps it is disrespectful for her to criticise her father to an outsider and a relative stranger. Perhaps the moments are too painful to discuss. As Maya Angelou remarked when discussing her own approach to autobiography:

> Some (events) were never recorded because they were either so bad or so painful that there was no way to write honestly and artistically without making them melodramatic (in Tate 1985:7)

In Vietnam, the Chinese settlers maintained a clear sense of identity and My tells of the language that was spoken called Dong, which was central to the Chinese-Vietnamese identity:

> ... It has a history ... from, you know last century or something like that, but it's actually slowly dying out. Because when we left in 1979, there was a war because the Vietnamese who didn't want to become communist were becoming anti Chinese ... They sanctioned the schools (sic). All our tradition and slowly all our whole identity was being erased. They were trying to make us Vietnamese rather than ethnic Chinese-Vietnamese. So that's when it started ... that we had to move out.

This adds another level of complexity since, as My observes, her family already had a hyphenated identity on their arrival in Britain. In terms of education her parents were keen for them to develop all sides of their identity, not for ideological reasons but in pragmatic ways. They themselves were multilingual in Cantonese, Vietnamese, Dong and Mandarin.

> For my father and mother, they knew English was important ... But they knew that if we let go our language, then they wouldn't understand us. So what my father did, instead of ..erm.. We were talking our home language, but because there's no written form of our home language ... my mother and my father actually saved up a lot of money and bought us a video and through that they rented videos ... Cantonese videos and that's how we learned Cantonese ... And when we moved up to London, my father enrolled us into Saturday schools.

Coupled with this was real sense of urgency that they should also do well in English. My relates how her father bought a book by Enid Blyton from a second hand shop, which she had to copy for handwriting practice. This chimes in with Eve Gregory's work (1993) which explores different culturally formed conceptions on the nature of literacy. Getting the characters drawn very precisely is essential in Chinese ideograms. A slight difference can render a wholly different set of meanings.

> ... So he was really huge into neatness and even though he couldn't hear us read, once we finished our writing he told us to go next door and read it to the neighbours.

Her father also supervised the homework in a very formal way:

> Each night, after we had dinner ... he would set up the table, a huge table and I've got ... three brothers and three sisters ... We would sit around the table, the six of us and he would sit there and watch us do our homework. And he would help us out with our maths and when he couldn't with our English we had to work it out together ...

This communal approach is quite different from the more individualistic approaches usually adopted by many English and American children, although My seems to see it as her father's individual idiosyncrasy rather than a culturally specific approach.

> I don't think it's part of a tradition ... more my father being scared that we wouldn't do well in our ... education. He knew that being in a new culture we had to work extra hard. And that was his way of making us do it. So he was very strict on us and if we didn't work properly then we were punished for it.

As My tells it, this mixture of coercion and self sacrifice on her parents' part coupled with proper attention to her culture and identity in her schooling has enabled her to feel comfortable with all aspects of her identity. She could see value in each of the different cultural approaches. She mentioned that although she admired the individual freedom implicit in European culture, she thought the

Chinese respect for elders was a value which should be retained. As I was leaving she put it succinctly

I have three strands to my identity: my Chinese strand, my Vietnamese strand and my English strand. If you take one away there is no My.

Olgun: Contradiction and conflict

Olgun's story, too, is of an identity born out of civil strife. What is different is that he moved backwards and forwards between Cyprus and England. His family are Turkish Cypriot and he grew up in a place where the Greek Cypriot population were in the majority. 'There was about a thousand Turkish Cypriots and about ten thousand Greek Cypriots'. Because of the continuing conflict, his family felt overwhelmed. His father was an Anglophile, who with immense energy and enterprise had built up a business making quilts:

He would actually make them ... a single or a double one. Have any kind of design and he would make it with his three fingers ... some incredible designs ... That's how he started off ... at the age of twelve.. then he went into sorts of food ... and other utensils. He had three shops before '63

Olgun's father lost everything in the war of 1963. Starting from scratch he rebuilt his business and in less than ten years had five shops. Olgun describes the outcome of the war in such an enclosed community as somewhat surreal. They had to move to a different part of their own town.

Some people were living in a big school and they just had sheeting between them. So they were almost refugees in their own town ... Families were living and cooking in a hall. Different families and this is obviously coming from an Islamic kind of thing where women and men have their separate ... you know women are protected by their culture.

Olgun spent his formative years in this environment. As a result he has an identity which has been defined *against* Greek Cypriot people, who he saw as the enemy, who denied his family basic amenities such as electricity. As a boy he remembers when he and his friends used to smash the porcelain cable holders on the pylons that diverted the electricity to the Greek villages.

He was taught in a small village school. One of his uncles was a teacher there. It was a very traditional education with a strong nationalist ethos

... incredibly nationalistic. I mean the Turkish flag and all the Turkish books from Turkey ... Attaturk and the war of independence in Turkey and we were all part of that ... a continuation, an extension of Turkey ... .we weren't Cypriots.

Although his identity is strongly defined against the Greeks, his family were traditionally great Anglophiles. His grandfather was in the British army. Ironically he was fighting *for* the Greeks. His uncle was also in the British army and had settled in Charlton in South-East London. His father also had a profound respect for British medicine, which he thought was the best in the world. Therefore it wasn't surprising that when Olgun needed an operation at the age of eleven, he came to Britain for surgery.

Olgun found life with his aunt and uncle in London surprisingly different. He had been used to living in a relatively small rural community. Now he found that he lived in a built-up area, which had a different set of sights and smells for him to become accustomed to. His uncle owned a fish and chip shop and a dry cleaning business. It seemed strange to him that people queued for cooked food in the middle of the day. He also found it difficult to settle in school. Although the teachers were friendly and welcoming, he found the rowdiness of some of the pupils difficult to understand.

The school tried to pair him up with another Turkish Cypriot boy, but it didn't work out since the boy had been brought up in England, could not speak Turkish and knew very little about Turkish culture. This demonstrates the complexity of the notion of diaspora. Olgun made good friends eventually with two boys who had been adopted. Being isolated from his own family, he possibly had found a different kind of common experience and thus a common identity. Later on it was suggested that the aunt and uncle adopt Olgun.

At school he encountered several racist bullies, one of whom later became a bank robber and ended up being shot. However, he stood up to the bullies who subsequently left him alone. It was at school that he found some comfort in his academic success and by the time he was sixteen, he was first in his class.

At this point he returned to Cyprus. His aunt and uncle had decided to emigrate to Australia. They intended to visit Cyprus, driving through Europe down to Turkey and visiting Olgun's family in Cyprus. In Turkey the car broke down and Olgun had to spend some time with his aunt, while his uncle tried to find someone who could fix the car. It was here where he realised differences, which disturbed him deeply. He was disgusted by the harassment his aunt received from Turkish men on the street.

> ... Even though they were from the same culture, they were different to us ... we felt very threatened by it ... It was awful ... I've never felt like this in Britain.

When they finally arrived in Cyprus, he decided he wanted to stay with his family. 'This is where I belonged. I wanted to stay there,' Not long after this he was sent to a boarding school where again he found some aspects of life different and difficult. Interestingly to he defined himself against the other boys in the school and he missed the privacy and the material comforts of living at his aunt's.

> I never felt so lonely and depressed ... I went to that place and there were sixteen of these dirty boys in this room ... 'Cause here, I was at my aunt's, I had my own room. I had my own encyclopaedias. I had my music(al) instruments. I had everything I wanted. It was mine ... I had my own television ... everything you know.

However, by contrast, he thought the education there was far better. He said, 'I feel that, if there was a peak in knowledge absorption, that was it.' He settled into his new surroundings and was about to take examinations when a devastating event occurred. His village came under attack from the Greek Cypriot forces and he was conscripted into the army.

> Just give me a gun and the next thing I know I'm like in the army fighting the Greeks ... I was taken prisoner of war for three months ... and I was beaten up and I saw people wounded next to me ... I was about 16 ... 17 ... yeah, I didn't even have a beard.

Although it must have been a terrifying experience, he went numb. 'It wasn't (terrifying),' he told me, 'you're not there ... you're outside ... you're there..' Reflecting on the experience he still has very ambivalent feelings. He has a rational and political opinion on the events. He doesn't generalise these negative feelings to all Greek Cypriots. However, he has some real doubts too:

> It was just weird looking back ... all those events ... and when I came here I was involved in left wing politics ... I wasn't ... I couldn't ... you know say if the Greeks was you know ... people ... brothers ... then why was this happening ? ... yeah ... even though I met at college ... Greek Cypriots who were friends ... there was this part that I couldn't just throw away

His identity is complex and contradictory. It is an unfinished story, which he is still trying to understand fully. At the time of our conversation he was completing an MA course and had chosen Cyprus as the focus of his dissertation study. Although his identity has a strong Turkish element, his liberal values lead him to question a narrowly defined view of this identity. Like most of the others in this study he says he received no confirmation of his identity in school. Towards the end of our conversation he declared without bitterness or irony:

> No confirmation on the part of the school. I was just another face, you know.

In this respect his story has considerable overlap with Michael, who is in his mid thirties and was born in Dominica in the Caribbean.

Michael: resisting racism

In Britain the statistics concerning black African Caribbean boys and schooling make extremely depressing reading. They are the largest group to be excluded from school. Official statistics estimate that they are at least four times as likely to be excluded as their white counterparts. They consistently underachieve in examinations and are under represented in most professional jobs. So Michael is an exception. He works as a research fellow at a college, which is part of London University and has embarked upon a PhD, in which he is studying the reasons for the level of academic underachievement among black youth.

His father came from the Dominica, where Michael spent his early years. As well as English his family spoke a French based Creole. In his story he points to the extreme contrast of his father's life in the Caribbean and the conditions in England when he came to join his brother. In the Caribbean Michael's father had been the manager of a large estate. He was a keen gardener who worked in the botanical gardens. He was a well-respected man in the Caribbean:

> He had a very outward personality. Well liked ... Everyone knew him from one end of the island to the other ... Very popular ... They called him 'The Brain' because he seemed to ... well ... was knowledgeable about most things ... The problem was when he came here ... he had different things to contend with ... and his status declined dramatically and his self-perception declined ... how he perceived himself declined, because he was no longer the big man. He was no longer the person he was in the Caribbean. He was looked down on. He was abused. He faced a lot of physical and verbal abuse. He ended up in a job he didn't like. The job he wanted he couldn't get. Absolutely couldn't get ... He became a changed man.

Michael sees that this is a common story for people from the Caribbean, who had to suffer extreme racist abuse:

> We lived in Canning Town. A very racist place. Extremely racist and ... erm ... I mean ... there are times ... as a kid, as a child growing up ... . I mean I came across a lot of it myself. I mean at school, I came across a lot of racism. Extreme racism..

This was from 1971 onwards when the flames of racism were not only being fanned by far-right organisations like the National Front, similar messages were coming from Members of Parliament like Enoch Powell. Michael describes an incident when he and a friend were badly beaten by a gang of racists. They were travelling home from school, when they were involved in an argument with a man who accused them of throwing a stone at his car. They denied they had done anything. Several minutes later, they were

> ... surrounded by these people ... Grown men. I would have thought that these people knew better ... you know ... kids ... We were kids, you know, we've come from school. Typical. We got books and stuff like that ... So they surrounded us and really laid into us ... Broke my friend's arm, broke his jaw ... Struck me with a metal bar across my head. I lost consciousness ... Nothing happened with the police ... My father was beaten up twice ... and throughout their life in Britain they had to put up with that.

This situation proved doubly frustrating since the family had to deal with the outcomes of his father's frustrations:

> So, you're doubly abused ... What that does to you is you feel yourself constantly under siege ... Because you go to school ... you face racism. Out in the outside world you face racism. You come home you have to face up to your father who feels that all his ... you know his belittling at work ... he's got to find an avenue to let it out.

Despite this Michael still respects his father enormously. In a later part of the conversation he states that, 'My father taught me everything I know.' Moreover, at this stage he has a deep understanding of his father's intolerable position. He dealt with the dilemma by withdrawing:

> I mean you have friends and they rally round. But you know ... the only way I feel how I dealt with it, I think, was to go into myself ... I became withdrawn ... I kinda became totally absorbed in myself ... I read a lot ... I wrote ... I drew ... you know ... Anything that meant that I was alone and I could speak to myself ... I read a lot of fantasy books ... If it wasn't reality based ... I liked it. If I didn't have to face up to reality ... what was around me. I mean if you gave me a book ... a realistic book, I would throw it back at you ... I had to feel I was somewhere else. I had to feel that I was different ...

Despite all the constraints upon him, Michael did well at school. He attributes this mainly to his love of reading and his father's strong belief in education. This belief was not founded on the premise that it would be an automatic passport to a better material existence or a more interesting job. Experience had taught him differently.

> Education as a way out doesn't always get you what you want, because it didn't get him what he wanted ... Because you still have to face up to prejudice. But education in itself is good ...

His conception of education is of acquiring self-knowledge:

> You know who you are. You know what it is that you're about. I can deal with you on an equal level. I don't have to put up with your nonsense.

In reality this manifested itself in the form of a 'crisis' where Michael had to resolve several contradictions, mainly between schooled learning and his own experiences. Despite his success, he did not stay on at school after 16, but embarked upon an electronics course. He quickly became bored with that and went to college to study three subjects at 'A' level. Again he dropped out of the programme, because he was experiencing what he describes as a 'crisis'. This centred round his fundamental questioning of basic issues regarding the way he was being taught history. It was also something of a crisis in terms of religious imagery. He felt that the school and the church had 'fed (him) too much nonsense'.

Having been brought up in a Roman Catholic family, he had been surrounded by the standard iconography, which portrays all the principal people as white, blue eyed and blond haired. He saw a contradiction that 'the very image which oppresses me, I have to go home and worship. The image is the same as the person who is oppressing me on the street'. Much of this he worked through and continues to work upon in his writing and art. I talked to him in his home and saw that the walls were covered with biblical images featuring black people. He now believes that history and religion are not embedded in rock. This also caused him to question the dominant historical discourses. It was at this time that he began reading more internally persuasive writers, Malcolm X's autobiography, Water Rodney, and Franz Fanon. He also mentions Karl Marx as a significant influence. For him Marx put things into a context that enabled him to see social relationships and to examine 'why things are the way they are'.

This 'epiphany' caused him to change direction and study literature. His MA was in literature, examining the representation of black people the Western canon. Although he sees his own identity as a complex management of many different strands, he feels there needs to be a central core to a person's identity:

> You need to have a concrete identity. You need to have a core identity. Like a sun and all other identities revolve around that sun.

Whilst he thinks that even that core is not finalised and determined, he believes that there has to be some stability and continuity. Although superficially he seems to have an essentialist view of himself in comparison with the other participants, his narrative of his own identity is not simple and certainly not unproblematic.

I have devoted this chapter to the broader aspects of the six interviewees' stories to retain a coherent, complex, contextualised and I hope, faithful view of their courageous, candid and deeply reflective accounts of their lives. I want to conclude this piece by delineating some emerging patterns.

Emerging patterns and questions

All six stories demonstrate the complexity of the process they have lived through. All six seem to echo Ien Ang's (1994:18) conclusion to her elegant paper, 'On not speaking Chinese':

> This post-modern ethnicity can no longer be experienced as naturally based upon tradition and ancestry, it must be experienced as a provisional and partial site of identity, which must be constantly (re) invented and (re)negotiated ... In short, if I am inescapably Chinese by descent I am only sometimes Chinese by consent. When and how is a matter of politics.

I cannot claim that the group is a representative sample. However it is interesting to note the connections, especially as they are from different heritages. Also interesting are the issues of class and gender raised by their stories. All six are qualified teachers and half of them have broken from family and community traditions and values in fundamental ways. This marks them as exceptions rather than the rule. However, their stories do show those tensions in a clearer light. Considering that they come from such different cultural backgrounds, there are remarkable similarities in several significant areas. All demonstrate:

- Similar patterns of family settlement – rural to urban – economically supported by family and community

- Conceptions of identity as fluid and mobile

- A strong sense of history and affiliation with heritage cultures

- Ambivalence to and questioning of value systems of the heritage culture and wider society

- Looking outside 'community' for life partners

- Influence of the mass media on their sense of identity

- Strong influence of peer group as a support network

- Frequent visits to 'homeland'

- An ambivalent attitude to living in the 'homeland'

- An enjoyment of schooling and learning, but no ostensible examples of how this connected to their daily lives

- Liberal, tolerant values and a critical outlook generally associated with aspects of a Western, liberal humanist education

- Identification with other oppressed or marginalised groups

The first three people I interviewed were born and brought up in Britain. At the time I noted that they exhibited a critical distance from several aspects of both their home cultures and the discourses of the dominant culture. Although the final three exhibit a critical stance, it has a quite different inflection: they are more firmly located within the traditions of their group. Some of this could be explained by the fact that a substantial part of their childhood was spent in their parents' country of origin. I shall explore these patterns in more detail in part three.

When I embarked upon this journey of discovery, I wished to investigate the idea of cultural change and the complex syncretism involved in that process. The following exchange between James Clifford and Stuart Hall (Clifford:1997: 44) suggested that it might also be fruitful to examine the corollary. Hall asked: What remains the same when you travel? Clifford replied:

> What stays the same even when you travel? A lot. But the significance may differ with each new conjecture ... Are we to think of a kind of kernel or core of identity that is carried everywhere with them? Or is it something more polythetic, something more like a habitus, a set of practices and dispositions, parts of which could be remembered and articulated in specific contexts? ... Obviously the issue is a crucial one in discussing diaspora cultures. What is brought from a prior place? And how is it both maintained and transformed by the new environment?

This led me to seek out frameworks by which I could discover what persists over generations of settlement. Family narratives play a central role in the process of maintaining continuity across generations.

What has been interesting for me about the life stories has been the wide variety of approaches they exhibit in dealing with their dilemmas. Although they appear to have reached similar points in their lives and share very similar political views, their routes are different and highly individual.

They also vary according to their widely different approaches to the telling of their stories. Their narrative styles range from the measured to the passionate. They appear to retain a music and cadence which relates to their cultural heritages, as they creatively rework their memories. This process entails not only the 'what' (the content) but the 'how' (the form).

I shall systematically analyse their stories in part three to reveal how their identities are produced. However, first I need to say something about how identity has developed in Western thought and look at some of the basic problems of researching identity in empirical ways.

PART TWO:
THE RIDDLE OF IDENTITY

3

Pure is a Bore:
The Riddle of Identity

*... identities are never completed, never finished; ... they are always,
as subjectivity, in process* Stuart Hall (1991)

Introduction: Setting the Context

Part of the difficulty in theorising issues of culture and identity in education over
the past three or four decades has been finding conceptual frameworks which
acknowledge specific heritages while at the same time avoiding the pitfalls of
over generalisation. The way educationalists have traditionally framed issues of
culture and identity has tended to be based on empirical research of a positivistic
nature. During the sixties and seventies, this led to oversimplifications about
how children operate at home and school. Although the research was intended
to counter racist stereotypes, one set of misleading generalisations often re-
placed another. The main reason is that the bulk of research was carried out by
behavioural psychologists, who were seeking precise and unambiguous definitions of complex and often contradictory phenomena.

Their approach lacked any sense of context or acknowledgement of social
change. Culture and identity were often conceived in fixed and biologically
determined ways (see Rotheram and Finney, 1993). As a consequence much of
the research conducted during that period seemed to mirror the static conceptions of openly racist genetic scientists, who sought to justify colonialism,
through quasi-scientific assertions of the genetic inferiority of the 'other' (see
Simon (1971). This was a necessary, perhaps inevitable, stage for those wishing
to develop antiracist approaches. It exposed the poverty of the arguments and
methodology, of those who saw IQ as biologically fixed and culturally inflected
(e.g. Jensen, 1969). It also celebrated diversity and questioned ethnocentric ap-

proaches in the field of education. However, in the field of educational research there has been little rigour in exploring the concepts of community, culture and identity, particularly as they impact on the curriculum. This is surprising since, in other fields such as art, anthropology, sociology, social psychology, literature, history and primarily in the relatively new area of cultural studies, such considerations have been a central and invigorating force.

It is no coincidence that community, culture and identity have been foregrounded in recent decades. From certain perspectives traditional societies appear to be threatened by the massive rifts, fragmentations and realignments taking place in our social reality. Cultural theorists are attempting to analyse the resulting complexity. Far from being viewed as fixed and immutable, the concepts of community, identity and culture are seen as fluid, multiple, hybrid, syncretic and often contradictory. Many theorists (eg Pieterse and Parekh, 1995) are now recognising that, like globalisation, these are not necessarily new phenomena, but have been part of a shared and common history of conquest and colonialism. The concepts of culture and identity are born out of and defined by those very conflicts.

However, debates by cultural theorists are generally conducted at fairly high levels of abstraction. What is missing from much of the current research is a detailed picture of how this process is working through the lives of the people involved.

Pure is a bore: the literature of identity

So much has been written on the subject of identity that it would be impossible to include everything. However it is possible to trace some general patterns chronologically. Like all such chronologies, it is messy. One development does not neatly follow another. Nevertheless, they can be organised into **four** broad categories:

- **bounded identities**: where people are believed to have a fixed individual identity with a theoretically unproblematic relationship to their culture and community. This is **the rationalist view** which derives from the 'Enlightenment' philosophers, principally John Locke

- **socially constructed identities**: following the works of Freud, Marx, Mead, linguists (eg Saussure) and the study of anthropology, this view recognises the powerful influence of others on our sense of identity

- **postmodern identities**: Postmodern thinkers eschew grand narratives of historical progress and see identity, culture and community as mutable, hybrid and diverse and open to conscious change

- **'storied' identities**. This is **the social psychologists' view**, which examines the notion of how collective memories are constructed, how predominant narratives gain a purchase on the individual's sense of self and, following Vygotsky, questions the distinction between individual and social identity. The construct is of a continuous, ever changing narrative for which Sarbin (1986) coined the phrase, 'storied lives'

Bounded Identities: The Lone Ranger: cherishing individual souls

Phinney and Rotheram's work (1987) is based on the 'Enlightenment' notion of fixed identity: a self-contained individual with a direct and largely un-complicated relationship to his/her culture. In attempting a definition they cite Shibutani and Kwan (1965) who describe an ethnic group as 'those who conceive of themselves as alike by virtue of a common ancestry, real or fictitious, and who are so regarded by others'. The conclusion they reach is that 'ethnicity includes group patterns of values, social customs, perceptions, behavioural roles, language usage, and rules of social interactions that group members share.'

In contrast, Wagley and Harris (1958) see ethnicity in relation to minority groups within the dominant culture and indicate that they are a subordinated group and characterised by traits held in low esteem by the dominant group. This eurocentric perspective is countered by Phinney and Rotheram (1987), who assert that not only minority groups, but also dominant groups in a country, for example White Americans, are ethnic groups. It is in such statements that we can perceive the mirroring of ideas. Phinney and Rotheram's (1987:12) conceptions are equally crude and stereotypical and they conclude in tautological fashion, that 'the term ethnic group is used to apply to any collection of people who call themselves an ethnic group and see themselves as sharing common attributes'.

This view underlines the problematic of the notions of identity. They are premised on the assumption that there is a clear cultural identity, which is in opposition to mainstream culture in consistent and unproblematic ways. Minority and mainstream groups both are depicted as sharing sets of common values and common language systems, each based on a common history of struggle. Each is hermetically sealed from the other.

In such a framework the ways minority and mainstream groups relate to each other are described in similarly unproblematic ways. Generally it is assumed that there are three types of contact (Padilla, 1980): assimilation, acculturation or accommodation and pluralism.

- **assimilation**: this is linked to the idea of a melting pot, where minority groups' values and identities are subsumed into the national majority culture

- **acculturation/accommodation**: this implies reaching some form of equilibrium after contact, conflict and adaptation

- **pluralism**: this assumes a valuing and recognition of the various customs, languages and traditions of different cultural groups. None are seen as being intrinsically superior or inferior

In their own time, these were useful categories for articulating a certain kind of strategic cultural politics. Use was made of such approaches in the formulation of multicultural and antiracist policies. They provided an analytical framework to support struggles for social justice. However, they were crude conceptualisations of complex social realities. They could capture neither the contradiction of their theory in such phenomena as mixed-race children, nor the complexity of personal histories or asymmetries of power and wealth both within and between so-called minority and mainstream cultures. Whilst there is little doubt that many subordinate groups do articulate a collective resistance to dominant values and approaches, they do not occur in such neatly defined ways. The danger is that there may be a residue of crude stereotyping in research that espouses a liberal view. For example Sue and Wagner (1973) suggested that Asians are a 'model minority' since they have an achievement orientation which coincides with the values of corporate America.

Phinney and Rotheram (1987) identify several components to ethnic identity:

- **ethnic awareness**: understanding of one's own and other groups

- **ethnic self identification**: the label used for one's own group

- **ethnic attitudes**: feelings about one's own and other groups

- **ethnic behaviours**: behaviour patterns specific to an ethnic group

Again, their arguments and definitions are generally drawn from positivistic research studies which rely upon a static conception of self and/or culture. They quote Erikson (1968), who 'outlines identity as an evolving sense of the individual that is expressed differently at each developmental period, but that is rooted in one's culture'. Frances Aboud (1987) takes as one of the criteria of ethnic self-identification 'that one's ethnicity must remain constant, that is, to be both consistent across changes in the context, and to be consistent over time'. The problem is that their research tools are ultimately blunt and crude instruments for investigating phenomena, which are so dynamic and sensitive.

As Aronowitz (1995:125) notes the positivist/rationalist approaches to identity derive from John Locke in *An Essay Concerning Human Understanding*. Locke himself thought that identity was an aspect of human consciousness which remained static and stable throughout the life of an individual:

> Thus it is always as to our present sensations and perceptions: and by everyone is to himself that which he calls self; it not being considered in this case, whether the same self be continued in the same or diverse substances. For, since consciousness always accompanies thinking, and thereby distinguishes himself from all other thinking things, in this alone consists personal identity, i.e. the sameness of a rational being; and as far as this consciousness may be extended backwards to any past action and thought, so far reaches the identity of the person; it is the same self now it was then; and it is by the same self with this present one that now reflects on it; that the action was done.

This connects to Locke's view that the mind is a *tabula rasa* upon which experience writes, making the link between culture and identity a simple one involving memory and experience. We see this view echoed by the empirical researchers whose work is described above. Although such ideas maintain a strong currency in educational circles, from the end of nineteenth century they were being challenged by such thinkers as Marx, Freud and, subsequently by Saussure and George Herbert Mead. In cultural terms the works of Vygotsky, Voloshinov and Bakhtin challenge the notion of the self contained persona at its very core.

Socially Constructed Identities: Legion live in us

Legion live in us
I think or feel and don't know
Who is thinking, feeling
I am merely the place
Where thinking or feeling is

I have more souls than one
There are more 'I's than myself
And still I exist
Indifferent to all
I silence them: I speak
Ricardo Reis (Heteronym for Fernando Pessoa)

As Hall (1991) notes, Marx unsettled such essentialist notions of identity:

> ... having lodged either the individual or the collective subject always within historical practices, we as individuals or as groups cannot be, and can never have been, the sole origin or authors of those practices.

He goes on to describe how this is further unsettled by Freud's 'investigations into the great continent of the unconscious'. Freud's concept of the super ego emphasises the social aspect of the construction of consciousness. This goes beyond Locke's notions of Laws which constrain individual action: those of 'God ... politic societies ... and the law of fashion or private censure.' For Locke the latter was more pressing. He states that 'no man escapes the punishment of their censure and dislike who offends against the fashion and opinion of the company he keeps', in short 'the condemnation of his own club. ' Locke's view mirrors the views of other philosophers of the Enlightenment such as Descartes, who proposed a dichotomy between the individual and society.

Freud produces a more complex theory in which views of significant people and important events are internalised and become important parts of an individual's psyche in ways the person is often only dimly aware. William James (1890) views the issue from another perspective, which is particularly relevant to the six individuals I talked to. It is the question of how individuals in complex societies negotiate different social networks. Since industrialisation, people have had to form into groups, which are not organic. It is often described as social frag-mentation. We often have little or no knowledge of the lives of people we work with and only a superficial understanding of their beliefs or values. Different groups may hold different values. Yet most people manage to belong to various networks and maintain an integrated identity.

> Properly speaking, a man has as many social selves as there are individuals who recognise him and carry an image of him in his mind ... He generally shows a different side of himself to each of these different groups ... from this there results what practically is a division of man into several selves; and this may be a discordant splitting ... or it may be a perfectly harmonious division of labour. (1890: 295)

It is not coincidental that James should choose to use an industrial metaphor to describe the phenomenon. In 1887 the German sociologist Ferdinand Tonnies (1971) analysed the effect upon the construction of individual identities of the rational approach to labour brought on by industrialisation. Comparing pre-industrial to post-industrial forms of social organisation in Europe, Tonnies made a distinction between two forms of social organisation, which he called *Gemeinschaft* and *Gesellschaft* and which have already been discussed.

Gemeinschaft refers to the kind of organisation prevalent during the Middle Ages: an organic community form of social solidarity, based on the fact that individuals shared a common history and common traditions. *Gesellschaft*, on the other hand, describes the rational relationships of industrial production, which is reflected in the contractual and instrumental relationships which form the bedrock of corporate society, Western industrial society. As Scollon and Scollon (1995:136) point out, this is a useful framework to analyse the different discourse systems prevalent in the West.

> One learns one's community, one's gender, and one's generational place in life processes through processes of socialisation or enculturation; that is one learns to be a member largely through naturally occurring non-institutional forms of learning. On the other hand, membership in goal directed discourse systems such as the academic discourse system or a corporate structure comes more often through formal education, training and institutionalised learning.

Since the end of the Middle Ages, Western individuals have had to negotiate a variety of different situations in which they have to build up multiple repertoires of identity, depending on the formality and the cultural framing of the context.

If both psychologists and philosophers had already unsettled essentialist notions of identity, linguists added a further set of complications. Experience is almost always mediated by symbolic forms. Humboldt and Saussure unsettled the Seventeenth Century rationalist view, espoused by Locke and the Port Royal Grammarians, that there was a direct correlation between language and experience. In fact they called into question the existence of an objective reality so beloved of the rationalists. They achieved this by noting that language was already there and we must enter a pre-existing discourse.

This raises the complex issue of how identity relates to culture and cultural memory. Language is one of the most sensitive indicators of our identity. Kenneth Goodman (1989) once remarked that, 'The way we speak is an emblem of who we are'. Both Vygotsky (1978, 1986) and Bakhtin (1981) inform us of the deeply social nature of the process of learning to mean. We internalise the symbolic forms we have learned in social situations and use those signs and symbols to construct our own independent meanings. As Bakhtin (1981) remarks, we do not learn our words from the dictionary but from other people's mouths, serving other people's intentions. It is from here that each speaker must take the word and make it their own.

Vygotsky (1978) makes a similar point. The symbols we learn in social contexts operate as both tools and sign. Although the signs are socially constructed, they are not immutable. We use them as tools for gaining an understanding of the world. For Vygotsky they are the cornerstones of memory. This in turn is the key element of the perpetuation of the phenomena of culture and identity.

The place of memory, both individual and collective, and how these two aspects relate to each other in the formation of personal identity has not, as yet, been well researched and even where it has been, the role of the emotions in it remains largely unexplored. Rosen (1996: 21) in his paper on 'Autobiographical Memory' revisits the work of Bartlett who:

> restored to the study of memory the context in which remembering is done. Where and when we remember affects how we remember. From what sociocultural location do we speak?

Bartlett's (1932) work involved asking people to retell a quite complex Native American tale. They brought different cultural and individual understandings to the process. That is, they made active interpretations. This led him to the view that:

> such actual traces of the past become interwoven with reconstructions of memory ... that memory functions by interpreting the past in order to give it meaning. Moreover, that interpretation and meaning, conscious and unconscious, emerged from the culture of the person telling the past. Rosen (1996: 22)

Any consideration of the way that individuals engage in the process of recreating their identities by continually reflecting upon their lived experience, is largely missing from current research. A point that Rosen (1996: 23) illuminates further when he says:

> This is memory structured somewhat like geological strata, each with its own characteristics and fractures but collaged together in conscious and unconscious manoeuvrings and therefore posing a hermeneutic challenge to anyone attempting to dissect and analyse it.

The problems of understanding and elucidating the notions of culture and identity are further exacerbated by the fact that they are both moving targets. Not only are they intimately interrelated, they are also in a process of constant flux and change. Moreover, it is not only through the symbolic forms that we achieve a sense of belonging, but in the day-to-day experience of our lived existence, which we frame within those symbolic forms. Because identity is essentially 'dialogic', it is not a static phenomenon.

As Berger and Luckman (1966:194) point out, identity evolves out of social processes, but it is not wholly determined by them.

> If one is mindful of this dialectic one can avoid the misleading notion of 'collective identities' without having recourse to the uniqueness, *sub specie aeternis*, of individual existence.

Identity is Janus faced. It not only indicates belonging, it also signals difference. It is not only how I describe myself, it is how others describe me. It is not only how my social group expect me to behave, it is also influenced by wider institutional expectations and constraints. It is not only of the moment and in a continuing stage of development, it also has a history and continuity beyond the boundaries of my own life. It is not only influenced by the intimate detail of my everyday life, it can be profoundly altered by events that take place far away and beyond my immediate control.

We are born into a pre-existing situation, which is not only where we learn our language and what is allowed and prohibited, what is valued and what is despised; we are born also into a site of struggle. Our sense of place is not merely geographical; it is also hierarchical. Our life chances are constrained or privileged by accident of birth. We learn through this not only 'where we are at', but also 'where we are from'. We learn about the power differential between ourselves and others. How we choose to negotiate these aspects is a key element in the construction of our identity.

Further eruptions came from those most directly involved in the study of the concepts: the anthropologists. As Lavie and Swedenburg point out (1996) early excursions in the field were imbued with the values of the colonial enterprise from which they sprang. Notions of high and low culture permeate the works.

> They had divided their world into the world 'Here' and the world 'Out There' ... The world Out There was 'scientific culture' ... It was colourful, but only in shades of dark. This world of tribes was governed by principles of kinship and recitation of genealogies to sustain them. It was a world of orality and tradition ... ..we were taught rows of books with titles such as *Anderman Islanders, Coming of Age in Samoa, The Lele of Kassai, Bedouin of the Negev*. Between the covers we found maps and photographs that fixed culture into a given, well-bounded place.

Such a tradition also informs the work of Eyesenck, Arthur Jensen (1967) and to a slightly lesser extent the work of Phinney. Lavie and Swedenburg trace the historical process of anthropology as a discipline. In their view it never was able to shake off its colonial antecedents. In its development they assert that it developed a pseudo-scientific aura in order to garner respectability in the academy:

> The scientific allegory served as a textual vehicle to rationalise and legitimate the US-European colonial hegemony of the West over the Rest.

This was because of the creation of the non-European 'other' who exists in the works as an objectified and racialised subject. The narrator becomes invisible in the cloak of pseudo-science.

> This was a process whereby essentialising the relation of a culture to a place positioned it beyond history and time. People were then abused as analytical tools for cross cultural comparison ... Thus the various alleged primitives were textually produced as hermetically sealed entities adequate unto themselves and explicable solely in terms of their own dynamics.

These are notions which are examined from a different angle in Geertz' *Works and Lives: The Anthropologist as Author* (1988), in which he views the texts as creative constructions. Through analysis of various ethnographers' methods and approaches, he unearths their underlying presumptions and values. Geertz' work has been seminal in questioning of the precepts and practices of ethnography in fundamental ways. Although *Local Knowledge* (1983) is, at one level, a comparative ethnography, Geertz uses the papers to explore underlying philosophical dilemmas. The very structure of exploring such things as art or common sense as 'cultural systems' allows him to consider in depth the problems of cross cultural understandings. He not only recontextualises ideas in complex and interrelated ways, he is also able to point ways out of the cul-de-sacs which seem to appear. In the process he is continually debunking essentialising myths about culture. At the same time he is careful not to ignore the immense variety of ways that human beings get things done. In *After the Fact* (1995: 23) he makes the following observation, which pinpoints the difficulties of writing about culture and identity:

> Coming to a country, any country ... is an experience palpable enough to be felt on the skin, and penetrant enough to be felt beneath it. The difficulty lies in articulating that experience, making it available to the common view. Impressionism produces an ethnographic telephone book. And thematicism ... produces historical opera.

Postmodern identities: a point in every direction is the same as no point at all

Throughout the '60s and '70s, in many fields of Western European academic life, fundamental understandings were being questioned. This was precipitated through the rise of social movements intent on social justice: eg antiracism, feminism and ecological movements. In the sphere of education there were struggles over the form and content of curricula. In the arts and humanities there was a grudging recognition that previously marginalised voices should be included. As Brah (1996) reflects, many of these movements were, in retrospect, somewhat naively optimistic in their approach. This should not diminish recognition of real achievements, however, notably in feminist thought and writing.

But the breakdown of the post-war liberal consensus in the late '70s and the rise of multinational companies, coupled with the explosion of highly sophisticated technological inventiveness, provoked a profound crisis. The phenomenon of globalisation has altered the geopolitical arena in fundamental ways. The collapse of directed economies in the former Soviet Union and Eastern bloc, the pervasiveness of market system, the success of the capitalist project in dismantling the institutions which traditionally protected the interests of the poor (at least in Western democracies) and the dynamism of what Giddens (1991) has called 'High modernity' have had profound effects on our notions of identity. Giddens observes that the construction of identity is increasingly a 'self reflexive project'. He notes that

> The self is not a passive entity, determined by external influences; in forging their self-identities, no matter how local their specific contexts of action, individuals contribute to and directly promote social influences that are global in their consequences and implications (1991:2)

Giddens talks of the dynamism and the pervasive nature of capitalism. He also talks about the disembodying mechanisms of the international standardisation of time and space, through mass media and the mechanical clock, which facilitate the notion of interconnected globalism. In such a context, it is no accident that identity has become a preoccupation of academics from many major disciplines. It is quite simply symptomatic of a crisis of identity. We can no longer rely upon the apparent certainties of the colonial era to define ourselves. Using the theoretical work of French structuralists and post-structuralists and the psycho-analytic theories of Lacan (1981), a more fluid, mobile, hybrid concept emerged. Responding to this changing context in the '70s a 'new' discipline of cultural studies was formed. It is within this field that some of the most exciting ideas on identity are being generated. But it is a young discipline and there are many conceptual problems to be faced. As with anthropology before it, there are dangers that its findings may unwittingly serve the power structures it seeks to undermine and criticise.

Cultural Studies is in itself a hybrid. The political struggles of the late sixties in the US and Europe had revealed that complex issues of cultural difference could not be dealt with through simple melting-pot analogies. People brought different histories and subtly different values and expectations to the struggles. As Avtar Brah (1996) points out, this could have debilitating consequences. Issues of personal history, class and gender lay submerged, but not resolved. Out of such dilemmas cultural studies was born. Stuart Hall in his paper, 'Cultural Studies and its Theoretical Legacies' charts the development of an area which 'has multiple discourses; it has a number of different histories ... .it include(s) many different kinds of work ... Although cultural studies as a project is open ended, it can't be simply pluralist in that way.'

For cultural theorists like Stuart Hall the notions of culture and identity have always involved and included issues of power. Using a variety of disciplines from politics to literary theory, attempts were made to unriddle the complexities of questions of culture and identity in this era of globalisation.

The changing global scenario provided a backdrop to the rise of cultural studies as an academic discipline. The social and political context was changing rapidly too. Following hard on the heels of sixties radicalism in the west was a vigorous response from the New Right, particularly the reformulation of political power structures. This was both manifestly ideological and strategic. In Britain it became known as Thatcherism. In Gramscian terms it was a hegemonic struggle, which culminated in the destruction, or reduction of the power, of major institutions (eg trade unions and welfare state) which protected the poor from the worst excesses of capitalism (now re-described as the 'market'). It was a cultural enterprise also. As Hall (1988) indicates, it was a strange amalgam of nineteenth century liberalism and traditional conservatism. It is testimony to Thatcher's skill and energy that she was able to articulate these two somewhat contradictory positions as a coherent philosophy with widespread popular appeal. Its appeal was due in part to the energy and sense of possibility it seemed to promise.

It was a major cultural shift in terms of values; a shift from the liberal to the libertarian. There was an appeal to individual greed and enterprise. This was welcomed by people who craved the wealth such individual endeavour promised. A major contradiction of Thatcher's approach lay in the fact that although there was an appeal to Victorian values in terms of culture and tradition, in the market place it did not matter 'where you were from'. If you had the energy and enterprise, you could succeed.

This era was characterised by enormous social, political and cultural change. This is particularly evident in the changes in the nature and scope of paid employment. These changes have been precipitated by shifts in social, political and economic power. Such changes have been intensified and sustained by the rapid development of sophisticated and pervasive technologies that are relatively cheap to produce. There was also a relaxation of the laws and constraints upon employers to have ethical obligations towards employees in terms of pay and conditions of employment. Borders of countries are now, in certain respects, more porous to the flow of goods and capital.

Moreover, we now have only one system of financial process. In such circumstances the nature and purpose of the nation state becomes more ambiguous. This in turn threatens the security of the idea of a national identity, hence, the very public debates about these issues in relation to the National Curriculum. Moreover, in cosmopolitan centres the sheer variety of personal histories which collide on a daily basis in the school, the workplace or the job centre unsettle easy and self-contained notions of community. We are cocooned in media technologies, often controlled by a handful of wealthy individuals and largely based in the US (Postman:1985, Fitzgerald: 1996, Shiller: 1996. Everard: 2000, Klein: 2000). At present we are only dimly aware of how we relate to each other through the new technologies, or how this process affects us and our social reality as it reflects back to us a highly selective surface of our world. In terms of identity we are only beginning to be aware of the influence of media and the fashion industry in framing important aspects of our daily lives. Giddens (1991:103-108) has pointed to the correlation between the rise of supermarkets and eating disorders such as bulimia and anorexia, which occur predominantly in young women. Klein (2000) examines the insidious intermarriage of media, fashion, big business and popular culture. It appears to generate a narcissism and a cult of celebrity, where advertisers and consumer oriented magazines bombard us with a range of desirable, 'branded' lifestyles and 'off the peg' identities.

Such a context takes the complexity of issues of culture and identity way beyond, the distinctions of *Gemeinschaft* and *Gesellschaft*. In educational terms this has precipitated a hegemonic struggle within the academy itself. The debates around 'the canon' and issues of 'political correctness are at the heart of the struggle. In her paper 'Multiculturalism and the politics of identity'. Joan W Scott (1995) states:

> What we are witnessing these days is not simply a set of internal debates about what schools and universities should teach and what students should learn. Journalists and politicians have joined the fray and added a new dimension to it. There is more at stake in their campaign against political correctness than a concern with excessive moralism, affirmative action and freedom of speech in the academy. Rather the entire enterprise has come under attack, and with it the aspect that intellectuals most value and that the humanities most typically represent: a critical, skeptical approach to all that society takes most for granted ... We are experiencing another phase of the ongoing Reagan-Bush revolution which, having packed the courts and privatised the economy now seeks to neutralise the space of ideological and cultural non-conformity by discrediting it. This is the context within which debates about political correctness and multi-culturalism have taken place. (1995: 3-4)

Although cultural studies has embraced this sense of complexity and many of its adherents, like Hall, have approached it from a leftist perspective, it has not as yet articulated any arena of political engagement. In fact one of the greatest achievements of the New Right is that they have obscured the areas of productive political engagement. The mechanisms of the market are not only pervasive, they appear uncontestable in quite persuasive ways. This poses a central problem in the question of identity. If the independent nuclear family is the basic unit, as was reiterated by the Thatcherite doctrine, if the workplace is disappearing as a place of organisation of struggle, then who do we relate to? If, as Klein (2000) insists, shopping malls are privatising what were once public spaces, where is there room for dissenting voices? If the curriculum is driven by content which leaves teachers little autonomy, where is their space for intellectual engagement and debate? How do we articulate not only 'where we are from,' but also 'where we are at' and relate those understandings to 'where we want to go'?

In terms of identity politics, the strength of the post-modern dimension of cultural studies is that it identifies and describes diversity and growth in the current climate. It recognises that the powerful consumerist forces have a deep effect on our notions of identity. Its weakness is that it does little to describe or articulate a counter-hegemonic strategy. The post-modern, sometimes breathless, celebration of diversity of some writers, whilst being exhilarating, can end up in the enemy camp. Its celebration of individual creativity disguises the pain of the current transformations in the lives of individuals. It often avoids uncomfortable issues of values in favour of an empty rhetoric of pluralism. As Harry Nilsson once intoned, 'a point in every direction is the same as no point at all'(1971). In this respect it is scarcely different from Fukayamas' 'end of history' argument. It mistakes defeats in hegemonic struggles for a permanent condition. Klein (2000) helps to explode the post-modern myth which portrays the predominance of radical and black urban style as a cultural victory, by revealing that it does little to alter the powerless condition of the majority of black youth in the US and that the production of the fashion items are sustainable only through the most ferocious and wilful exploitation of young women in such places as Indonesia and Mexico.

Sometimes this aspect is recognised by cultural theorists such as Hannerz (1992: 107), who states that: 'This, however, is no egalitarian global village. What we see now is quite firmly structured as an asymmetry of centre and periphery'.

Rattansi (1996:15) gives a critical overview of the 'post-modern frame' in which he looks at both its strengths and limitations as a critical structure. He acknowledges that 'there is much bold, innovative theorising the relevance of which for understanding racialisation and ethnic and national mobilisation is becoming apparent and is clearly in need of greater exploration and development'. He also values 'the greater interdisciplinarity in social sciences and humanities, since it creates 'opportunities which allows old questions to be considered in new ways and points up the manner in which racialisation and ethnic identifications may be taking new forms'.

In common with other commentators, he points to a central, 'performative contradiction' in Lyotard's founding text. In eschewing the 'grand narrative' approach to history, he is in effect creating his own meta-narrative: postmodernism itself. Rattansi critiques the postmodernist debate from several perspectives, not least because of the ethnocentrism of their arguments and the contradiction that although, for example Giddens, Baumann, Foucault and Derrida discuss the limitations of Enlightenment rationalism, they nonetheless use it as an analytical tool. He goes on to raise a number of epistemological issues. He asks:

- is there a contradiction involved in interrogating the nature, foundations and limits of Western modernity while still using some of its own logics and devices?

- to what extent does the questioning of modernity and its characteristic rationalities and epistemological foundations ... of many of the post-moderns as defined here collapse into a self-defeating relativism, an 'anything goes' nihilism and 'irrationalism'?

- how distinctive is the 'post-modern' frame as a form of theorisation separate from other modes of analysis current in the social sciences and humanities?

There are many benefits to the post-modern frame in terms of analysing the profound changes occurring in the conceptualisation of personal and social identities in the face of the relentless onslaught and global reach of contemporary capitalism; the pervasiveness of late capitalist production and distribution of goods, which are symbolically inflected; eg Levi jeans, Coca Cola, designer labels; their mediation through television, newspapers and advertising; the fact that they connect on an emotional level with our deepest dreams, desires and our sense of self and worth cannot be ignored (See Klein: 2000).

Further, post-modern frames help us to understand that notions of culture and identity are not fixed. This allows space for the creation of new cultural forms and expressions. Alongside this is the celebration of diversity, cross cultural invention and the possibilities for change and renewal. There has also been a blurring of genres and a loosening and interpenetration of academic disciplines. In short there is an implicit set of attitudes, which are culturally liberal.

However, post-modernism is by its nature not a coherent philosophy. Although there are common strands and similar areas of interest, there is lack of political strategy. Interesting ideas are generated but fundamental questions are often sidestepped. There are profound political questions to be asked. However, there is a general refusal to problematise issues in strategic or political terms. It avoids any critical response to the rational marketplace. It notes responses through cultural invention, but has lost sight of the battleground. It lacks any thoroughgoing political analysis of the role of mass media in the construction of identity. Fitzgerald (1996:112-113) sees this development as precipitating a fundamental change in the way we relate to each other:

> Groups whose place was formerly shaped by physical isolation ... are no longer segregated from larger social groupings. Aspects of identity that were once dependent on particular physical places and experiences available to them have been permanently altered by electronic media (Meyrowitz 1986:125) The concepts we use to define ourselves are influenced today by the media as a symbolic place

Because it does not accept the notion of 'grand narratives', there seems to be a lack of acknowledgement in post-modern theory that the individualism of the enlightenment, the essential self, remains the dominant narrative, purveyed through film, television and popular song. Klein (2000) demonstrates that this manipulative aspect is not an unconscious accident but is central to the thinking of executives in corporate America, who want to sell us Branded Lifestyles. She cites Levitt (1983) (see Klein 2000:116), who argues that 'the world's needs and desires have been irrevocably homogenized ... The global corporation operates with resolute constancy – at low relative cost – as if the entire world ... were a single entity; it sells the same thing in the same way everywhere ... Ancient differences in national tastes or modes of doing business disappear.' Klein also demonstrates how such channels as MTV, set up by American Express and Warner Communications, feed into this branded culture. The paradox is that underpinning this homogenisation is that the goods themselves promise choice and a rugged individualism. In reality this frequently degenerates into a debilitating narcissism, the cult of celebrity and a worship of glamour and fame for its own sake.

But such developments are not new in the US. Holstein and Gubrium (2000:5) trace the genesis of this isolated sense of self through the conditions of economic liberalism in the United States during the nineteenth century. It is a curious combination of independent self reliance and extreme conformism where

> ... individual agency combined with social feedback yielded a self which could move completely and confidently through the world both reflecting and responding to changing needs and circumstances ... The social self was remarkably versatile ... a mutable self was essential for complex and changing times

Here we experience an eerie sense of deja-vu. Similar arguments are being put forward today. It is not that writers like Stuart Hall, Paul Gilroy or Homi Bhabba do not have a sophisticated political grasp of the issues at hand. In recent years those issues have become fuzzy and unclear at the edges. Forms of dominance and oppression in the New World Order have become more complex and contradictory. This is why the issue of identity has become foregrounded in recent years. Where does the individual locate himself or herself within the new and rapidly changing alignments of political and economic power? How does that positioning relate to individual or collective histories? For illumination it is worth consulting the social psychologists who are currently exploring these facets.

Storied lives – new moves in social psychology

Missing from the much of the post-modern research is any systematic analysis of the influence of collective memory, the role of the media and affective aspects of social groupings on identity. There is an ethical vacuum at the heart of it, which depoliticises and weakens it as an approach. Kenneth Gergen (Shotter and Gergen 1989: 70-80) poses the question and reveals that he is willing to tackle issues of culture and power in a more explicit way. He asks: 'How are we to understand the origins of our vocabulary of self-understanding and the elaborated discourse into which it is woven?'

Taking this as his starting point he examines how certain discourses become privileged and how this, in turn affects our sense of self. He goes on to propose

> ... that in important measure the mental world becomes elaborated as various interest groups within a culture seek to warrant and justify their accounts of the world. In effect our vocabulary of self shifts as pragmatic exigencies dictate ... given the range of competing constructions, and sufficient stakes in the outcomes, there may be brisk competition over whose voice is honoured.

> Whose voice prevails in a sea of alternatives may be critical to the fate of the person, relationships, family life, community, and in a significant sense to the future of humankind.

A similar case could be made about the tendencies which in recent decades have come to underpin the ideals of the rational marketplace. Certain warranting discourses have always been predominant in the mass media. They have intensified since the collapse of communism in the Eastern bloc countries. In her paper, 'Values in a World in Transition' Maria de Lourdes Pintasiglio (1994) enumerates them as:

- competivity, which permeates all spheres of doing

- the centrality of the ego

- a confrontational mode of expression

- having rather than being

- a dilution of the frontier between what is and what appears to be

- the marginalisation of the weak, vulnerable and disorganised as some form of dysfunction in society

She goes on to argue:

> Overarching economy and politics, the archetype of the winner shapes aspirations and desires. The spiral of power and visibility, having the winner at the centre, conveys equally with it the marginalisation of the weak, vulnerable, disorganised. The freedom leading to the struggle towards democracy creates, paradoxically, social zones of dependency or of outcasts. Both mechanisms are driven by the motto of 'always more': more things, more freedom, greater speed. The empire of MORE, of quantity, annihilates judgment. In the name of freedom [there] ceases [to be] the evaluation of each new situation and its components.

These values underpin the prevalent discourses which inform our present world-view. The main source of power in the construction of dominant discourses lies with media institutions. Although they are not totally monolithic, they do set certain norms and values which have great influence. Media institutions certainly have a role in manipulating desire and manufacturing consent. There is a powerful connection between media and desirable material lifestyles. (see Klein (2000); Herman and Chesney (1997); Miller (1989); Wolf (1999)). They inform attitudes and habits of speech. Gergen (1989) even gives examples of how various schools of philosophy have constructed dominant narratives to safeguard their own position.

The problematic of identity is central to any resolution of these issues. How we orchestrate the competing and conflicting voices, how we find effective and collective ways of resisting the untrammelled wishes and desires of the powerful and how we attain any meaningful way of ensuring social and economic justice are dependent on how we resolve the dilemmas.

What recent work in social psychology has added to our understanding in this debate is the recognition of the central place of self-narrative in the process of identity formation. Through its emphasis on memory, there is a recognition of a continuous, yet changing sense of self. In many ways this has been a result of an ongoing debate within psychology concerning the nature of memory. Laura Otis charts this debate in her book *Organic Memory* (1994), where the argument for genetic memory, which rose rapidly in the 19th Century, has been steadily been losing ground to more social constructions. During the past hundred years the arguments for genetic or race memory have been used to justify the rise of nationalism since the mid nineteenth century. Many social psychologists now argue that our lives only achieve meaning as stories, life histories, self narratives or autobiographies (Holstein and Gubrium (2000): Rosenwald and Ochberg (1992); Sarbin and Schiebe (1983); Freeman (1993); Ezzy (1998); Randall (1995); Linde (1993) Carr: (1986)) and that the 'self is constituted in and through language usage, and more particularly through self narration' (Kerby 1991:125). We do have an active role in the construction of our identity, through the narration of self. However, we need to keep in mind the central paradox in this process, as it is illuminated by Suzanne Langer (1952:262):

> Virtual life as literature presents it is always a self-contained form, a unit of experience in which every element is organically related to every other, no matter how capricious and fragmentary these items are made to appear, that very caprice and fragmentation is a total effect which requires a perception of the whole history as a fabric of contributive events. Actual experience has no such closed form. It is usually ragged, unaccentuated ... But there is a normal and familiar condition which shapes experience into a distinct mode, under which it is apprehended and valued: that is memory ...

> Memory is the great organiser of consciousness. It simplifies consciousness and composes our perceptions into units of personal knowledge. It is the real maker of history ... to remember an event is to experience it again, but not in the same way as the first time ... most events are recalled as separate incidents, and can be dated only by being thought of in a causal order in which they are not 'possible' except at certain times.

This is why even conversations focusing on life stories have a defined and coherent narrative shape. Without such shaping and polishing they would be essentially meaningless. David Carr (1986) gives narrative a central place in our shaping of experience in general. Like Hayden White (1981), he argues that we don't experience reality as 'a mere sequence without beginning or end', that the whole process is a quest for meaning:

> what stories and histories represent is not purely physical events but human experiences, actions and sufferings, including the human activity of projecting meanings onto or finding meanings in physical and other events. (Carr: 1986:19-20)

This chimes with Barbara Hardy's famous assertion that 'narrative is a primary act of mind'; a primary way of organising experience. Such narrative shaping is culturally learned (cf Neisser:1982) and is not, as a strong reading of Hardy would suggest, a natural, biological impulse

The approach of the social psychologists is much closer to Bakhtin's (1981) dynamic, organic and elaborated view of the interelationship between language and individual consciousness. Throughout his work, Bakhtin, emphasises the social nature of consciousness. His work is a response to the structuralists and formalists, whose work deeply influences post-structuralist and postmodernist ways of thinking. It is a more sophisticated and less mechanistic view than that of Saussure, the founder of structuralism.

This is why I have based my own analyses of the life stories on a framework based in turn upon Bakhtin's view that individual consciousness results from the interplay of three elements or perspectives:

1. **Others for self**: How we are influenced by other people or dominant narratives

2. **Self for others**: How we present ourselves to the the world. Our social persona

3. **Self for self**: How we view ourselves from the inside

One of the main strengths of using such a framework to analyse the narratives is that it makes the process of integrating the competing forces and of identity construction clear. If memory is mainly rendered, maintained and reworked through culturally learned narratives as some researchers (Schank and Abelson: 1995; Barsalou: 1988; Barclay: 1986, 1996; Barclay and Smith: 1992; Gergen and Gergen: 1988) argue then the framework described above has the potential to make the process visible, since it reveals the relationship between the social and the individual in the six narratives in this book. In fact it is premised on the understanding that the narratives are a product of complex inner dialogues where the different, often conflicting discourses, are orchestrated into a coherent sense of self. As Rubin reports:

> The narrative structure of autobiographical memory appears indistinguishable from the narrative structure of other social communication, and the recall of autobiographical memories is usually a social act (Hirst and Manier: 1996) that can define a social group (Bruner and Feldman: 1996) ... An especially interesting social situation is that of parents teaching their children narrative conventions used in telling and therefore having autobiographical memories ... For example Fivush et al 1996) observed longitudinal changes in parent/

child recall of unique family events such as trips taken during vacations (Rubin, 1996).

Such research confirms Bakhtin's assertion that 'I realise myself initially through others; from them I receive words, forms, tonalities for the formation of my initial idea of myself.' It is interesting to note that in Rubin's (1996) review of recent research studies on the biological and physiological dimensions of memory, including studies of the brain remain at best inconclusive.

Conclusion

In summary, the debate concerning the self rages in many academic areas, each with a different approach. In this chapter I have tried to isolate and analyse four main approaches which affect our work as teachers.

- **The enlightenment concept** of a self-contained individual acknowledged that we experience reality in a unique body which has a certain degree of continuity. This released people from the notion of a natural order of things. It undermined the oppressive nature of the philosophy of the Great Chain of Being (ie that we occupy a preordained position in the world), with its deeply hierarchical and entrenched view of power. *What it didn't account for was the social nature of identity*

- **The social models of identity** attempted to address the problems of the nature of identity and in many cases overestimated its social nature. The more negative forces *worked against a recognition of the individual's ethical responsibility for their own actions or their part in the construction of their own identity*

- **Postmodernist models of identity**: This view posits a creative, and constantly changing, view of self as we respond to rapid social and technological changes. However, *it underestimates the force of cultural memory, and the need for a coherent and continuous self*

- **Social psychologists** have posited theories of 'storied' identities, by which we make sense of our past life and the present by constantly updating our narratives to produce coherent narratives of self

Most current empirical research in the area of identity concentrates on single groups and often is directed at youth culture. Much has been written about rap and dance music. These are adolescents in the early stages of identity formation and where a sense of belonging is frequently in a volatile state of flux and confusion. Very little work has been done with first generation British-born adults. Moreover, what is missing from the research is any systematic cross cultural study that seeks to analyse how these complex constructions of identity are achieved in first generation British-born people who have reached adulthood and have integrated the various competing forces acting upon them in a way which is rare in adolescents. In Part Three I put some flesh on the bones by analysing the life stories of people who are experiencing this process at first hand. However, first I must say something about the problems involved in researching identity in empirical ways.

4

Honour and Authenticity:
analysing life histories

Full accountability, of course, like the dream of self knowledge, is elusive
James Clifford 1997:11

Introduction

As the last chapter showed, notions of culture, community and identity are complex, multifaceted, often contradictory and difficult to describe. And the ways in which research is conducted are becoming increasingly problematic. This is particularly true of ethnographic studies which seek to provide a platform for dispossessed and marginalised groups: members of the community whose voices are sidelined or diminished through powerful institutions such as the media. Often works in the field of ethnography try to present a collaborative approach. My research project follows such a pattern. Collaboration has a cosy ring about it. But like its travelling companion, partnership, it has some troubling aspects. Both notions raise deeper and more aggravating questions about the aspects of power which tend to lie, unexamined, at the heart of the research.

Some of the major issues in conducting ethnographic research are:

- Who owns the research?

- How can the work be conducted ethically?

- How far can it be truly collaborative given the in-built discrepancies in the power relationships?

- How can we ensure that our joint efforts compose as authentic a picture as possible of such a complex social reality which links history, culture, identity through the mind and memory maps of individual consciousness?

As Clifford Geertz (1995:2) put it:

> When everything changes from the small and immediate to the vast
> and abstract – the object of study, the world immediately around it, the
> student, the world immediately around him, and the wider world
> around them both – there seems to be no place to stand so as to locate
> just what has altered and how.

It is clear that such research must be fully contextualised. So before examining
the methodological issues, here is a brief outline of its genesis.

The story of the research

The roots of this book are deeply embedded in my personal history and the complexity of my own identity, and the book is also connected with my professional
work as a teacher and teacher educator. But I didn't perceive it as such at the start
of this research. As with the participants and their stories, it is only with
hindsight that I can make a coherent narrative of that sequence of events.

A more immediate and chance event determined the work's direction and progress. I had been invited to run a workshop at Middlesex University on the place
of multilingualism in the 1995 version of the National Curriculum, following the
Dearing review. At the end of the session one of my ex-students came up to express interest in my talk and told me that, if I wished to conduct further research
in the area, I should contact her to interview her about her own experience of
being bilingual. She became the first participant in my project.

Conduct of the interviews

I took up 'Aliki's' offer to interview her in April 1996 but did not complete the
final interview with 'Michael' until March 2000. During those years my
theoretical understandings gradually became more sophisticated and the interviews assumed a comfortable pattern. A productive rhythm for them emerged
and I was able to discover certain enabling questions and approaches.

But there are other dimensions to the difficulties I faced. In the course of collect-
ing life stories from people in Britain from so-called ethnic minority groups (a
problematic term) I encountered several dilemmas. Some are ethical. Others are
pragmatic. Most of my 'collaborators' grew up in Britain and have achieved
success within the state education system. All possess at least a first degree. My
original intention was to discover how their success linked to their experience of
schooling. I wanted them to be able to set the agenda. This is why I followed the
phenomenographic approaches recommended by Hazel Francis (1993: 70).

> The aim of the interview is to have the interviewee thematise the
> phenomenon of interest and make the thinking explicit (1993:70)

The risky nature of this approach calls for the researcher to adopt a more spontaneous and conversational attitude. Although, superficially, this seems less rigorous than the formal structured interview, it has yielded rich results and has forced me to reappraise the original direction of the study in fundamental ways.

For example, I noticed that as my interventions became less sure and articulate, the interviewees become more sure and fluent. I also realised that, through my reading and previous experience in this area, I have access to information the interviewees do not. They on the other hand have a lifetime of lived experience and deep and often painful reflections upon what it means to negotiate complex networks of people and signs, within layers of history and, sometimes conflicting, traditions. Where we connect is where we are trying to unriddle these complex processes of cultural change we are living through. What concerns me here is how we, as researchers, can engage in a fruitful dialogue in which we neither overplay our knowledge and stifle the conversation nor underplay it and miss opportunities to widen the parameters of the picture. In short, how can such encounters be as authentic and honourable as possible?

Some of the problems we face lie in the methodological tools we use. It is not they are no longer fit for purpose. But we need to examine some of the purposes they have been put to in the past and adapt the tools to our own uses. James Clifford (1988) offers a clear-eyed critique of certain ethnographic methods and approaches. For me, the tools themselves are not neutral or innocent but have accrued notions of investigating culture which derive from their colonial heritage. So they must be handled with care.

Partial truths and serious fictions: an outline of the methodological problems of analysing life histories

Even the seemingly most individualistic interpretations of the world are never truly and thoroughly individual and unique. On the other hand, the 'deep structures' of culture only exist as people act and behave in accordance with those structures or make use of them in their activity. Indeed the line of inquiry known as cultural studies is perhaps best described as a crossroads, the arrival, through the application of concepts from various disciplines, at a shared view that it is useful to study cultural distinctions and meaning systems from the point of view of both actors and structures. Alasuutari (1995:35)

Let me state at the outset that notions of cultural purity are of little interest to me. Issues of culture and identity are messy and puzzling phenomena. Constantly in motion, they are difficult to pin down and describe. There are no conceptual nets fine enough to capture such complexity. Many of the theoretical tools we have at our disposal are crude and blunt. But if we apply them with sensitivity and are candid about how we apply them, we can build up helpful and distinctive pictures of the period of profound social and cultural change we are currently experiencing. I also think we need to be candid about the conduct and context of the research. A 'warts and all' approach which includes an admission of the messiness of the process can help to do justice to the complexity of the phenomena we are describing. We are an important part of the research and it is much more useful if we do not cover our tracks. Those tracks are central to the story.

Being here: Research as a problem of writing

All research is our account of 'what is going on around here/over there' or 'what was going on around here/over there'; our effort to get to grips with a phenomenon, which fascinates, irritates or obsesses us – or sometimes all three simultaneously. It is generally a problem of writing. Italo Calvino (1996) gets to the heart of this matter. In his final and incomplete book *Six Memos for the Next Millennium*, he points to a fundamental dilemma of being human, which illuminates the central problem we face in conducting our research:

> Mercury and Vulcan represent the two inseparable and complementary functions of life: Mercury represents *syntony*, or participation in the world around us; Vulcan, focalisation or constructive concentration. Mercury and Vulcan are both sons of Jupiter, whose realm is that of consciousness, individual and social ... Mercury and Vulcan are both contrasting and complementary. I have begun to understand something ... about myself and how I would like to be; about how I write and how I would like to write and how I may be able to write. Vulcan's concentration and craftsmanship are needed to record Mercury's adventures and metamorphoses. Mercury's swiftness and mobility are needed to make Vulcan's endless labours become bearers of meaning. Calvino (1996:53)

This is the dilemma facing all researchers as they choose their research tools and write their interpretations. A healthy balance is required because if we veer too far into *syntony*, we could end up with 'undifferentiated continuity' of living spontaneously. On the other hand the extreme of *focalisation* can end in 'egocentric isolation'.

I quote this at length because I think that consideration of these two aspects is helpful to us in the choice of research tools. It also helps in bridging the somewhat false dichotomy between quantitative and qualitative approaches. As Alasuutari (1995:2) points out, ' ... the real gist of cultural studies is to make use of all useful theories and methods in order to gain insights about the phenomena one studies. By avoiding the accusation of being eclectic, one may end up theoretically correct but intellectually boring ... Cultural studies methodology has often been described by the concept of bricolage: one is pragmatic and strategic in choosing and applying different methods and practices'. It is not about seeking out absolute truths but contributing interesting viewpoints and insights to an ongoing public discourse. Therefore we need to be clear about when quantitative and qualitative methods are useful in unriddling a given phenomenon.

Life History? Whose story?: the strengths and limitation of life histories

My approach was never going to be strictly ethnographic, even though each of the interviewees has strong links with a well-defined community group. If it is ethnography, it is ethnography in a comparative sense. I am probing ethnographic issues such as culture, community and identity, through the life histories of individuals. From their stories we gain a great deal of information on the families and communities which share sets of assumptions and values which are described, sometimes critically, by the individuals themselves.

As with ethnography, there are problems and dilemmas involved in making sense of the stories themselves. To begin with it is worth examining the obvious advantages to this approach.

> Life history and narrative offer exciting alternatives for connecting lives and stories of individuals to the understanding of larger human and social phenomena.

> A life history is composed of self-referential stories through which the author-narrator constructs the identity and point(s) of view of a unique individual historically situated in culture, time and place. (Hatch and Wisniewski 1995)

It is also a critical approach. As Goodson (1995) states:

> These approaches offer a serious opportunity to question the implicit racial, class or gender biases which existing modes of enquiry mystify whilst reproducing (See Giroux, 1991). Storying and narratology are genres that move researchers beyond (or to the side of) the main paradigms of inquiry with their numbers, variables, psychometrics, psychologisms, and decontextualised theories.

But Goodson warns us to be vigilant of 'the tyranny of the local' (Harvey: 1989) and cites Denzin's timely advice that:

> The cultural logics of late capitalism valorize the life story, autobiographical document because they keep the myth of the autonomous

individual alive. The logic of the confession reifies the concept of self and turns it into a cultural commodity ... The recent return of the life story celebrates the importance of the individual under the conservative politics of late postmodernism. (1992: 8-9)

This is one of the major problems of postmodernist theorising. The lack of a grand narrative or even a clearly delineated set of common political and social aims or values can put you in the camp of the people who have come to dispossess you.

As with the problem of 'informants' in ethnographic research we must be cautious about generalisation we can make from these sources. In their paper, 'Life history and narrative: Questions, issues and exemplary works', Hatch and Wiseniewski (1995) asked narrative and life history scholars to comment on their own work. From their analysis, they raised a number of interesting issues and perspectives,

- life histories as a type of narrative

- stories as ways of knowing

- life histories as individual, contextually situated stories

- how life histories are distinguished from other types of qualitative research by their:

    focus on the individual
    the personal nature of the research process
    the emphasis on subjectivity

In common with ethnography, life history is a genre developed through a Western/European literary tradition. It is not natural and unselfconscious, despite its personal form. In the earliest writings, lives of public figures were formal and exterior, revealing little of the individual's private and personal thoughts. As Bakhtin (1981) notes the ancient Greeks did not use the form extensively. It was only during the later Graeco-Roman period that autobiography developed, and even then Ovid, Horace and Juvenal tended to treat the form ironically. Confessional literature only really began with St Augustine. So the model we have internalised stems directly from him. Much of the commentary on the development of the genre of life history has been in the field of literary criticism. It is closely related to the autobiographical novel, or 'spiritual autobiography' of such writers as Defoe.

Eighteenth century excursions into this form bear all the hallmarks of the Enlightenment conception of a human being. Karl Weintraub (1978) in his book the *Value of the Individual* saw the genre emerging in parallel to Western culture's celebration of the individual. This point is endorsed by Buckley (1984), who sees it as the development of the subjective impulse in literature since 1800. Rousseau's philosophical autobiography attempts to move in two directions at once:

- tracing a historical succession of experiences, which formed his character

- attempting to discover in the same experiences his transcendent 'natural' soul

Spengmann (1980) traces the evolution of the autobiographical form and notes that:

> ... we must view autobiography historically, not as one thing that writers have done again and again, but as a pattern described by various things they have done in response to changing ideas about the nature of the self, the ways in which the self may be apprehended, and the proper ways of reporting those apprehensions.

He summarises the historical evolution of the genre, from Augustine's Confessions onwards, and identifies four categories which have developed:

- **Historical self explanation** – 'To say more than human things with a human voice' (Spengmann, 1980): originating in the Renaissance and enlightenment period. eg Dante, Bunyan and Defoe. Linked to the rise of individualism.

- **Philosophical self-scrutiny** – 'To say human things with a more than human voice' (Spengmann, 1980): which developed in the later 18th century. eg Rousseau. The Enlightenment dichotomy of mind and spirit, it represents a critique of the society of the time.

- **Poetic self expression** and

- **Poetic self invention** – 'To speak humanly from the height or the depth of human things' (Spengmann, 1980) which developed through the 19th century. eg Dickens' several past and present selves are worked through the characters in his novels in a poetic form.

Spengmann points out that these developments were cumulative and have added to the richness of the genre, also that they reflect the local and current preoccupations. He makes the interesting point that Augustine's work identified problems in the conduct of autobiographical writing, problems only too familiar to me, as I attempt to unriddle the interviews. They are:

How can the self know itself? Can it be achieved:

- by surveying in the memory its completed past actions from an unmoving point above them

- by moving inquisitively through its own memories and ideas to some conclusion about them

- by performing a sequence of symbolic actions, through which the ineffable self can be realised?

Such problems are closely linked to the identified categories: historical, philosophical and poetic.

Olney (1972) refers to autobiography as 'metaphors of self'. He refers to Heraclitus' view that every cosmology begins in self knowledge. This chimes in with Gramsci's view (cited in Said, 1978:25) that:

> The starting point of critical elaboration is the consciousness of what one really is, and is knowing thyself as a product of the historical process to date, which has deposited in you an infinity of traces, without leaving an inventory ... therefore it is imperative at the outset to compile such an inventory.

There is a central paradox in autobiography in that: 'Without a self one cannot write about it, but whatever one writes will be about the self it constructs' (Olney:1972).

Because 'our actions write an autobiography, which is of course a fiction' (Regis Michaud), the particular interpretation we make tells us about the self which is being described. Tagore (1917: 3) underlines the creative process involved in autobiography:

> ... it is almost a truism to say the world is what we perceive it to be. We imagine that our mind is a mirror, that is more or less accurately reflecting what is happening outside us. On the contrary, our mind is the principal element of creation. The world, while I am creating it, is being incessantly created for myself in time and space.

Michel Leiris (1946:13) raises an interesting point about the purposes of writing autobiography, which is essentially confessional literature:

> What I did not realise was that at the source of all introspection is a predilection for self contemplation, and that every confession contains a desire to be absolved ... .To expose myself to others ... was an attempt to seduce my public into being indulgent, to limit the scandal by giving it an aesthetic form.

For most commentators autobiography was seen as a sub-category of biography and it is only since the 1960s that interest has focused on the text itself. It is now a complex and pervasive genre. Rosen (1998) identifies a wide range of manifestations and variants. He subdivides types of autobiographical discourse into three sections: written autobiographical acts, spoken autobiographical acts and types of approaches to the study of autobiography.

1. Written autobiographical acts

    • the major literary work

    • memoirs

    • diaries, journals, collections of letters

    • embedded autobiographical writings

    • autobiography in canonical literary genres eg:

        • autobiographical fiction

        • autobiographical poetry

        • autobiographical drama eg Wesker

    • autobiographical travellers' tales

    • some forms of journalism eg Tom Wolfe

    • the curriculum vitae

2. Spoken autobiographical acts

    • attempts to speak a life eg the work of Studs Terkel

    • framed episodes

    • oral personal story on demand or under duress, eg police interview

3. Types of approaches to the study of autobiography

    • literary criticism/theory

    • the ethnographic tradition

    • the psychological tradition

    • social and cultural history

Life histories are not exclusively autobiographical texts, although they contain strong autobiographical elements and clearly individuals employ most or all of the narrative conventions analysed above. However, interviews add another dimension and make the process a dialogue rather than a monologue. Different sets of problems emerge. Equally, different sets of possibilities also become apparent.

Hatch and Wisniewski (1995) identified other issues connected with life history or narrative work, those I raised at the beginning of this chapter: Who owns the stories? How authentic is the representation? Whose voice is privileged? How do we balance individual stories and the social context? What criteria do we have for judging quality?

The question of ownership is a difficult one. As Paul Munro notes (cited in Hatch and Wisniewski (1995: 119)

> ... a central tension in life history is the desire to 'give voice' without producing the very unequal power relations we are critiquing. How does the notion of 'giving' voice actually underscore our perceptions of those with whom we conduct our research.

How collaborative is this act?

> How do we carry out a collaborative, mutually beneficial project while working through issues of knowledge, power, control and privacy: how as a researcher, can I contribute as much as the subject of my work is giving?

These questions were uppermost in my mind as I conducted the interviews, transcribed the tapes and wrote up my version of events. The slow, laborious process of transcription, revealed a different dimension to the stories of the transitions. What comes forward very strongly is the pain of the process. Linda Tillman Rogers (in Hatch and Wisniewski: 1995: 119) charges researchers with the responsibility for that pain.

> Reflection is a powerful tool; the researcher, simply by being there causes a form of knowing an 'event' differently. Many people survive or, indeed, endure by deliberately not being aware of all the complexities and dangers ... The reflective act does make clear the nature of the problem, but existential reality – what we really do and really know— is often not comforting ...

Life histories, if they are to have any depth, need to enter this unknown and potentially dangerous territory. Although we need to tread sensitively and carefully, there may be a way of reading the oversensitivity of the statement above as condescending, as if the interviewee has neither the strength nor the desire to discuss difficult issues and dilemmas. Handled with sensitivity, making sense of difficult aspects of their own life may be the richest reward for the individuals themselves. This is the point which tests all our integrity not only as researchers but also as human beings.

Problems of validity and reliability

Issues of sensitivity are important, but work on self-narrative always encounters the more common problem of validity and reliability. Therefore I need to state my position on this matter before proceeding with the analysis. As Langer (1952) and Carr (1986) argue, memory of any event is always something of a fiction.

For my information I relied upon interviews in which first generation British born individuals narrated what they saw as key episodes in their lives related to issues of identity and schooling. This poses methodological and epistemological problems. The representational crisis and legitimation crisis in researching in the social sciences has been thoroughly explored by such researchers as Denzin.(1991,1993,1997); Derrida (1978); Lather (1993); Atkinson (1992); Lincoln and Guba (1985). This is not merely a methodological problem; it is a fundamental epistemological problem which questions the very nature of know-ledge itself. If, as some writers suggest, everything constitutes a text, which is then open to numerous interpretations, how are we to make any kind of useful sense of our own and our collaborators' reflections and observations? Are there an infinite number of possible interpretations? Or are they limited by the mean-ings articulated by the writer? Denzin (1997:9) locates the central issue when he states, 'If validity is gone, values and politics, not objective epistemology, govern science'.

Denzin not only analyses the crises in legitimation and representation, he locates them in the historical context of ethnographic investigation in the West (Denzin: 1997: 16-19), which closely parallels the history of the concept of identity out-lined in the previous chapter

- **The traditional period**: early 1900s to end of World War Two: Following Rosaldo (1989) Denzin states that 'Qualitative researches wrote 'objective' colonialising accounts of field experiences reflective of positivistic social science paradigm. They were concerned with offering valid, reliable and objective interpretations in their writing. The other who was studied was alien, foreign and strange'

- **Modernist phase**: (1945-1970s): Builds on 'the canonical works from the traditional period' but attempts to formalise 'factist' approaches (Glaser and Strauss: 1967). 'The modernist ethnographer and sociological participant observer attempted rigorous, qualitative studies of important social pro-cesses ... clothed in the language of positivist and post positivist discourse'

- **Blurred genres**: (1970-1986): More pluralistic, interpretive perspectives (See Geertz: 1973:1983 and Alasuutari: 1995). Researchers using a full range of paradigms, methods and strategies to 'unriddle' (Alasuutari: 1995) the situation being observed

- **Crisis of representation: 1986 onwards**: Several writers articulated this moment (Marcus and Fisher, 1986; Turner and Bruner.1986; Clifford and Marcus, 1986; Geertz, 1988; Clifford, 1988)

The problem is not the traditional one of validity, since the notion of objectivity has been called into question. It is rather one of giving a clear, contextualised and recognisable picture of what is being analysed and at the same time being candid about the subjectivities which exist in the final text. This allows the reader to read it critically from their own standpoint in the light of their own histories and experience.

However, personal accounts of experience differ in so much as memory is considered to be notoriously unreliable in terms of accuracy of recall. People forget chronological details, invent reported dialogue and maliciously distort events and actions. Often they will present a rather idealised and favourable version of themselves. Even self-deprecation can be seen as an engaging narrative device, which seeks to portray the speaker as modest. There is no harm in this – we become the hero (or even anti-hero) of our own stories. However, it could be argued that this invalidates research of self narratives. It could be justifiably asserted that this will not give an accurate picture of the person telling the story. As Gide (1955) says in his autobiography:

> The most annoying thing is to have to present as successive steps, states that occurred in confusing simultaneity. I am dialogical; everything in me fights and contradicts itself. Memoirs are only half sincere, no matter how great the concern to tell the truth: everything is always more complicated than one supposes. Perhaps we get closer to the truth in the novel (1955: 245).

> My memory of a place does not often fail, but it confuses the dates. I am lost if I confine myself to chronology (1955:22).

By way of reply to those who seek objective truth in autobiography, I need to make several observations. Firstly there is the issue of 'good faith'. I am well aware that in the space of a short dialogue I am not going to have anything resembling a complete life story. It will be a selection of a limited part. Consequently, the major issue in conducting this kind of research is establishing veracity or validity. In such intrinsically subjective territory, this is a minefield. Nevertheless, we are able to recognise internal consistency of the narratives.

Secondly, the narratives are also constrained by the nature of the encounter. My own interests, which I made clear to all participants at the outset obviously did much to frame their responses. Allied to this there is also the consideration of audience, which is common to all utterances, whatever the level of formality. The fact that most participants knew me already will also have affected the stories. Moreover, the narratives are co-authored, in that we both shaped the narrative through the course of the conversation. No one had any real idea of the outcome as we progressed through it. Although this act of shaping is spontaneous and improvised, it is not random.

There are positive aspects to working with people I already know. I can attest to their trustworthiness and ethical outlook. The people I selected are unlikely to deliberately mislead me on any major issue. I took what they said in good faith and gave them some degree of editorial control by returning the full tapes so they could amend, add or ask me to omit details which they felt were inappropriate, damaging or potentially embarrassing. I do not share the mass media's current enthusiasm for conflating truth with voyeuristic entertainment.

In terms of recall there are constraints in terms of selecting episodes and rendering experience through narrative. My view is that the constraints of time can actually sharpen the selection process so that the most powerful or significant memories will come forward in the narratives. Listening to the narratives in detail and transcribing them, I was impressed by how much the individuals were able to share in such a short time. This concentrated potency is the underrated characteristic of the narrative genre as a resource for research. The narratives are richly contextualised and many layered. They are also holistic, connecting all aspects of experience: physical, cognitive and affective into an accessible framework. They are densely packed with information.

There is still the question of accuracy however. Neisser (1982) illuminated the problem in an original way when he coined the term 'repisodic memory'. At the time he was analysing testimony on the Watergate scandal. He was particularly interested in John Dean's testimony. Dean acquired some celebrity for his apparently acute memory. In fact he was known as the 'human tape recorder' since his recall of dialogue appeared to be exact. But on close analysis, the tapes revealed that his version of events was inaccurate in terms of both the words used and their gist. Neisser found that, although reconstruction played an important part in his account, he often compressed several similar encounters or events into a single dramatic episode. He was truthful, but not accurate. It is not uncommon for lawyers to do the reverse, ie compile narratives which though factually accurate are neither faithful nor true representations. However, when we are recalling events from various periods of our own lives we, like John Dean, tend to use 'repisodic' memory.

Lastly and perhaps most importantly, I realise that I am working with texts and that my task is an interpretive one. I am seeking pattern and illumination, not irrefutable abstract 'truth'. As Freeman (1993:30) points out:

> ..life historical knowledge, in so far as it is predicated on understanding rather than retrieval of isolated facts, should never – indeed can never – be judged according to its correspondence with what was ... Furthermore when considering autobiographical texts, texts for which the interpreter is at once reader and writer, subject and object, it becomes clear that the meanings one arrives at are as much *made as found*, the process of autobiographical reflection: a new relationship is being created between the past and the present, a new poetic configuration, designed to give greater form to one's previous and present experience. The text of self is thus being rewritten.

For such reasons I am much more interested in other criteria for the narratives such as apparency and verisimilitude (Van Maanen:1988), transferability (Lincoln and Guba: 1985) an explanatory, invitational quality, authenticity, adequacy and plausibility (Clandenin and Connelly: 2000).

Reissman (1983:64) articulates this position well when she states:

> The historical truth of an individual's accounts is not the primary issue. Narrativisation *assumes* point of view ... Narratives are laced with social discourses and power relations over time ... *Trustworthiness not 'truth'* is the key semantic difference. The latter assumes an objective reality, whereas the former moves the process into the social world. (my emphases)

Reissman's (1983) position, like Bakhtin's and Vygotsky's, assumes that human consciousness is a deeply social creation. She suggests that we seek illumination of this complex phenomenon in our research and do not limit our investigation to the construction of narrow paradigms which exclude 'point of view'. She goes on to suggest four criteria for approaching validity in narrative inquiry:

persuasiveness: is it reasonable and convincing?
correspondence: can it be taken back to the researched?
coherence: does it provide a coherent picture of the situation described?
pragmatic: to what extent can we act upon it?

I think there are ways forward with research of this kind which can avoid being recklessly risky or condescendingly anodyne. I argue that we need to establish relationships with the individuals which encourage mutual trust and respect. To my mind it is not about method but about the need of us as interviewers to put ourselves as much in a position of risk as our 'subjects'.

Honour and authenticity: context and conduct of the interviews

Aliki is in her late twenties. Her heritage is Greek Cypriot. She was born and brought up in Hackney and is now Head of Drama at a Secondary School. To set the context more fully, I need to give a few background details to the interview. Firstly, I knew Aliki reasonably well before I interviewed her as she was a student in my educational drama classes at Middlesex University. I had developed an interest in issues of culture and identity over many years and Aliki knew this and obviously knew something of my position on the main debates in the area. I feel that these factors are important for any reader to know in order to make sense of what follows.

When I began the work I was aware of some of the dilemmas involved and I wished our conversations to be as informal as possible, but also I had questions and hunches of my own which I wished to explore. I sent Aliki a copy of questions which I wished to explore. But I wanted her to feel free to take up any angle she wanted, so the conduct of the interview was unstructured, and I tried to ask open questions.

I already had experience of unstructured ways of investigating issues from my work in educational drama. For example I was not afraid to wait for replies. I knew that this often led to fruitful and thoughtful responses in drama sessions. Complex ideas often need careful thought.

My first question elicited a response that, I can see with hindsight, changed the course of the study. After a false start I reformulated the question I had really wanted to ask

> C: ... What I really wanted to do is to ask you to travel back in time to your first glimmerings of memories. What are they? ... You know ... to do with culture and language and identity. What are your first remembrances?

After a long pause, lasting more than twenty seconds, she gave an unexpected answer

> A: ... mm ... very first? ... I think ... I know what's happening here. Because I'm thinking, 'Oh, is that because of my sister?' Cos you know I've got a sister who has cerebral palsy ... erm ... and I think this is something, I'm still coming to terms with. Trying to work out in my own head, years and years later. When I think of my behaviour or how I was as a child, I either put it in terms of culture ... Right? That was because I was of that culture and I didn't feel that I fitted into that culture. Or that's because we felt ... *I* felt uncomfortable not being part of a normal family. Because I had a sister who could not walk. So, we didn't do normal family things. So I think you're

going to have a problem with me because some things relate to my ... in terms of my language and ... erm ... ability and confidence and self image and some of it relates exclusively to my culture, but it's just trying to identify which ones do, but ...

This radically altered my understanding of the nature of identity. At that time I saw it as neither fixed nor rigid but as a set of repertoires. However, I had still underestimated the kinds of ambivalences which stem from conflicts within the layers of Aliki's personal identity. I was not until I started to transcribe the materials that I began to understand the extent of the pain involved in those processes.

My stumbling line of questioning also produced several insights for me which I now see changed the course of the research in fundamental ways. As I transcribed and analysed my interview with Aliki, I began to trace the genesis of my approach. My 'technique' was not conscious or deliberate but originated from my own work in educational drama and as a practising teacher interested in encouraging sustained oral responses from children and students. From Dorothy Heathcote's work (see Bolton, 2003; Wagner, 1976 and Johnson and O'Neill, 1984) in particular, I had learned to take on different positions within the drama and often encouraged children or students to assume 'the mantle of the expert'. Heathcote was always seeking ways of repositioning herself at different levels of power within the work while still assuming responsibility for the shape of the drama and the social and psychological health of the group. The mainstays of her approach were: allowing people time to formulate responses; taking the role of naif; asking participants in the drama for directions and advice; challenging contradictions by playing devil's advocate. Her strongest tool in the creation of meaning was the reflection upon the action, the teasing out of dilemmas contradictions and knotty ethical problems, by asking that small, but all-powerful, question, 'Why?' These are all approaches which align her work strongly with Brecht's conception of theatre. Without consciously planning to follow Heathcote, each device is apparent in my conduct of the interviews.

Researchers always bring their own histories to their work and this was mine. Also, educational drama was a history I shared with Aliki. I don't claim to have known her well. I only taught her for one term. But we did work with a shared set of assumptions and values, which perhaps explains why she responded in deeply reflective ways despite minimal clues in the questions. The stumbling nature of my approach was not merely due to the fact that it is difficult to formulate interesting questions while simultaneously engaged in listening to interesting and highly personal responses. I was being tentative about probing further so as not to abuse the power position I had as the interviewer. I was signalling my interest and at the same time allowing an escape route for Aliki should she need it.

The other main lesson I had learned from my interest in educational drama was that the best sessions happened when students took control of the direction of the drama. They had ownership, which is the cornerstone of motivation. This is a difficult path since it means that we must tolerate experiment, 'failure' and find ways to edge the work forward tentatively. Once teachers have taken a leap of faith, these approaches can yield exciting possibilities in terms of learning. I find evidence of the same things in the interviews. It is often when I am at my most tentative that a sudden, articulate and profound response arises from the other person. I could point to many examples of this throughout the interview. One of my favourites is when Aliki puts a stop to my over-tentative ramblings by saying firmly 'Go for it!'

In the early parts of the interview she alludes several times to when she wanted to be English or was jealous of friends who were blonde and blue eyed. On the second occasion she raised this point, we had the following exchange:

C: That's the second time you've brought that up ...

A: Yeah

C: There's that image that you wanted to be like this other ... the other..

A: Yeah..yeah..

C: It must have been ... I know that it couldn't have been quite like that ... but it must have been distressing in a way..

Here, I border on incoherence. But in the context of the interview, this is a real turning point. From here on, Aliki takes over. Her stories become more confident and candid. Her unprompted observations and reminiscences become longer and more detailed. They also give deep insight into how she is learning to maintain a sense of integrity and dignity within the web of conflicting forces influencing her. She is making sense of her personal history. In the interview she charts the changes in detail. In response to my rambling she replies:

A: I think I carried that through all the way through until the end of my degree.

C: Really? ... That far? ...

A: Yeah. And it wasn't until I came to do the PGCE that things started really, really changing ... rapidly erm..I came out of a long term relationship that was quite oppressive in that ... you know ... and I think that has completely changed me absolutely now.

When I probe this further it is apparent that her own teaching helped her recognise her own situation clearly. She describes how her teaching:

> ... suddenly made me realise that you couldn't put people in boxes and deny them who they were. Because with some kids ... I'd think, 'I know why they're doing that' and in terms of drama, I know why they've got their sentences mixed up there and it sounds awkward and gawky and that's why the other kids don't want them in their group. And then it just clicked and I thought,'That's me!' or 'That's how I perceive myself! and that's why I can't move forward because I let everybody else ... sort of say, 'No you can't come in because your sentences aren't..I mean but that's really extreme but that's the example I could think of.

She goes on to compare this with the oppressive relationships she was in with a middle class English man who told her she was aggressive.

> Whereas now I look back and when I started changing I started thinking, 'Well actually it's not aggression, it's just me and it's part of my culture. We're like that, y'know.

Although the interview and subsequent analysis tends to fragment the narrative, when viewed as a whole the stories and reflections provide a coherent and surprisingly detailed account of the whole of her life. It is also interesting that she also fulfils the three different strands of autobiography described above.

> **Historical elements** are apparent through an elaborate chronology which follows her early childhood in Stoke Newington, the move to Tottenham and finally to Enfield. This coincides with the traditional route out of the city to the suburbs of many Greek Cypriot families in North London.

> **Philosophical elements** are apparent through all of her narratives,which trace her political and ethical understandings as they grow and develop through analysis of her personal experiences and her work in drama.

> Drama also provides examples of her **poetical** working through of experiences. Three major and illuminating works are described on the tape:

> - Her first memories as a baby in her cot and her early relationship with her mother have been written up as a play

> - In the face of an instance of racism at her drama college she wrote a play which tells of sweatshop workers from different cultural backgrounds who work together but do not get on (analysed in Chapter 7)

> - In her final year at college she wrote a one-woman piece set in Cyprus in the future, in which she articulates the dilemmas and choices facing

those who have diverse cultural and linguistic repertoires and are subject to complex political, social and economic forces (See Chapter 5)

I have concentrated on Aliki's story mainly because it was the first and most exploratory of the interviews. In the process my focus shifted from language to broader issues of culture and identity. This is partly because many of my respondents have lost much of their facility in their heritage language. More importantly, Aliki's story alerted me to levels of complexity of which I had only an inkling. It also forced me to examine my methodological tools more closely. There are parts of ethnography and of life history which are useful and productive. I have also found cultural studies an invigorating and exciting field. My work is to make connections between their speculations on the bigger picture, the broad sweep of recent history and how this articulates with the lives of individuals.

My subsequent interviews had a more structured beginning: I would ask each of them to tell me something about their family histories. It has been a productive opening, since it gets to the heart of the matter quickly and painlessly. It also gives them the initiative quickly. Several have said how interesting this process has been and that they have never done it before. Asif, in his interview, spontaneously breaks off midway through his narrative to exclaim, 'This is quite interesting, actually!' This is praise indeed from Asif, the master of understatement!

Conclusion: the role of the researcher

Even though I have taken a highly critical view of the academy in research of this kind, I am not at all dismissive of the important role researchers play in bringing these complex narratives and perspectives to the light of day. We have a great deal of knowledge and experience in unriddling these complexities and contributing to the ongoing dialogues. There are, as I see it, several preconditions which can help to make our work more exciting and effective.

- firstly, we must examine the tools we use critically

- secondly, we must be open and candid with the people who agree to collaborate with us

- we must seek ways of diminishing differences in the power relationship

- we must genuinely seek to work towards practical resolutions of dilemmas unearthed by our research. We must be participants, rather than merely participant observers in a political sense. This demands courage and commitment. We have a responsibility not to let it slip into mere voyeurism or careerism

- we must be aware of the epistemological issues raised by our work and work to more democratic notions of what's worth knowing

As Dorothy Heathcote used to say, we must take responsibility in shaping the work in ways which put us at as much risk as our collaborators. Such a route is exciting and illuminating. It is play and fun. It is a never-ending story. It is being human.

5

The Patterns that Connect:
The Content of the Narratives

To return to the past is not sufficient, nor is it possible in the dynamic process
of cultural formation. However, the past does supply powerful and important
connections that are essential to the revisioning of ... identities.
Terry de Hay *Narrating memory* (1994:29)

Introduction

Identifying patterns in human behaviour is always a complicated business.
Patterns tend to imply precise congruence. When applied to human affairs they
can mislead and make life appear tidier than it actually is. With moving targets
like culture and identity it is even more problematic. However, we need to engage in this pattern making to create even the most basic meaningful pro-
positions. Abstracting formal patterns that connect is therefore useful only as far
as we remain alert to the limitations of such an approach. Clifford Geertz
(1996:3) describes the problem in this way:

> To form my accounts of change, in my towns, my profession, my world
> and myself, calls not for plotted narrative, measurement, reminiscence
> or structural progression, and certainly not for graphs; though these
> have their uses (as do models and theorisings) in setting frames and
> defining issues. It calls for showing how particular events and unique
> occasions, an encounter here, a development there, can be woven to-
> gether with a variety of facts and a battery of interpretations to
> produce a sense of how things go, have been going and are likely to
> go. Myth, it has been said, I think by Northrop Frye, describes not what
> happened but what happens. Science, social science anyway, is much
> the same save that its descriptions make claim to solider grounding
> and sounder thought, and aspire to a certain dispassion

To reveal the complexity of the patterns in their stories I use a great deal of direct quotation to bring out their distinctive voices. This reveals the rich diversity of motivation and action beneath what appear to be broadly similar stances and viewpoints. As with all self-narrative, such quotation is not merely descriptive, it is interpretative. Freeman (1993:29) reminds us

> Memory, therefore, which often has to do not merely with recounting the past, but making sense of it – from 'above' as it were – is an interpretive act the end of which is an enlarged understanding of the self.

Self-narrative is always about point of view. This is what makes it such a rich resource. The layers of context, action and evaluation, reflection, philosophy and standpoint are contained within the attractive, familiar, ordinary and accessible framework of story. Although I concentrate on the *content* of their self-narratives, it is clear that embedded within the anecdotes are their own well-articulated, evaluative arguments.

For the sake of clarity I present the main patterns as sets of the relationships. I chose to begin with the family, which is generally where the most intimate and formative relationships occur, and work outwards in what I consider are widening spheres of influence. They are:

- **Relationships with families**

  - fathers as a dominant influence
  - families' interest and involvement in education

- **Relationship to cultural heritage**

  - patterns of family settlement
  - a strong sense of history of heritage culture, involving formal study
  - regular visits to 'homeland'
  - ambivalence and questioning of the heritage culture
  - ambivalent attitude to living in the homeland
  - ambivalent attitudes towards community schooling
  - finding life partners outside the community

- **Relationships with peers**

  - gender differences in attitudes to peers

- **Relationship to the dominant culture**

  a) General
  - a liberal, tolerant attitude and critical approach
  - ambivalence and questioning of values of dominant culture
  - an explicitly political and critical view of capitalism

- identification with other marginalised groups
- a wide knowledge of the debates surrounding culture and identity
- experience of various forms of racism and adoption of different strategies for dealing with it

b) Mass Media
- a recognition of its powerful influence
- differing attitudes towards it

c) Education
- an enjoyment of schooling and learning, but only one ostensible example of how it connected to their daily lives
- a period of crisis with dominant educational values and precepts in late adolescence

At the end of the chapter the six individuals explicitly describe their own identities. Obviously these stories are constructions of their individual identities at the time the interviews were conducted.

All six were familiar with much current academic research in the area of identity. All had read the history of complex post-colonial struggles and additional knowledge about them was garnered from family histories. Moreover, all six have researched them as part of their formal education. As a result they are informed about the mechanisms of power involved in the struggles and all espouse a similar political position in relation to this. By the same token, all are critical about aspects of both their own heritages and the dominant discourses. A complex syncretism is achieved through their stories. In this chapter I describe the constituent parts of those syncretic process and in the next two chapters I look at how those syncretic process work through the lives of the individuals: how they orchestrate the different and often conflicting elements into a coherent sense of self.

How similar their stories are is striking, given that they come from a variety of cultural heritages. The most important feature for me is the profound influence of family members, especially fathers, evident in the narratives. By comparison, other supposed socialising influences, such as peer groups and schooling, pale into insignificance. Sometimes I had to try to draw from them information about schoolteachers and school friends.

Relationships with families
Parents as a dominant and often pervasive force in the narratives

I realise myself initially through others; from them I receive words, forms, tonalities for the formation of my initial idea of myself. The elements of infantilism sometimes remain until the end of life (perception and the idea of oneself, one's body, face and past in tender tones). Just as the body is formed initially in the mother's womb (body), a person's consciousness awakens wrapped in another's consciousness. Bakhtin (1986:138)

The central influence of families in the stories poses a formidable challenge to many post-modern thinkers. It would seem that the grand narratives of family life have a profound and pervasive effect on them, constraining the self-conscious reconstruction of identity. The postmodernist theoretical viewpoint grossly underestimates affective aspects of the development of identity. Desire is sometimes mentioned but there is far more to affect than desire in the complex politics of family life. Moreover, there are significant gender differences in how fathers are portrayed in the narratives. All the women's fathers tend to be portrayed as authoritarian patriarchs, insensitive in many ways. Nandine remarks that:

> I've always felt this sense of responsibility towards my family or ... In communities where it's very close knit, you know it's rural ... sort of traditional family set-ups or behaving to parents in a certain way ... because I think outside of that I can be assertive with people older than me ... (but) ... Even now when I've spoken to my father, I just cannot express myself articulately ... Because I'm still bound by all that ...

The ambivalences run deep, since shortly after this she says in a very quiet voice, 'Although in other ways, I don't have very much respect for my father.'

Aliki's narrative is characterised by similar deep ambivalences towards her father. She dislikes his macho attitudes. At one point she portrays this relationship as one of confrontation between her sisters and mother on one hand and her father on the other. It has certainly deeply coloured her world-view. A basic theme, reiterated throughout her conversation, is that she will never marry a Greek man. Nevertheless the relationship is complex and ambivalent. Since she has become successful and has achieved the post of Head of drama in a large secondary school, her father's attitudes towards her has changed. His respect for her has grown and they now have a much better relationship.

By way of contrast, My reports her father's autocracy in a neutral, dispassionate tone, when she describes the family homework ritual:

> We would sit around the table, the six of us, with my father at the top end and he would sit there and watch us do our homework. And he would help us. With our English, we had to work it out together. He knew being in a new country, being in a new culture we had to work extra hard. And that was his way of making us do it. So he was very strict on us and if we didn't work properly, then that was it. We were punished for it as well.

The men's attitudes are much more ambivalent and their responses vary widely. Michael acknowledges his father as an extremely powerful influence in his life, even declaring at one point: 'My father was my school'. His whole narrative is soaked in references to his father, who he sees as a quite exceptional person, despite having had difficult period with him when he first came to England.

> My father, despite everything that happened, was a good man ... there was something fantastic about him, but something, I think, in this society poisoned him.

Asif describes his father as energetic, enterprising and courageous in many respects, particularly as he dealt with racism experienced whilst working for the water board. On the other hand he also has deep disagreements with him, particularly in relation to his view of traditional heritage values, which manifest themselves in discussions and arguments about culture and religion.

Olgun admires his father's energy and ambition.

> ... he was an intelligent man. After losing that business in '63 ... he came to Turkish side and and he built five shops and several houses ... and he wanted every one of us to succeed.

But this energy and enterprise also had a negative side:

> My father had always ... (indecipherable, very quietly) ... and he was such a strong domineering sort of person and he dominated my life. He dominated everything you know. For example in Cyprus he wouldn't let us play ball or anything like that and I'm not into sports now at all because of that.

Even when he came to England and stayed with his aunt and uncle in Charlton, his father continued to exercise a great deal of control.

Mothers, however, are portrayed as almost invisible. They certainly assume minor roles in the narratives, in comparison to the fathers and in some cases (Olgun's, Michael's and My's) are reduced to mere ciphers. At one point Olgun declares that he never knew his mother, but he must have lived with her until he was at least eleven and again upon his return to Cyprus.

Asif's mother also has a subordinate role in his story. Born in Delhi to a family of wealthy socialites, she studied medicine. By 1948 she had become a midwife.

Her family lost everything following Partition, when she made the Long Walk to Pakistan. When her father died her mother had to take in sewing to feed her family. It was in Karachi that she met and married Asif's father, who was working as a pharmacist in the same hospital. He was from the Punjab. On coming to Britain she appears to have assumed a completely domestic position. Early in the conversation Asif talks warmly of how she presided over his early education. Thereafter she disappears from his narrative almost entirely.

Nandine had a close relationship with her mother during the years when she assumed the traditional role of the dutiful eldest daughter in her Bangladeshi-British family. In her reflections it is a position she held with great resentment. She pinpoints the moment of this realisation vividly, when she first took on these responsibilities:

> Well my mother was ill or she was having the baby, so I had to do that [vacuum the dining room]. And while she was in hospital I had to take on that role. I was very angry about it ... Even now I remember I was very angry about having to hoover the dining room ... It seems weird doesn't it, but I just remember it so vividly.

Her resentment is compounded by the fact that she thought she got scant recognition for her work from her mother:

> It's funny because, you know, often people would come round and say, 'Oh..your daughter works so hard..' and my mother would turn around and say, Oh, she's only doing that because you're here' or 'They have to learn', and I used to think, 'She never ever praised me in front of my face. Never ever!' and I used to resent that so much.

Obviously such observations have to be taken in their context. Shortly before the interview, Nandine had been disowned by her entire family for not submitting to a second arranged marriage. Instead, she decided to marry out of her cultural and religious tradition. She is now married and has a child.

Aliki's mother figures much more prominently. Again this was an arranged marriage, as is true for the majority of the cases presented here.

> That's really undermining to my parents' relationship ... when I look at it there's nothing apart from obligation to each other and the children.

She is portrayed as long-suffering, having to put up with her father's absences from home and general neglect or subservience to him.

> Dad was never around. There was no father there. It was my mum all the time. Dad used to go on gambling binges and stuff like that away from London and when he did come back mum and dad were either arguing or he'd be down the road at his brother's house.

Her mother speaks very little English. So she feels isolated. This has been compounded since Aliki has lost her fluency in Greek and at the end of the interview she reflects that her main reason for wanting to learn Greek is so that she can have a proper conversation with her mum.

> I feel really ashamed when I go to Cyprus. I can't have conversations with my family ... It upsets me that I can't do this with mum... The main reason (for wanting to learn Greek) is so that I can talk to my mum properly.

Language could be seen as a factor in this case in terms of the invisibility in the narratives, but it does not really fit with the patterns of language competence for all of the others. My and Olgun are, by their own estimation, fluent bilinguals who would find little difficulty communicating with their mothers. Both Asif's and Michael's mothers are fluent in English. Nandine's mother has a high profile, yet their relationship is at its lowest ebb. Ironically, it is Aliki, who has most difficulty in communicating with her mother, who mentions her mother most often. One can only conclude that there are other reasons why they have such a low profile, which they do not explicitly state.

It is interesting that families continue to exert such a powerful influence on each individual's sense of self. It demonstrates very clearly the limits of postmodern thinking. Theorists such as Iain Chambers and Homi Bhabha (1996) and others who regard identity as a social construction need to be aware that there are limits to how far we are able to consciously construct or reconstruct ourselves. Holstein and Gubrium (2000:4) begin their book, *The Self We Live By* in the following way

> Hopefulness versus disintegration , presence versus imagery, narrative inventiveness versus discipline. How can we reconcile these competing messages? What's the point? Is it that the self continues to significantly inform experience, but is now more narratively complex than ever? How can we be both selves and the stories of selves? What social processes make it possible? These are questions this book aims to answer, beginning with a story of a social self that some say has retreated from the spotlight of social psychology into nihilistic postmodern disarray ...

The production of new discourses is certainly possible and new attitudes are often born out of the kind of ambivalences, resentments and dissatisfactions to which these stories bear witness. However, these are difficult moves. Those influences have deep roots and change is a painful process, since it has profound social consequences. Dissent can be a lonely and trying business. It is also significant that fathers still remain a dominant force in the narratives, often embodying the very conservative attitudes which are limiting to social and cultural change.

It is remarkable that families continue to exert such an influence on these people, even though all are highly critical and analytical people. All have independent means and are successful in their careers. This affective dimension is grossly underestimated by many postmodern theorists. A force field of influences constrains our ability to merely reinvent ourselves afresh. Relationships within families are often very powerful and breaking away from communal traditions is frequently gained only at great emotional cost. The roots of tradition are very deep and pervasive. Even in this era of the supposed disintegration of the family, families continue to exert a mysterious, almost primal power over our creation of identity.

Families' interest and involvement in education

Apart from Aliki's, all the stories bear witness to their parents' desire to see them succeed at school. But here again there are different emphases. The parents of Olgun, Asif, Nandine and My were all very concerned that their children should do well at school in order to enhance their chances of a better material standard of living.

Asif talks about the time when he was at primary school and his mother was dissatisfied with the educational system and hired a tutor. His mother's expectations of the system were far higher than she felt were delivered.

> That was tricky for her and that was ... I can remember being 5 or 6 and there was a retired teacher in our road and one or two afternoons a week my sister and I would be sent there to go and do things and so we carried on with that. It was deemed necessary even at 6 or 7, because I think there were concerns about my primary school.

Nandine speaks about how she was explicitly told that she needed to achieve at school. When she encountered difficulties with her 'A' level studies a tutor was promptly recruited. As described earlier, My's father not only closely supervised his children's studies, he arranged for them to read to an English neighbour and sought out English reading material for them.

Olgun also speaks of pressure from his dominating father to succeed at school. He talks about his aunt taking over this role when he came to England. All these reports demonstrate the phenomenon of 'prolepsis', described by Cole (1996). It is only Michael whose father had a different idea of the purpose of education.

At one point in our conversation, Michael comments rather surprisingly, 'My father was my school.' His admiration for his father is apparent throughout the conversation and certainly his father was keen for him to achieve at school. Prolepsis, in relation to educational success, is common to all except Aliki. But, when I probed Michael to see if his father saw education as a passport to material success, a much more complex view emerged, which was located in issues of history and identity. Again this sprang from his father's attitudes:

> There was something in him that made me and my brothers realise, and my sister realise that education was important. You had to succeed..er ... and there was no ... You simply had to move on. You can't sit on your butt

But education is good in itself, not merely for social advancement because

> ... as a black person you can have as many certificates as you need ... it often doesn't get you where you want to be. You always have to end up slightly lower ... .but it is good in itself ... because if you've got it then you know who you are. You know what it is you're about. I can deal with you on an equal level. I don't have to put up with your nonsense ... I will see you for what you are and I can choose to deal with you or not. I've got that freedom. ...That is one of the things my father taught me.

So though the parents were generally keen for their children to succeed, they placed their emphases slightly differently.

Relationship with cultural heritage
a) *Patterns of settlement*

Memories framed in stories are integral to identity. Some stories extend beyond the borders of our own lives, so that 'our histories begin not in memory, but in the stories told to us by others. Indeed these become our past' (Freeman:1993:53). As a child, Michael knew his father only by his impressive reputation, as he had already settled England.

> In the Caribbean he was the big man. He was called 'the Brain', because he had a personality ... He had a very outward personality. Well liked. Everyone liked him. Everyone knew him from one end of the island to the next.

Although the other five did not experience this early separation, all have close connections with their parent's 'homeland'. Their patterns of family settlement are similar. They all moved from a rural location to an urban one. Their migrations were economically supported by their families and communities. The period they have lived through has also coincided with a general and continuing expansion of agribusiness. Wedded to fast and pervasive technology, it is mediated through a kind of bare-knuckle marketplace capitalism that responds rapidly to privileged consumers' whims. This in turn has transformed the production and distribution of foods, forcing many rural communities off the land often to eke out a meagre living in a variety of demeaning ways in the cities. This pattern of migration to Western cities has characterised the post-colonial period since the end of the Second World War. Flight has often been accelerated through civil strife in post-colonial states. The family histories of all of the participants are in some way framed, often directly, with such struggles. All report that their parents initially had to find work which was lower status and more badly paid than the careers they had followed in their country of origin. Apart from Aliki, they all came from fairly middle class backgrounds. Even Asif's father who had come from a farming family had become a pharmacist. So the pattern in terms of class backgrounds coincides with the majority of successful pupils in Britain. Even here class appears to be a strongly determining factor.

b) *A strong sense of history of their heritage culture*

Demonstrating the importance of wider events, Asif begins his narrative with allusions to Partition and the Great Walk, which effectively dispossessed both parents. Similarly, My describes her experiences as a five year old when her whole family had to make a harrowing journey out of Vietnam. Aliki's parents fled Cyprus, when Turkish troops invaded their village. Olgun's family were based in an area which was predominantly Greek Cypriot, where they were denied basic amenities such as electricity. At sixteen, he was conscripted on his return to Cyprus. He was taken prisoner during the fighting and witnessed violence and brutality at first hand. These events have coloured his sense of identity in profound ways:

> I'm not saying all Greek Cypriots but those extremists were actually ... electricity pylons passed through the middle of our town, but we didn't have electricity.

His experiences raised profound doubts that have continued to plague him:

> It was just weird looking back ... all those events ... and when I came here I was involved in left wing politics ... I couldn't ... you know ... say if the Greeks was you know ... people ... .brothers ... then why was this happening? ... .yeah ... even though I met at college ... Greek Cypriots who were friends ... .there was a part I couldn't throw away ...

It is particularly difficult to discard memories of such events. They tend to become inscribed in family histories and often acquire almost mythical proportions. On the other hand, Nandine's and Michael's families came to seek a better or at least a different way of life, although their own histories are also realised against a background of colonialism. Throughout his narratives Michael, like the others, demonstrates a strong sense of history and affiliation with his heritage culture. His identity, which is powerfully defined by the extreme racism he and his family encountered in Canning Town, has even deeper roots in the Caribbean. He talks of Dominica with exceptional fondness, makes frequent trips to the Caribbean and is the only person in the sample who would still want to live in the homeland. He also sees the whole issue of racism in terms of deep historical connections:

> The relationship that our ancestors, both black and white, carved out something for us. For good or ill they locked us into this kind of struggle ... My history is your history ... So whether you repatriate me or not you will always be conscious of me ... History is memory and you know ... You will hear about me in books and you will see me in films. You will always be conscious of the other.

Here he demonstrates that, far from assimilating the dominant discourses of history and culture in the West, he is examining the process critically and drawing on other black intellectuals, such as Fanon, to articulate his own perspective and political point of view. He represents what Gramsci calls an 'organic intellectual' (Gramsci:1988:300-311). This committed, critical and knowledgeable approach to the history of their respective heritages is a common strand through all of the narratives. (Asif also cites Fanon as an author whose arguments he found 'internally persuasive'.) Their narratives are suffused with a deep knowledge and understanding of 'where they are from'.

For many of them this aspect has determined the direction of their later academic work. Michael's MA concerned the representation of black people in the canon of English Literature. His comments carry the resonance of his study. My studied the language teaching in Britain received by Chinese-Vietnamese settlers who fled Vietnam at the same time as her own family. Nandine studied bilingual Bangladeshi-British children in Tower Hamlets and worked on a research project which compared differences in conceptions of reading between mainstream schools and Arabic classes in the Mosque schools. Olgun's own MA dissertation involves close study of his own background. Aliki's theatrical work is an exploration of identity that draws strongly on the history and tradition of her own cultural heritage. Although Asif has not engaged in study for an award-bearing course, he describes how he read systematically and widely in the area.

Their informed interest in their own backgrounds adds to the rich complexity of their understandings, which is also shared through countless litanies of family histories in informal settings. It is easy to imagine conversations full of amusing anecdotes, farcical encounters, misunderstandings, family disagreements, tragedies and scandals. Each anecdote would be redolent of context, people, events, foods, smells, sights and sounds. Each would be described and savoured. Such stories may also be a source of mirth or embarrassment to adolescent sons and daughters. They will eventually be weighed against their actual experience gathered during their, often frequent, visits to their parents' homeland. A truly polyphonic inner-speech.

c) *Regular visits to the 'homeland' and ambivalence towards living in the 'homeland'*

With the exception of My, all have visited their parents' country of origin many times. However, it is precisely in their references to the these visits that the most powerful ambivalences arise. Asif explains how his father sees the post-modernist position of identity as shallow and rootless.

> This idea of broadness ... it's a strange ... or is it that you've dissipated identity so much that you have nothing and you're lost, which is what my dad would suggest to you ...

However he is wary of returning to his 'mythical homeland':

> I wouldn't mind being buried on our plot on our farm in the Punjab ... So I like holding on to that idea of a base, but not an awful lot else. I think it's more of a romantic notion and nothing else.

At one point he did toy with the idea of return to Karachi, where many of his relatives live and taking the Civil Service Exam. However his distaste for the political situation and the day-to-day life prevented him. He talks about the bribery and corruption he experienced from even minor officials and the extremes of poverty and resulting brutality. Comparing it to Britain, he says 'I do get very angry about the poverty in Britain but when you see people with their limbs hacked off by their junkie dads which is what you see a lot of in Karachi. Karachi ... where my dad's family is from, is the major heroin export. It came from the Afghan thing. So there's a lot of drugs, a lot of crime and it's a very, very dangerous city.'.

Although less dramatically, Nandine expresses a similar dilemma with regard to day-to-day life in Bangladesh:

> I've thought it would be nice to go back and teach there but I'm very parti-cular about things like ... my grandparents now live in Dacca, but they've got open drains and ... I just can't ... I found that very hard when I went last time ... The last time was '92 ... I just thought there's no way I could put up with things like that and the dust and the heat ... I suppose that's a bit superficial, but ... and you don't quite fit in anyway. It's not like ... it's your motherland, but it's not really your ... you are sort of straddling two countries. And I know this one infinitely better than that one and again I do stand out as well ...

She goes on to say that she identifies more with young Asian people in Britain

> ... with the younger Asian generation coming up ... and other peers I have ... What I see in the media and what I see in literature, I see the emergence of a young Asian culture that's changing and new and I can identify with.

This contrasts quite strongly with Michael's attitude. Having spent his childhood in the Caribbean, he carries an image of it, which he cherishes and describes in a lyrical way. The Caribbean landscape fills him with wonder and nostalgia.

> My playground was the sea ... the rivers ... the forests ... the birds were my friends ... your pets and you would go in the mountains and make traps with your friends and you would trap a bird which would become your pet and other animals ... Space ... . and sunshine ... Colours, ... colours you know ... Green, gold, you know ... fantastic! I lived ... I mean my house was there ... and five seconds you're in the sea. You can hear the sea washing ... while I'm sleeping ... .Then if you contrast that with here. It's like you've entered a dark tunnel ... You can see the light at the other end. But then you're walking, walking, walking, walking, a totally different ... way of living and way of being.

At another point he talks about witnessing traditional storytelling and dancing during his childhood and how this left an indelible and far reaching impression on him:

> Well every day at a certain time the villagers would gather in the square and the storytellers would tell stories, traditional stories and the kinds of stories and other kinds of stories. And there would be dancing; traditional dancing. And this would happen with the moon, which, I remember being really bright, as a kid. It was as if you didn't need any other kind of light. It was so bright. And with the sound of the sea in your ears and you would sit there really kind of enthralled by it, really kind of awed and listen and soak it all in ... And today I still hear the stories. I still visualise those images in my mind and again they are sustaining things. And being a creative person a lot of those things have crept into my stories.

It is interesting to note his difference from Aliki, who also uses knowledge of her own heritage in her creative work to explore dilemmas of identity. Michael's experience of virulent racism has possibly meant that he recalls his homeland in a nostalgic and more affectionate way. This marks out a significant difference between those who were born in this country (Aliki, Nandine and Asif) and those born in their parents country of origin (Olgun, My and Michael), even if they came to Britain at a relatively early age. They remain much closer to the heart of the tradition, in terms of both their bilingualism and their attitude. It is also interesting to note that those born here have either made partnerships with people from outside their own community (Nandine and Asif) or intend to (Aliki).

However, Olgun's story adds another layer of complexity. Although he has very close connections with his own heritage and has married within his community, he does demonstrate ambivalence toward his own cultural background on two occasions. In the first is where he describes his journey through Turkey with his aunt and uncle at the age of sixteen. The car broke down and while it was being repaired Olgun was delayed for several days in a hotel in Istanbul. What comes out most forcefully in this section of his narrative is his deep distaste of the treatment his aunt received from the Turkish men on the street.

> ... We couldn't go out ... How shall I put it? We were really afraid of going out ... the Turkish men ... we tried to go out with my aunt one day and all the men were just looking at her ... I don't know, it was weird ... Even though they were from the same culture, they were different to us ... We felt really threatened by it ... .and Istanbul is such a massive place, you know, and my uncle had to be out there, just trying to get this part and you know when you walk down the street and they were just looking at us ... just looking ... and you know you feel really threatened ... And these Turkish people and I thought ... you know ... and I thought, you know, 'I hate you ... Leave us alone' and we went in a restaurant..and a man came and he was chatting up ... trying to chat up my aunt. I hated him, you know ...

In the second instance he refers to the time when he had to attend a boarding school in Nicosia. He disliked having to share a room, especially with 'sixteen of these dirty boys in this room ... The room wasn't dirty but they were'. Like Asif and Nandine, he missed the comfort and privacy of his life in England. However, he thought the standard of education he received was far higher than in Britain.

Aliki's ambivalences about her own heritage run much deeper and are a prominent theme throughout her narrative: her distaste for many aspects of Greek Cypriot culture, her determination not to marry a Greek man and the poor self-image she had for much of her life. At the end of her narrative she reveals however that she is beginning to reconnect with that aspect of her identity in more positive and constructive ways. But she needs this to be on her own terms:

> As soon as this year's out I want to go to Greek school and learn my language properly. I also want to spend weekends with my mum getting the recipes from her so that I can cook Greek, but that doesn't mean to say that I want to marry a Greek man. And that's what I keep telling my mum, because she keeps ... Every time I get encouraged about my culture, she says 'Oh yes. A nice Greek man is in sight, I feel' and I say, 'No, that's not what that's about. That's, you know, about me having to identify with my identity, and that's part of my identity ...

> I think I want to work in Cyprus for a few years. I want to teach out there for a couple of years. Not forever. But I would like to do some sort of drama

out there ... Something. That's not the main reason. I think the main reason is so that I can talk to my mum properly.

So perhaps this too is a romantic notion of return. Michael is the only one who harbours any serious notion of return and this would be for only half the year. My's position is different: migrants to Vietnam from China do not have the same attitude towards the 'homeland'. But the Chinese Vietnamese community has one of the strongest infrastructures in terms of community schools. One of the first things her father did on moving up to London from Devon was to enrol the children in Saturday schools. Many of the Chinese-Vietnamese settled near Deptford. My's narrative is very different to the others in so far as she voices no discontent with either her heritage culture or her experiences of Western culture. She readily admits to an English strand to her identity, but nothing further is specified. However, when asked directly what she thought were the relative strengths of each of the facets she replied that the good thing about Chinese culture was respect for elders, whereas the good thing about English culture was the amount of individual freedom allowed.

d) *Ambivalence towards community schools*

Community schools are regarded as an important resource for many communities in terms of maintaining language and identity. Up until the late 1980s local authorities gave space in state schools for mother tongue classes to be conducted during the evenings and at weekends without charge. As early as 1935 the first Greek school was set up in Camden Town. They are often well subscribed and well attended. But there has never been a close connection with mainstream education in terms of administration or teaching style. The state is reluctant to officially fund such schools. Equally, communities seem to wish to maintain independence in terms of curriculum and teaching approaches.

Neither Olgun nor Michael, who arrived when they were about ten or eleven years old, attended community schools in this country, although Olgun had attended, a Turkish school in Cyprus which had a very nationalistic outlook.

> incredibly nationalistic. I mean ... the Turkish flag and all the Turkish books from Turkey ... Attaturk and the war of independence in Turkey and we were all part of that ... a continuation, an extension of Turkey ... we weren't Cypriots.

Out of the four people who attended community schools, only My sees it as a positive or at least unproblematic phenomenon. She attended from a relatively early age and her parents were keen for her and her siblings to maintain their home language and culture. My describes it as part of her parents' wider agenda or 'prolepsis' to use Cole's term.

For my father and my mother, they knew English was important ... But they knew that if we let go of our language, then they wouldn't understand us. So what my father did, instead of ... erm..we were talking our home language, but because there's no written form of our home language ... He actually ... my father ... my mother and my father actually saved up a lot of money and bought us a video and through that they rented videos out ... Cantonese videos out and that's how we learned Cantonese, through listening, through the films and all that. So that's how we learned our speaking Cantonese. And when we moved to London ... my father enrolled us into Saturday schools. It was to learn Cantonese. So I can write a little Cantonese now and I do speak Cantonese fluently.

I had assumed that Nandine had learned Bengali in a similar manner. This pre-conception was based on the fact that she had worked on a research project on reading styles in community language schools and acted as an interpreter. How-ever, when she talks about it a different picture emerges:

C: What about ... Did you ever get into Bengali literature or ... ?

N: I can't read Bengali!

    ... ...

C: I didn't realise, I thought you were biliterate as well ... No?

N: No ... when I was at school there weren't many Bengali ... and there weren't any community schools at that time. And my parent were just more keen that we were learning English and we started with the Arabic later.

In contrast, both Aliki and Asif have late, brief and negative experiences of com-munity schools. With the benefit of hindsight they are now highly critical of the methods of teaching, which were highly structured and formal. Asif remembers teasing the elderly teacher to relieve the boredom:

... dad sent me to the local mosque to the Islamic school ... (laughs) ... which was a complete riot ... We'd just have some poor duffer who was about 60, who could barely stand with a big beard and a stick. And he had about 30 of these 8-10 year olds who just wanted to play and run around. And it was quite good fun to be chased by him with his walking stick. You know. He liked to use it a lot and we enjoyed being chased by him.

As for the teaching methods he says that it was 'Sit down. Everybody get the same thing out. I'll read a line. You read a line. You follow with your fingers.' So it was a sort of sing song'.

He was not aware of the differences in terms of learning as a child, however. He continues:

But ... erm ... I don't think it struck me as odd. At that point, as a child, I didn't really have set views on what learning was. I assumed that this was learning, I guess and I was prepared to trust the adults that that was happening. But now looking back I think it's very odd that, one, it wasn't in Urdu, it was in Arabic. The language we were singing to each other in was Arabic. I had no idea what it meant.

He didn't attend for long. His parents were not so committed to the idea of community schools as My's. Again it points to the dangers of visualising a community as a uniform and homogenised whole. Aliki and her sister were sent to their local community school when she was about eleven or twelve:

We were there every Saturday for a whole day and we hated it because we hated the Greek girls and we said we hated the Greek boys but we kind of fancied them. But me and my sister Maria would never admit to each other that we did ... erm ... and we used to bunk off and erm ... there was a place where they had Space Invaders and we'd spend the afternoon in there. Then we'd quickly go back and wait for mum to pick us up or get the bus back.

Later in the conversation she talks explicitly about her negative feelings towards the other Greek girls:

Because they were ... they all looked so Greek and the way they dressed was all so ... They were confident ... (pause) ... I think that's the word ... they were confident and we weren't. You know they talked to the boys with ease ... You know they talked to the teachers with ease. They felt comfortable about being held by their parents and we didn't.

Their relationship to their culture is therefore a complex internal dialogue. What both Aliki and Asif cannot understand or engage with is the bland unquestioning nature of the process from *their point of view*. For Asif the meaninglessness of chanting in a language he doesn't understand is odd. They are however both insiders to the culture and, in Adorno's (1978/1951) terms they are 'hating tradition properly' and attempting to achieve a new synthesis. This is not to say that My's approach is merely total compliance, that may be a facet of her narrative style. This is an issue I explore in more detail in the next two chapters.

e) *Life partners*

One of the significant differences between the three people who were born in Britain and those born in their parents' homeland is the issue of partners. Those born in Britain have either committed to someone outside of their own cultural heritage or intend to. Throughout her narrative Aliki is insistent that she will not marry a Greek man. Nandine has been ostracised by her family for refusing to agree to a second arranged marriage, and Asif lives with an Englishwoman.

Both Olgun and Michael have married women from their own cultural backgrounds. My did not speak about her personal relationships.

Relationships with peers

In the mythology of popular psychology, peers greatly influence the construction of our identity. Peer pressure is seen to exert a powerful force, especially during the maelstrom of adolescence, when the importance of social belonging is a troubling and confusing experience. The fashion industry and the 'star making machinery behind the popular song' (Joni Mitchell:1975) certainly exploit this. So again I was surprised by how little it is mentioned by the thirty-somethings in this study. I was even more surprised how little peers seem to discuss their cultural heritages with each other. Perhaps this second point delineates one of the dilemmas. Elements of one's own heritage may be traded for academic success. Perhaps the norms of the dominant culture embarrass people so much that they conceal their allegiances with their own families. This is certainly true for Aliki, as is evidenced from anecdotes reported earlier.

When I asked her about this explicitly she replied:

> A: Yeah ... I think so. Because if I'd have gone for my own culture. I'd be married now ... I didn't want to go that way (pause)
>
> C: Do you think there was anything conscious in there even at that very early age?
>
> A: Yeah ... about I don't want to get married and I want to be academic or I want to achieve something before I get married ... Yeah
>
> C: Where did that come from?
>
> A: Dad was never around. There was no father there ... .

So it links back to the earlier quotation in this chapter. She surrounded herself with a group of school friends from different communities, including Kula, who she didn't realise was Greek.

This seems less surprising when she explains that:

> We never talked about our families. Our mothers, our dad. We never talked about our brothers and sisters with friends ... . don't know what we talked about but we never ever ... I certainly remember not talking about mum and dad and I can't remember them speaking about mum and dad.

Nandine goes further with the surprising statement:

> N: I don't have many Bengali friends or friends from my background
>
> C: Yeah? Does that go back a way or is it recent really?

N: No, it goes back a long way really because you could never really trust someone from your own circle ... So none of my close friends have been Bengali

C: Right ... why did that happen?

N: You just knew if they were from another family ... Families were the most important thing and your friends came second. So if you were making friends ... And I did have my fingers burned, because there were some girls who I was friendly with when I was younger. So one day I was moaning about my mum. 'My mum always makes me do the housework.' They'd go back and tell their mum, who'd tell my mum and then ... So then I began to realise that you can't trust someone in your own circle.

Although these stories are superficially similar, the motivations for avoiding any relationship between their peers and their cultural background are distinctly different and individual. One is to do with self-image, whereas the other represents a desire for privacy in a close-knit community. Olgun's narratives add another twist, which illustrates the complexity of the notion of diaspora. When he arrived in Britain, the school showed concern and thought it a good idea to pair him up with another Turkish Cypriot boy, Hussein. However this did not work out as planned, since Hussein 'couldn't really speak Turkish, he was born here...' But the first day went well. Hussein knew how to say hello in Turkish and taught the class this greeting. Olgun confirms this as a good experience, 'the fact that Hussein was there and they all looked and smiled ... and they tried in my language to say 'Hello' to me was something special'. School was generally a positive experience

> ... apart from the ... Well, I didn't know about the bullying but that came later ... But, as I say I didn't know any English, so I didn't know what was going on. It was a class of 25, 26.. and I was sitting with Hussein and ...er ... he wasn't telling me all the things ... and he couldn't anyway ...

They fell out because Hussein submitted to the school bully and was giving him 'lots of money'

> ... So I said 'I'm not giving him money' ... I just started moving away from him, Hussein and I think it was then that I ... and there were two brothers and they invited me to their home, Ian B and Victor B. They weren't really brothers. I found out later.. They were actually adopted ...

It would, of course be wrong to read too much into this in psychological terms, but the two new English friends were in a similar position to Olgun. The friendship lasted some time.

During the four year period that I was at secondary school I was in the same class with them ... Of course, we had our bust ups now and again but generally we were sort of, like together ... (but) ... again my aunt was very strict with me and she wouldn't let me go out in the evenings and on Saturdays I had to go and work with my uncle.

As with many aspects of this study there appear to be significant gender differences in the stories of relationships with peers. Aliki and Nandine talk of their relationships with their friends in closer and more affectionate terms. Asif occasionally mentions friends and Michael is rather dismissive, often preferring his own company. It is a surprising aspect of their self-narrative, since all are now gregarious and sociable people.

Following the brutal attack on him by racists on his way home from school, Michael withdrew into himself. He preferred to deal with this situation in isolation. He makes lukewarm responses to questions about friendships:

I did know a lot of kids ... you know ... your friends came for you. You didn't really want to go, but you went. And when you went you had a good time. You got up to mischief ... er... er ... went to discos. The usual stuff ... If you were to ask, I would have preferred to be on my own. But I did anyway. And when you did it, it was fun you had a laugh, you came back I would prefer to be on my ... This is still the same today, you know. I see myself to be very much of a lo ... I mean I socialise when I need to. (laughs)

As a boy from an Asian background, Asif found himself in the minority in a predominantly white school in Swindon. He talks of some rather humiliating comments he had to tolerate to become included in the social life of the school, which I guess is common to many 'survivors' in such situations. It had at least a temporary effect on his fluency in his home language. Following a question I ask about maintenance of Urdu, his heritage language, he replies that although he did maintain his home language at primary school,

I think in secondary ... When there's that social identity finding: Where do I fit? What do I speak? What am I? And being one of two Asian boys in this school in Swindon and ... 'You're not a Paki, you're just like us, really!' and I sort of bought into that, wanting to be part of the group, so I'd subsume my national identity to be part of that group identity. I think that had effect on my language ... Even now I'm out of practice, but I make a point now when I go home ... but say the turbulent stage of teenagehood from thirteen to about seventeen.

However repellent this manifestation of racism was, in the long term the effect on his sense of identity has not been totally negative. Like his father, he seems to have dealt with it with both integrity and dignity, never surrendering completely to the ignorant and superficial view from the outside.

> Then suddenly the use of Urdu again is a cultural thing that I'm trying to grab hold of once again to sort of rein that in ... I'm not rejecting it as a blanket rejection of whatever this cultural melee is, but I'm very clear of where I fit within that, but I use my parents, my father in particular to bounce ideas off and to clarify those ideas for myself ...

As an adult the experience has given him a sharply critical understanding. His experience has also given him a facility to be sociable and strategies to be included.

> English has had ... *occasional* detrimental effects on me or being exclusive and not including me through other means. So that through race I've been excluded. Through speech, education, personality or whatever reasons I've been included. So it's a complex one there. But you know it's also the way it's excluded my family. So I identify very much with the excluded groups ... so, all non white groups really. So ideas of racism are quite strong for me and I'm very conscious of that ...

Both Aliki and Nandine have encountered similar experiences which have put them in a similar position but unlike Michael or Asif or even Olgun, they have used their friendship networks for support. They both had networks of friends in primary school. At a later stage both experienced more indirect forms of institutional racism which they dealt with together with their friends and established a sense of social solidarity, which they express in less abstract terms than the men.

During her sixth form years Nandine attended a Roman Catholic private school. Her parents thought this would enhance her chances of academic success. Having been considered good at English in her previous state school, it came as some surprise that her abilities were greatly underestimated by her new teachers. But even from the first day she experienced the negative attitudes of her fellow pupils. She describes the humiliating experience:

> I can remember the first day. I was taken to the sixth form common room and Miss D, the Headteacher, introduced me and no one came and spoke to me and I just wanted the earth to swallow me up. It was just one of the most awful experiences I've had. And I just walked over to the window and stood there ... Because they'd all ... They were all in their cliques and there were five of us who had just joined the sixth form and we made our own ... kind of outcast group.

These were important friendships for Nandine:

> I'm still in touch with one girl and she's Hindu ... She's a doctor now ... And there's a Ugandan girl and I've lost touch with her ... She's a lovely girl ... She was one of my best friends. Another Afro-Caribbean girl. She went to Scotland ...

For the first time in her school life Nandine had difficulties with work, particularly in her favourite subject, English. She could not understand the religious and cultural references in the texts they were given to study: Blake, Gerard Manley Hopkins and Browning. This was exacerbated when the teacher predicted low grades for her and her African-Caribbean friend, Tracy.

> ... we were predicted. Both of us ... Tracy was predicted an E and I was predicted an E. The other girls were predicted Bs and As. I was just beside myself, you know. But they kept saying, 'Well you know ...' just talking about the difficulties I was having interpreting 'x' and blah. blah ... My essay writing was poor ...

As in Asif's case, her parents found a suitable tutor and she succeeded in getting a B. But the episode left a bitter aftertaste.

> I went back the next year and told Miss O (that she got a B), who said, 'Well I knew you'd do that anyway' ... It was an outrage ... Tracey got a B as well and I was so angry, because I just thought ... if I'd have had a bit more encouragement and a bit more prompting, it would have just meant so much more to me.

The effects of teacher expectation are well documented and there is no need to rehearse the arguments here. What is clear is that students from marginalised groups need a great deal of grit, determination and support from other sources to overcome the deeply embedded and subtle forms of institutionalised racism. Although peer group support has worked well for the women, the men see the struggle as a very individual one. It does form their basis of how they themselves view the dominant culture.

Relations with the dominant culture

a) Liberal tolerant values and a critical outlook

As can be seen from the values that are implicit in their arguments, all six individuals have a liberal, tolerant attitude and a critical outlook generally associated with Western liberal humanist education. Their critical outlook means that they question many aspects of the dominant discourses, which they have gathered from the mass media and through their education. It is most likely that all have encountered racism of varying degrees of intensity. I say most likely because it is not common to all the narratives. Five speak openly about racism but it entirely absent from the transcript of My's conversation. In this section I examine their attitudes to schooling and look at what some of them have to say about the media before looking in some detail at their different ways of coping with racism.

b) A critical questioning of the values the dominant culture

Most have found the eurocentric educational experience interesting in its way. Helped by the attitudes of their parents, they have been prepared to go along with this approach, being on the whole willing and well motivated pupils in the school system. However, all view the dominant culture in critical ways. There is a common pattern of crisis in late adolescence, which has been witnessed from many of the anecdotes and reflections cited so far. There is also evidence in the evaluative parts of their narratives that they have a great deal of knowledge of the power relationships in the history of colonialism. The three men and one of the women explicitly refer to the way that Marxism and other socialist thinking has influenced their own world view. Moreover three talk explicitly about the effect of the media in terms of (mis)representations of marginalised groups. Two speak explicitly about success as being personal success and not just academic achievement.

The crises talked about by Aliki, Michael and Nandine have been provoked by profound dissatisfaction with **both** their heritage culture and their experience of dominant white middle class culture, which permeates the media and schooling. Michael articulates this candidly and forcefully. Being a religious person he also includes, within his account, his crisis of faith.

> You were being taught historical facts which when you begin to grow up ... you begin to question those historical facts and I want more. I don't want you to say to me ... 'Well, this happened.' You need to tell me more. You need to tell me why and how.

Being dissatisfied with the dominant discourses he began, like many others in a similar position, to look elsewhere for alternative, internally persuasive discourses.

> ... I began to read..Malcolm X ... Things that were not really in keeping with things that I was taught at school as the facts ... You had to accept certain things, but I've never been a person to accept things. So after a while you question. You say to yourself. 'Is that so? Is that the way things are? And of course, Karl Marx ... strangely enough ... He put things into a context I was able to use and to really kind of see the social relationships which govern ...

Here he rearticulates a position which is close in its perceptions to Aliki's and Asif's and reiterates a political standpoint held by four out of the six. All have a deeply critical take on the power mechanisms of capitalism in its current form.

They have an equally critical view of their heritage cultures. Asif's arguments with his father and uncles over religion focus on the political dimensions (see Chapters 2 and 6). Some of the more explicit questioning of dominant values comes through discussion of the media.

c) Schooling

Although they have all entered the teaching profession themselves, their experiences of being at school are not entirely positive. Whilst most agree that their schooling was on the whole a pleasant and enjoyable experience, there is only one instance where teachers are reported to have connected with the cultural experiences they brought to school. When I embarked upon this research, I had expected My's positive experiences to be echoed by others. Following her immersion classes in Thorny Island her family moved to Launceton in Devon (described in Chapter 2). The LEA had organised a thoughtful and enlightened approach to the education of the Chinese-Vietnamese children, where they were allowed to use their home language for part of the time and at other times were put into contexts where they had to speak English. In addition their whole sense of culture and identity was supported. My's teacher encouraged the children to talk about their experiences and she also took the time to inform herself. However, My says that this was also an isolated experience. For her dissertation at university she interviewed Chinese-Vietnamese peers who had been educated in London. They had experienced less thoughtful and less sensitive programmes and took much longer to achieve fluency in their second language than she did.

Olgun has some fond memories of his schooling in England. He was treated kindly by all his teachers and received great understanding from the Headteacher. However, he describes it as a tough school He was very uncomfortable with the disruptive behaviour of some pupils and the disrespectful way they interacted with the teachers. Nevertheless, he achieved a great deal in the school and after only three years scored the highest marks in the class in his examinations. Yet he feels that school did not really acknowledge him as a person or make any connections with his culture: 'No confirmation on the part of the school. I was just another face you know'.

If individual teachers are remembered at all, they tend to be from primary school. Aliki has vivid memories of two of her teachers. She even remembers the name of her favourite infant teacher, who would play the guitar and sing songs. It was in this teacher's class that she first began to have ambitions to act, and she sees this as a turning point in her life:

> A: And those are really like quite vivid. I can even remember an image on the projector screen which is of a person a little person erm doing that (makes a gesture) and I remember saying to the teacher, 'Oh! I want to be that person on the screen' and that *really* sticks in my mind.

C: Why did you want to be that person on the screen?

A: Oh ... I don't know. That's a can of worms. I don't know

C: What do you mean can of worms?

A: I think it's to do with my perception of my sister and my family and me and how others perceive me and I don't know if it's possible at such a young age to have that ... maybe ... I don't know ... I certainly didn't enjoy going shopping at Sainsbury's at that very very young age, because people would look at us.

Aliki's memory is deeply but indirectly linked to questions of identity and how to hide her embarrassment about her sister's condition of cerebral palsy and the fact that her mum spoke Greek. Despite the obvious impact of the infant teacher she feels now that school had failed her and her sisters. She does not believe there was any connection with her own heritage:

I can't remember anything in terms of books or class discussions or ... ever relating to any other culture apart from English and that sticks in my brain. I don't know if that's just me as a grown up person sort of being defensive about it but (pause) I always thought that up to the end of secondary school that the whole thing had failed me and failed my sisters..erm..because I always had this 'But what about me?' ... Kind of thing ... 'What about me? Aren't I special? And if I am special, why am I special?' And I never identified that it was because I spoke another language or that I had another culture.

When her family moved to Enfield, Aliki moved to a secondary school which was even more eurocentric in its approach. She 'just went completely mad and rebelled against everything ... I kind of just lost hope'. Towards the end of our conversation I ask her what difference it might have made if teachers had understood and acknowledged her identity.

I think my self-image ... of myself and my family would have been a lot better than it has been because ... Not really by saying you're the best thing but someone acknowledging and respecting ... Not that it was disrespectful ... But in a sense it is disrespecting if you're not acknowledging it, not taking it into consideration, not encouraging it ... er, ... I think it would have made a huge difference ... I really do ... Yes!

Interestingly, she has a different take on success now:

I think ... erm ... I think I would have been personally more successful, because I think being academic makes no difference to me any more. I think it's about knowing who I am. What I'm about ... If I had had that initial input

I think I would have felt better about myself. And therefore I would just naturally achieved any way. I would have been more confident. I would have gone for things more ... I wouldn't have given up every time I came to confrontation or conflict ... ..

[.Formerly] ... it was frustrating. I couldn't do it ... I wanted to be good at the academic stuff but I couldn't because I didn't have the peace of mind and the confidence to do it ... to ... to see it through.

Michael has a similar take on the issue of success at school but gives it a slightly different spin. He is explicit about his views on his teachers:

C: Are there any teachers who stand out, who gave you support?

M: No

C: No?

M: Not one ... ... .I did very well at school. No thanks to teachers

Paradoxically, he talks throughout of his love of school and particularly his love of books.

I loved school ... when I was at school ... I loved ... you get me a new book ...right ... I just loved the feel of it ... I'd smell it and I couldn't wait to open it ... something fantastic to me and I couldn't wait to peek inside and see what's in it ... and yet I don't feel that the teachers did enough for people like myself to enable us to deal with school life.

Part of this was the teachers' failure to acknowledge the complexity of Caribbean creoles and recognise that they do constitute a different language system. This applies especially to his own linguistic background, which was the French based creole of Dominica.

It can't be just a different accent because the language I speak has nothing to do with English ...

In common with many Caribbean children of his generation, he was not clear about the rules of the game and the majority of teachers were uninformed about these linguistic subtleties. Therefore they were never given the appropriate support with their language.

... when I first came here I was ... I'm bilingual, I speak two languages and whilst I spoke English I still found English very daunting. Because when I came here ... if you was speaking to me now some of what you're saying would pass me ... you see what I mean, because my accent and my way of saying things would not be the same as ... So if you shoved a book in front of me ... there are certain things in it ... I would recognise it but ... That wasn't recognised you know. And there were quite a lot of Caribbean people in my school who did not have any other kind of support, who were not taken through the process. You were simply recognised as an English speaker and that was that.

Since Asif was one of the only two Asian pupils in his secondary school, no one took the trouble to build upon his cultural identity. In fact he felt he had to subsume this just to get by. I take this up in more detail in the next chapter in the analysis of his narrative.

Similar things happened to Nandine at school. She remembers individual primary teachers and was an avid reader, but the examples she gives are exclusively eurocentric favourites such as Roald Dahl:

> When I was younger I used to like reading lots. Even when we went to someone's house I'd end up finding a book and just sit there reading. So I was antisocial in a   way ... ..The usual stuff: comic books or novels erm ... I was reading things like *Charlie and the Chocolate Factory* and other Roald Dahl texts from when I was about ... er ... I suppose eight or nine ...

Like Michael, but for different reasons, Nandine used reading as a means of escape. When I asked her what appealed about those books she replied:

> Imagination. Just so much ... so much magic ... My life was so mundane and boring ... I'd just rather have my nose in a book ... Yeah, it sort of helped me balance the fact that I couldn't go out with my friends very much ... play on the streets ... things like that ...

She also enjoyed reading C.S. Lewis

> ... or there's something like *The Lion, the Witch and the Wardrobe* ... Sometimes ... we used to have this old big wardrobe and I used to think, God, if I could open that and disappear into this other land, you know.

There appear to be close parallels with Michael, who talks of his love of reading fantasy at a slightly older age:

> I was about ten ... eleven ... erm ... I loved comics..Superman ... I loved fantasy books I just chewed them up. One after the other. I loved science fiction. Anything that didn't have to do with ... If it wasn't reality based ... I liked it. If I didn't have to face up to reality, what was around me. I mean, if you gave me a book... erm ... a realistic book I would throw it back at you, because I didn't want to face up to anything that had reality in it. But it had to transport me somewhere. I had to feel I was somewhere else. I had to feel different.

However, the similarities are superficial. Michael's comments connect both to his earlier life in Dominica, listening to traditional stories suffused with magical realism and as an escape from brutal and violent racism he experienced in Canning Town and having to face the results of his father's frustrations.

> In terms of what that does to you is you feel yourself constantly under siege.

In contrast, it is boredom and drudgery that leads Nandine towards fantasy fiction:

> It wasn't that I was unhappy, that I was being abused or anything ... it was just, you know, the same old routine at home helping out. You sort of get into that. But I didn't question it at the time, 'Why do I read so much?' I just did it.

The by-product of this love of reading was that they both found it relatively easy to succeed at school work. Nandine was encouraged at primary school. Many teachers told her she was good at English. But there is no indication in her narrative that teachers made any connection with her heritage. In fact, when at sixteen she transferred to the Roman Catholic school for her sixth form studies, she experienced real difficulties for the first time and her parents hired a tutor for her. On the whole, however, there is no reference to any overt racism in the early years of schooling in any of her narratives.

In summary, when asked to talk about these issues explicitly the most common feeling is that these young adults have made it on their own, without much help from teachers. However, there is a significant gender difference when it comes to accounts of individual teachers. Of the men only Olgun mentions one by name: a headteacher who was particularly kind to him, whereas the women's narratives contain warm anecdotes about several teachers. My found her schooling a wholly productive and positive experience. Having said that, five of them explicitly talk about their love of school. Asif doesn't talk much about the detail of school, but concentrates upon describing his interaction with his peers at that stage. I found it surprising that five out of six successful people should have found nothing in their school life which connected with their heritage. Maybe this is inaccurate, but I am concerned less with the accuracy of their memories than with the narratives they have constructed. *Their* point of view. The stories they tell to others. *Their* history. In those terms they convey the *impression* that there was nothing. So that even if they did have teachers who in-tended to take account of their heritage, this was completely missed by those at whom it was directed. Moreover, these were not reluctant students. They were the kind of students who would be most open and receptive to such an approach. Therefore, because it is an unrepresentative sample this has wide implications for our profession. I return to this point in my concluding chapter.

The Mass Media

Although Asif was a media studies teacher he makes little explicit reference to the media in his conversation. One oblique reference is in his discussion of Islam. He is particularly scathing about the simplistic nations held about Islam by Westerners. In his view, there is a tendency to conflate it with a particular kind of fundamentalism. The media tends to concentrate on such aspects. This chimes in with Said's notion of Orientalism (1978). The Western media tends to perpetuate such mythologies. Asif observes that:

> ... when I have discussions with my dad and his friends it's about interpretations ... ie Turkey.. non-alcohol..Well it doesn't actually say non-alcohol (in the Qu'ran) it says 'Don't get drunk'. So the Turkish people drink ... yet it's an Islamic country ... So Attaturk and whatever he did in the twenties 'modernising' Turkey. Is it still an Islamic state and so on or, you know do we have to look to the Saudi experience? Who are the authentic holders of Islam? ... Or Singapore? Malaysia? There are lots of those countries which we're not actually aware of. Particularly in British culture, we tend to pick on a few ...

This question of stereotypical representation also bothers Aliki. From her child-hood she remembers that, if they appeared on television at all, people of her heritage were often lampooned in crude ways. After she talked about her poor self-image at the beginning of our conversation I asked her whether that was re-inforced by school. She replies:

> I think so yeah, yeah ... School and television, which may be why I was into drama and film and theatre. The fact that the images on television were not related, you know to the images around me, in my home and with my family ... And if you think that television is the be all and end all of how a child might see it, I probably thought, 'How comes we're not on television?' or our type isn't and when we were, we were funny ... I used to think, 'Oh, this is unfair ... I'd rather be English so that I could be on television' and if I were English then I would be on television and I think that translates into school...

As she describes it, this search for representation and a voice, this quest for in-clusion and acceptance, strongly influenced the direction of her life. Michael took this further in two directions. Part of his personal crisis as a religious person brought up in a Catholic family, was the popular image of Christ as a blue-eyed, blond-haired white man. This ubiquitous image, that appeared even on the walls of his own home, troubled him deeply. It is a powerful image and continues to exert a strong influence over many people even in these supposedly secular times. Combined with his experience of racism, the image was profoundly dis-turbing. He articulates the contradiction:

> I go out into the world ... I'm beaten up by white people. I'm oppressed. I'm told I'm a particular way. But that very image of whiteness is up on my wall. The very image which oppresses me, abuses me, I have to go home and worship. Now I've got to go in a church and worship him and I'm told that, 'That is OK'. That doesn't fit well with me. Do you see what I'm saying?

In his home, where I interviewed him, the walls were covered with representations of Christ and other biblical characters as black people. This problem of representation remains deeply problematic, although there has been some progress since his schooldays in the seventies. However, he sees that the media has extended the powerful dominant discourses of the United States, especially in the Caribbean, which has undermined the sense of community:

> ... what has happened is you have different cultures ... you have an American way of looking at things. Because what has happened is (that) before the American culture was not so dominant. Now you have a way of looking at life which is influenced by outside. So the unity and closeness, the way of looking at things is not the same ... it's crumbling away.

However, he is quick to assert that he is not against change *per se*:

> I think things will never stay the same. I'm not someone who believes that everything should stay. I think things change and they need to change. What I feel is that there are certain things that I'm seeing that are not very good ... I think they're destructive

He talks of the values which come through soap operas:

> ... it comes with all other things ... There is a glorification of certain values ... selfish values

He links this world wide phenomenon with the observation that there does not seem to be a viable alternative for the young at present.

Nandine, on the other hand, does not see the media as a homogeneous phenomenon. In her own position she has found alternative discourses which have been helpful and supportive in her dilemmas with her own parents and community. She talks about the television programme, *Goodness, Gracious Me*, which is written by Asian people and lampoons aspects of the British-Asian lifestyle:

> I mean there's some parts that are very badly done ... not very funny. But just the fact that there are, here, now a set of people that can laugh at things that are wrong with our culture without people being offended ... and there's a lot to go against.

She also talks about a documentary called *Inside Story*, in which the filmakers interviewed 'three Asian women who had chosen to be with English partners'. It had powerful resonances for her:

> ... the actual emotion they felt I could identify with ... you know, that separation. You know, having the complete ... being completely ostracised from your family ... and just to know that there are other young women out there who have experienced things like that ... Not having any sense of revenge or ... Just wanting to get on with life wanting them to accept and recognise that they have chosen something different, they haven't changed ... I just think it's very sad. But there are other women out there that are like...

C: And does that personally give you a lot of strength?

N: Mmmm..It does ... It does ... I felt very empowered by it.

Our relationship with the mass media is extremely complex, but it is maybe an extension of media which have always existed eg visual art and the written word. Plato criticised the medium of writing for precisely the same reasons that we criticise current technological advances.

The dilemmas outlined by Strange (1994:120), in her review of the 'knowledge economy' certainly need to be addressed. They reflect the thoughts explored by the three participants.

> Firstly there are changes in the provision and control over information and communications systems. Secondly there are changes in the use of language and non-verbal channels of communication. And thirdly there are changes in the fundamental perceptions of and beliefs about the human condition which influence value judgments and, through them political and economic decisions and policy. Strange (1994:120)

The question of value is a fundamental element in the six individuals' ability to create a coherent and satisfying sense of self throughout this complex period of change. The role of the media in the process of identity formation is clearly powerful and ambiguous. As yet research into people's relationship to the mass media is at an early stage. As Kathleen Hall (1999:13) points out, there are inherent limitations to what the media can do in its representations of 'real life':

> Media representations of 'real life' create a public 'space' where viewers in the privacy of their homes are brought into a zone of 'time-space compression'. In this space a fiction is created which seduces audiences into believing that they can know other realities by simply encountering them in a decontextualized media world ... programmes

> produce selective and partial ... views and interpretations of the complex cultural worlds they represent

Explicit views on identity

All six individuals have a fluid and mobile sense of identity. Through their study and reading most are aware of the current debates in the area . Being 'organic intellectuals' (see Gramsci: 1988:300-322) they also read these debates critically in the light of their own experiences. Each locates themselves in a slightly different position. In terms of allegiance Olgun, My and Michael seem to be near to their 'traditional' heritages, whereas Nandine, Asif and Aliki have broken with some of the basic premises of their heritage culture. It may just be coincidence that the first three were born in their parents' homeland whilst the others were not. Nandine is in the midst of undergoing profound, painful and fundamental changes in her sense of self. My says very little, yet her pithy comment that 'I have three strands to my identity, my Chinese strand, my Vietnamese strand and my English strand. If you take one strand away there is no My', points to a complex and intertwined sense of self.

Others are more explicit. Asif's musings have been detailed in this chapter and the last. His view embraces all aspects of his identity, but is informed by a critical stance. He sees himself as a 'European traveller'. His sense of self is complex and unfinalised and he has no respect for those who have taken on an English persona uncritically. A critical awareness is fundamental for him. In this he has a similar viewpoint to Aliki. Her theatrical work explores her own dilemmas in powerful ways. This working through was not an altogether deliberate or conscious act. When I asked her if this exploration of identity links to her quest for peace of mind she replies:

> I think so ... Yeah ... Maybe I'm ..I feel I'm trying to make sense of them for myself or ... I don't know ... I think it is ... Even when I do them., I don't realise I'm doing them. I mean, when I wrote it, that play, it didn't have as much significance to me as it does now.

This is further complicated in so far as both Aliki and Asif have made reconciliations with their families and the cultural legacy of their parents, but clearly on their own terms. Both see identity construction as unfinished business. Aliki articulates it this way:

> The way that I feel about it now is I don't think it's over. I think there's more to come. I don't know if it will rear its head when I'm in a position to marry, settle down with someone ...

Olgun continues to explore his sense of self through study for his MA, particularly his relationship to Greek Cypriots:

> I mean ... I chose to do it on Cyprus to understand why it happened and what are the reasons for it. I'm reading Greek books, British books, Turkish books and my experiences. I know more than..what I thought I knew ...

Formal analysis of history, memory and narrative is a validation of his own experiences – in Bakhtin's words, 'an internally persuasive discourse'.

As illustration of this complex syncretism, Michael offers an extended overview of how he sees his own identity, which is far more complex than the theorists' picture of identity construction. In his view there must be coherence and continuity. However, he does not completely dismiss the postmodernist position:

> '... you can slip in ... because I slip into identities ... But you need to have a concrete identity. By that I mean you need to have a core identity around which ... like a sun and everything else all other identities rotate around that sun ...

> C: What does that core consist of?

> M: It's my Caribbeanness ... fused in with a little bit of my Britishness and that creates ... but it's not ...

> C: But it's not an essentialist notion, then?

> M: It's something more abstract..it is an abstract treatment.. It is the sum of my experiences that I have chipped away at..throughout my growing up. I have fashioned a sense of who I am. Now that sense of who I am is something I have worked at. Chipped away at all the fogginess. Chipped way at all the nonsense. Chipped away at all the things that I feel are unnecessary ... What is left is me ... You know I have chipped away at all the nonsense values I was taught. I've chipped away all the nonsense histories. The nonsense religions. I chipped way all the nonsense things about what British is, all the nonsense about what it is to be Caribbean and what I am left with is something I feel is me. It is the core. It is all the crap thrown away.

> ... It is being grounded in a way of being that I feel is me. My ideas of what life is is not based on what others have told me, but what I have come to find out for myself ... and that has grounded me. It has rooted me like a tree.

> Now that rootedness does change, but then you'll always find your way back to that rootedness. That core of who you are.

So his view of the core identity is many layered and paradoxical. It changes, yet there is coherence. It is like our ever-changing physical appearance. It is neither random nor arbitrary. There is pattern. There is continuity. There are strands which persist and endure over time. Memory is the link. Memory is culturally learned and mediated. It is soaked in the grammar of our experience. It is shaped through the cadence of the narratives we create to make sense of it and to render it meaningful and manageable. How this is achieved is explored further in the next two chapters.

Conclusions

Although there are unmistakable patterns in each of their experiences, what is emerging is a fascinatingly complex picture, which demonstrates how these six people are reworking their understandings of each strand of their identity. Such identities are not hybrid grafts – they do not wear their English identity merely as a mask or a flag of convenience. I argue that they are working through complex internal and external processes by facing dilemmas which confront us all.

Each person has unearthed a complex set of allegiances and ambivalences regarding their heritage cultures. All take a critical stance and have balanced the issues in profound and individual ways. All 'bring home forcefully ... the paradoxical sense that ethnicity is something reinvented and reinterpreted in each generation by each individual ... Ethnicity is not something that is simply passed on from generation to generation, taught and learned; it is something dynamic, often unsuccessfully repressed or avoided' (Fisher, 1986:195). Even within the unmistakably common patterns, there are subtle and intricate differences woven through the fabric of their daily lives. They hold similarly complex allegiances and ambivalences to the dominant culture too; through schooling, the media and their differing experiences of racism and their diverse strategies for coping with this disturbingly pervasive aspect of modern cosmopolitan living.

So the pattern is complex and uneven. It certainly seems that routines learned early in life persist longer and allow people to engage with aspects of their heritage in routinised and unthinking ways. They may well be genuinely comfortable with this but it does chime in with Bakhtin's view of two types of action, which he calls rhythm and loophole. Rhythm consists of routinised patterns of behaviour, which we engage in without being fully aware of what we are doing. Most actions have some practical imperative. The danger with rhythm is that it becomes an uncritical way of behaving, where we do not take individual responsibility for our actions. It can be a dull and uncreative way of living. Loophole, on the other, hand means being fully aware and looking for ways of resolving the problems of living in ways which are dynamic, creative and ethical.

The problem the stories raise is whether it is possible radically and consciously to change our identity. Although identities are constructed, some elements appear more basic than others to their constitution. Although changes do take place over time the difficulties involved in consciously changing our identity should not be underestimated. Although it is liberating that 'postmodernist' thinkers have unsettled essentialist notions of identity and shown the creative possibilities offered by playing with identities, they have not sufficiently considered the 'residual' aspects of identity formation. Identities are still constructed within layers of historical experience and within specific political structures, hierarchies and struggles. As Nandine's account showed, identities cannot be shed for pragmatic reasons without great emotional cost.

Memory plays an important part in the process. Remembering is active, dynamic and creative. We are continually 'modernising the past' (Yourcenar: 1957/1994). Whereas memory's dark shadow, forgetting, is less amenable to conscious change. Often memories flood back unbidden to disturb our view of ourselves and the world. Several of the people involved in this study express disapproval of people they know, family or acquaintances, who try to alter their behaviour to gain material advantage in the workplace. They see them as denying aspects of their own history and heritage merely to gain promotion and recognition. All feel that contradictions need to be faced and dealt with. There is a difference between 'hating tradition properly' (to use Adorno's (1978/1951) phrase) and submitting uncritically to the dominant discourses of the powerful.

'Hating tradition properly' means maintaining a courageous and critical dialogue with our own heritage. It means being able to weigh and balance the positive and the negative of all the networks we belong to. In other words, maintaining integrity. Integrity is also the root of integration in terms of personality. Questions of differing values are a central problematic to cross cultural understanding. At present we appear to want to leave such difficult aspects of pluralism to one side, unexamined. But these are the issues which the people in this study are grappling with in their various ways. I have detected a strong emphasis on values throughout the narratives. Many of the dilemmas they face centre upon ethical issues and this is fundamental to the construction of their identities. This is not to diminish the problems which exist in terms of power and struggle. The dilemmas of identity are among the most challenging questions of our time.

All six individuals feel they are richer in a human sense for confronting their dilemmas with honesty and integrity. Having detailed and intimate knowledge of a range of cultural possibilities gives them distinct advantages, among them:

- a critical distance from social and political issues and an ability to make comparisons

- a more complex, yet integrated view of the self

- explicit understandings of the issues of identity

- a broader and deeper understanding of the current global situation – as Stuart Hall has commented: 'We're all diasporic now'.

- an understanding of the relationship between culture and power

- the development of radical values which go beyond and often conflict with values of the home culture and of the dominant culture. These values often draw on existing academic discourses and debates, most notably feminist discourses.

As their stories demonstrate, new formations in terms of identity are neither un-problematic, nor painless. However, far from being disadvantaged by this situation, the six individuals are open to a wide range of influences and are making critical sense of them. In the next chapter I delve more deeply into how they are actually constructing that sense of identity through their narratives. To look at the patterns of their 'storied lives' (Rosenwald and Ochberg 1992) and to examine how they use basic narrative devices, ie employment, character, scene, time and point of view (Clandenin and Connelly 2000:19) in order to recount and make sense of their lives, I use a framework I have developed from Bakhtin's (1979) consideration of character development both in the novel and in life.

6

Orchestrating Contradictions: Identity Construction

There were three men went down the road
As down the road went he
The man he was
The man folk saw
The man he wished to be
Source unknown

As the poem points out, our awareness of ourselves is at best problematic.
In fact it is a thoroughly complicated affair: many levelled, multi-faceted,
and ever changing. Randall (1997:345)

The flow of events forms our external life, while within us a series of
pictures is painted. The two correspond but are not identical.
Rabindranath Tagore (1917:17)

Why Bakhtin's triad?

This chapter examines how the varying elements, influences, discomforts and
ambivalences identified in the last chapter are woven into a distinctive identity.
It is clear that the construction of identity consists of much more than slipping
in and out of roles to negotiate many different social networks. Nothing works
in isolation. Each facet of a person's identity impacts on the others. This results
in complex inner and outer dialogues. Such syncretism is achieved by the
orchestration of different influences and significant events into a coherent sense
of self. This process of orchestration is clearly evident in the self-narratives of
the six individuals. Until now, the process has not been empirically examined
and analysed.

I had to construct a research tool to throw the aspects of identity construction into clear relief. I call this **whole dialogue analysis**. I needed a framework that was sophisticated, flexible and dynamic and, at the same time, relatively simple and straightforward to use.

For this purpose I drew upon Vygotsky's (1978, 1986) and Bakhtin's (1979. 1981, 1984, 1986, 1986a) idea that human consciousness is a product of the interplay between our internal consciousness and the external forces acting upon us, mediated by socially generated symbolic systems eg gesture, language, art, music, dance etc. Since I was analysing taped interviews, I concentrated upon language. The theories of Bakhtin and Vygotsky avoid the over-determination of rationalist/behaviourist models by returning to the individual the responsibility for their own actions. They also mitigate against the extremes of postmodernist thinking, which affirms that identities are constructed, but which greatly under-estimates the power and influence of external forces to constrain and shape our thoughts and actions.

I turned to an early work of Bakhtin (1979), where he first put forward his ideas of the relationship between insidedness and outsidedness in the development of human consciousness in an early work entitled, 'Author and Hero in Aesthetic Activity'. As Morson and Emerson (1990:179) point out:

> Bakhtin extends his ethical concepts into the realm of the aesthetic. Now his primary concern is not so much with individual responsibility and the ways we answer for ourselves in an act as with the ways in which we come to create images of others and ourself for others ... Bakhtin examines the process of self formation in both art and life ...

A Description of the Framework

Bakhtin suggests that the development of consciousness consists of a triad comprising the following elements:

- **others for self**: ('the man he wished to be') how others appear to me (influential people, role models)

- **self for others**: ('the man folk saw') how I appear to others (my social persona)

- **self for self**: ('the man he was') how I perceive myself from the inside

I used Bakhtin's categories to code and sort the interviews to demonstrate the development of identity in the six people in the study. The patterns were uneven. The differences appear to be linked to narrative styles and subtleties of social and cultural etiquettes. For example some of the participants describe their struggles and discomforts forcefully, while others have a quiet and understated style of unfolding their tale.

Such practices are learned in families and form basic constituent to our individual identity. The past exerts a much greater constraining force on cultural change than has been recognised by many postmodernist theorists. Using Bakhtin's categories to examine their life narratives revealed how deep the roots of tradition are. The individuals work through contradictions and ambivalences to gain an authentic and balanced sense of identity, whereby they acknowledge all areas of their social existence. This process consists of a constant rewriting of the self. Although identity, like the body, is always in the process of change, it does, like the body, have a recognisable consistency and continuity, which persists throughout life. Indeed, the body is an integral part of our identity. Coherence is achieved through the narrative devices by which we 'story' our lives and create our own mythologies of self.

Sorting the narratives

Once I had transcribed the conversations and coded various sections of the narratives, I transferred this contextualised information onto grids for analysis (for examples see Appendix 1). This clarified the developmental processes considerably. More specifically, it demonstrated how the different elements interact within the narratives. In short it became a **window upon the syncretic processes which were taking place in the life of each person** as they weighed and balanced the often contradictory events and discourses. The framework enabled me to trace the development of identity as it progressed through our entire dialogues. My original plan was to organise the material chronologically but this became unnecessary. In most cases, the stories tended to be told in roughly chronological order, allowing for the usual amount of room for flashbacks or projections into the future that occur in even the most straightforward narrative. Only Aliki's story is not strictly chronological.

Another reason I decided against presenting the narratives in chronological order is that, in common with many long narratives, the effect is cumulative. We see this in a coda to my conversation with Michael, when I asked him to re-describe a memory from his childhood in Dominica. He recalled his experiences of watching traditional stories and dance being performed on a beach in the moonlight. After describing this he went on to connect it with his earlier analysis of his own identity and his current work in fiction and poetry. He also connected the experience and the stories he heard with the magical realism of authors such as Gabriel Garcia-Marquez and Isabel Allende and the African writer Ben Okri. To try and separate these reflections would destroy not only the important connections he was making, it would also destroy its beauty and its meaning. I therefore decided to let the chronology of the recorded event take precedence over the chronology of the life described as this tells us more about the nature of memory.

The advantages of whole dialogue analysis

Using whole dialogue analysis I discovered that whole conversations on a single topic have a cumulative effect akin to a novel. Once the conversation is underway, certain basic premises and understandings emerge which are built upon and developed throughout the conversation. **Viewed from this perspective, it becomes clear that far from being shapeless and arbitrary, whole conversations have a definite architecture and follow precise narrative patterns**.

Although there are obvious differences in the narrative approaches of each individual, there are clear patterns too. By coding the various stages of development, I was able to summarise the information contained on the original grids ie using the headings which had emerged in my original sorting (See Appendix 2 for examples). This form of analysis gives a different perspective to the stories and links them closely to much of the theoretical and speculative in social psychology, where the self is viewed as being continually re-inscribed. (Freeman:1993) The same events are being rewritten over and over again from new perspectives.

Development of personal identity and the demands of the narrative genre

It also became apparent that the requirements of the narrative genre make it necessary for the individuals to present their memories in a rhythm of causal sequences. Personal development can be viewed most readily in the 'self for self' column. Periods of discomfort and crisis invariably precede moments of epiphany or temporary resolution. Crises are almost always precipitated by a dissonance or discomfort over the demands made by the social group which the individual finds uncomfortable or unsettling.

Finding meaningful categories

Once I had coded the stories according to Bakhtin's categories, I gave each section a heading which seemed meaningful. I wished for the categories to emerge, rather than to allow myself to get trapped in a rigid framework. Initially, I found that the categories I had used were not of the same order: eg 'role model' is not of the same categorical order as 'influence'. So I refined them, subdividing them into 'Aspects of outsidedness' and 'Stages of Development'(See Figure 1). I also found that it made more sense to employ them as a dyad, eg Role model/Influence; Dominant culture/Discomfort etc.

Most of the categories are self-explanatory, with the exception of 'epiphany' which I appropriated from James Joyce. I have used it to describe the breakthrough to a temporary and unfinalised sense of equilibrium between internal perceptions and outside forces, which results in an authentic sense of self. For

Figure 1. Categories for coding the narratives

Aspects of outsidedness/influences	Stages of Development
• Role model/Parent (RM)	• Influence
• Heritage:Community/history/tradition (H)	• Prolepsis
• Dominant Culture (DC)	• Ambition
• Alternative norms/role model (AltRM)	• Discomfort
	• Ambivalence
	• Reflection
	• Epiphany

example, when Michael realised that he did not have to put up with 'the non-sense he was being fed', he had found alternative models which in turn enhanced his own way of expressing himself, and contributed to his clear and distinctive individual voice.

Examination of the processes

To examine those dynamic processes at work in the narratives of two of the six individuals, I have chosen vignettes that centre round their individual epiphanies. This is where syncretic influences achieve at least temporary closure. The maps themselves help us locate these crucial moments in their current constructions of identity. They also reveal both the broader and more immediate contexts in which they occur. I analyse them in detail here to demonstrate how different and often conflicting elements are internally orchestrated to give an integrated and coherent sense of self-identity.

For the sake of clarity I begin each analysis with a brief summary of the relevant section of the conversation to be analysed. This is followed by the table showing a summary of the analysis of the section of the conversation. The detail of the analysis comes after the general maps.

Asif

When we spoke it appeared that Asif was in the process of making sense of how he related to his heritage culture. This was precipitated by recent events in his family. His father had recently returned to the Islamic faith, following a serious illness. He retells this as a series of epiphanies on his own identity. We can see how he stories the conflicting loyalties and understandings in a series of moves. The transcription of the section of the conversation summarised below took up eight handwritten pages of my quarto notebook.

Summary of the conversation

Asif begins by talking about the history of his family's migration from Dehli to Karachi. According to him it was a 'chain migration' of a large Urdu speaking community. He describes how the Urdu speaking community achieved economic power in Karachi and how this has caused friction with the indigenous population ever since 1948. He also speaks of the political movement the MQM, which represents the interests of this Urdu speaking community.

He then goes on to speak about how he wanted to travel to Karachi and thought that he would fit in easily. It was at this point that he had the rude awakening. He realised that his Urdu would not be adequate for him to get by. In addition it was not the majority language. At my request he talks about his fluency in Urdu, saying that he was fluent in primary school.

He then moves on to describe how as only one of two Asian boys in the school he rejected his linguistic and cultural background at secondary school. He describes how he is coming back to a recognition of his parents' heritage, but on his own terms. This process involves a great deal of discussion with his parents and his uncles. He talks of his father's illness and how it caused him to return to Islam.

Asif goes on to speak about his own experiences at Islamic school and how he didn't understand what was going on because the lessons were conducted in Classical Arabic. He ends by describing his present position as regards religion.

Map of Asif's conversation

When I analysed this section a clear pattern began to emerge:

Others for self	Self for others	Self for self
	Heritage/Influence	
	Heritage/Ambivalence	
		Epiphany
	Heritage/Influence	
	Heritage Culture	
	and Dominant Culture/Discomfort	
Heritage (school)/Discomfort		
(metanarrative)		
	Heritage/Ambivalence	
	Heritage/(school)/Influence	
Heritage/Discomfort		
		Epiphany

Observation

The first thing to notice is the movement back and forth in the narrative from outsidedness to insidedness. Moreover, most of the entries revealing outside influences are in the category 'Self for others'. Unsurprisingly, they all have 'Heritage' as their main focus. This is an epiphany about belonging (or not) to his heritage. His view of outsidedness is also evenly balanced between his influences and ambivalences. This reveals that this is no easy move, although there is no lack of clarity in the final outcome.

The way Asif presents his argument is also interesting. It is a conventional Western liberal humanist way of constructing an argument. He considers each side in an even handed and tolerant way and argues a rational outcome. A potentially controversial or seemingly insensitive remark often carries a rider. Where he speaks of his father's return to faith after a heart attack, he notes that it is a common phenomenon for people who experience serious illness, then adds, 'Maybe that's cynical on my part'. In his piece, such evaluations are quite often in the form of a meta-narrative, where he steps back from the story to give an additional, necessary context to the content or a reason for a judgment which will follow. Likewise he is keen to acknowledge the positive qualities of his heritage culture and in his first epiphany in the sequence he tells of his dawning understanding that he did not know his heritage culture as well as he thought.

Detailed analysis

If we break this conversation down further we see that his argument consists of two moves. In the first he distances himself from the way people behave in his parent's 'homeland'.

Others for self	Self for others	Self for self
	H/Influence	
	H/Ambivalence	
		Epiphany

This is achieved in quite a complex way. He begins by describing his heritage with some pride. He outlines the positive achievements of his heritage community in the homeland (H/Influence). He tells of the movement of his family's community from India to Pakistan, which he describes as a 'chain migration'. He describes how '... a lot of that was going on. One family would settle and say 'Life is good in Karachi' Come here.' So he sees this as an important part of his history and his heritage. The community became economically successful in Karachi and have formed a political group, the MQM (the Mahajar Qom Movement). Here Asif displays his knowledge of the political and economic background.

His narrative then charts some ambivalence in terms of his own knowledge, H/Ambivalence. He achieves this in a way that Labov (1972) would call 'complication', a standard narrative device where some issue of doubt or conflict is raised.

> I was shocked actually because I had had assumed that all Pakistanis speak Urdu ... I was going through a bit of independent travelling ... I thought, 'I'll go to Pakistan I'll just wander ... I look the part ... I'll be able to go anywhere.' But it's only the top 8%, who've got Urdu.

This first epiphany (Epiphany) is that he did not understand the culture as well as he thought he did.

> Urdu is the language of the educated and everybody else has got Punjabi or Sindi or Beluchi ... It scuppered my plans a bit because Dad speaks Punjabi, but I don't.

Asif is learning something about the complexity and contradiction of the relationship between the 'homeland' and the 'diaspora'. Ironically this discovery came from a *Lonely Planet* Travel Guide.

His second narrative move builds on the first:

Others for self	Self for others	Self for self
	H/Influence	
	H and DC/Discomfort	
		H/Discomfort
H(school)/Discomfort (metanarrative)		
	H/Ambivalence	
	H/(school)/Influence	
H/Discomfort		
		Epiphany

At my request, Asif talks about his competence in Urdu and he relates how he maintained it at primary school and how this has given him a strong base. (H/Influence)

> Within six months I'm sure I'd be speaking properly.

This leads to the next complication. (H and DC/Discomfort) Talk of secondary school triggers uncomfortable associations about conflicting loyalties between his own heritage and the dominant culture.

> I think in secondary, when there's that social identity finding, where do I fit? What do I speak? What am I? And being one of two Asian boys in this school in Swindon and 'You're not a Paki, you're just like us really' and I sort of bought into that wanting to be part of the group.

Here he demonstrates how he had to subsume the Asian strand of his identity in the face of racism from his classmates. It is interesting to note that he follows this progression through relating it to his attitudes to his heritage language:

> Say the turbulent stage of teenage-hood from say thirteen to seventeen, I didn't speak an awful lot, but obviously I listened.

The conflicting discourses of his family and his schoolmates are difficult to resolve and his narrative moves forward to the present, but still with some discomfort. He begins with language:

> Then suddenly the use of Urdu again is a cultural thing that I'm trying to grab hold of again to sort of rein that in.

This then broadens out into a discussion of wider considerations and residual discomforts with his heritage, which he portrays as an ongoing internal and external dialogue.

> I'm not rejecting it as a blanket rejection of whatever this cultural melee is, but I'm very clear where I fit in within that. But I use my parents a lot, my father in particular, to bounce ideas off and to clarify those boundaries for myself for what is and what isn't.

He talks of this in relation to his father's recent enthusiasm for Islam:

> So he's doing that and it's good for him, but he feels very bad that I'm not. And he feels very much that it was his cultural duty to do that. To actually get me involved in religion from an early age. And he did make a few little attempts.

This in turn triggers two memories which illustrate Asif's ambivalences (H/Ambivalence). One concerns the time his father bought him booklets introducing children to the Qu'ran, which he seems to have enjoyed. The other is a discussion of his time at the mosque school, which bored him, as he related in the last chapter. Both demonstrate how little Asif was affected by such teachings. He readily admits that that is not how he would have seen it as a child. At the time he was willing to go along with his parents' wishes (H/(school)/Influence). However, in his meta-narrative Asif is critical of such approaches from his perspective as a qualified teacher (H(school)/Discomfort (meta-narrative)). This shows the complex set of conflicting forces awaiting internal resolution. He then moves on to describe his own view. He remains unconvinced that he should return to Islam and argues the point with his uncles and his father (H/Discomfort). This leads to the second Epiphany where he describes his current position. He cannot admit to faith because he simply does not feel it. His interest is from a sociological/cultural/political perspective. Although he rejects the premises his family put forward, he is also highly critical of the stereotyped assumptions prevailing in most of the dominant discourses in Britain concerning Islam. He is interested that the complexity of the Islamic diaspora should be recognised and not just the narrowest and most illiberal manifestations which the media concentrate upon.

Summary and findings

One advantage of analysing the conversation according to the framework suggested by Bakhtin is that it reveals how the different elements of Asif's past experiences and present understandings are orchestrated in a complex and critical way. He is not simply shedding one set of self-understandings to take on another, even though some of the situations have forced him to make tough decisions and uncomfortable compromises. Cultural change as it manifests itself in an individual consciousness is a labyrinthine process. Both the internal and external dialogues are ongoing. The process is deeply social and complex.

Another advantage to using the framework is that the whole dialogue approach allows us to identify gaps in the narratives. This does not mean that they are real gaps in the sense that they have never been considered or addressed. Any narrative is going to be incomplete in some way. For Asif there is little reference to the dominant culture and only one example of discomfort in this area. His dealings with the dominant culture are perhaps an area that he feels he's already resolved to his own satisfaction. This is hinted at by the fact that he talks about strategies that enabled him to experience 'belonging' or 'inclusion' in areas where his family has been excluded. So it is possible that his relationship to the dominant culture is not the issue it once was. It plays a smaller part in his current narrative of self. Moreover, there are no alternative role models mentioned although it is clear that he is widely read and he does identify with the struggles of other marginalised people. He has read and been influenced by the same authors as Michael. Again we need to be careful about drawing any definite conclusion, except to note that these issues are not high on Asif's current agenda. They appear to have been integrated into his world-view. They are now normalised and taken for granted. What the extract does show is how he is re-integrating himself into his heritage on his own terms and that this is a very delicate process.

The other example I wish to analyse in some detail is Aliki. She demonstrates more explicitly how she deals with the conflict between their personal history and heritage and the dominant culture.

Aliki

Summary of a conversation

Aliki demonstrates a different approach in achieving her own syncretism. Like Asif she is attempting to reconsider her heritage on her own terms, but her route is markedly different. If we consider the map of her whole conversation, there are, in fact, marked differences from all the others analysed. Her epiphanies occur more frequently and appear earlier, both in terms of the narrative and chronologically. Her first epiphany relates to an event that happened in school when she was six. The teacher showed a picture of a performer on an OHP screen. The memory is so vivid that she even remembers the teacher's name. Her reaction was to tell the teacher that she wanted to be the person on the screen. This relates to her poor self-image as she interprets it now. At the time of the interview, she felt that the episode in the infant school put her on the path to being a performer and that this in turn led to her method of working through her dilemmas creatively. In the narrative she sees this as a real turning point.

Secondly, Aliki is the only one of the six who describes vivid eidetic memories, which occurred before she was able to talk. These memories are usually composed of images and sensations and do not have a narrative value, ie there is no 'point' to them. No tension. No resolution. They are even harder to corroborate than those related as a narrative. But they are laden with affect, as are all her narratives. She really feels her past as she relives it.

The third point is that her conversation is the least chronological. It tends to be thematic. The section we are about to examine is a typical example of her approach. She begins by discussing the poor self-image she developed at primary school. Her narrative then turns to how these negative feelings lasted for a long time, 'up to the end of [her] degree'. Then she gives an account of how the issue was resolved, by returning to episodes from different parts of her degree course. Part of this lack of chronology could be explained by the fact that this was the first conversation in the present study and I had not yet developed the strategy of asking her to tell me something about her parents' journey to Britain. However, I did ask her to think about her earliest memories. So perhaps this is a characteristic of her narrative style.

It would certainly fit in with the culturally based findings of Deborah Tannen's research (1980), with references to Greek women's autobiographical narratives conducted in the US. She compared the narratives of Greek and American women after viewing a film and concluded that the Greeks seemed to be 'acute judges' who recounted events and interpreted them, ascribing motives to characters and offering judgments, whereas the Americans were 'acute recallers' who gave more detailed descriptive accounts and were more concerned with accuracy of detail and chronology. While Americans focused on content, Greeks focused on interpersonal involvement. Though we must treat such generalisation with caution, Aliki's narrative bears out this approach in both its overarching structure and the detail of her observation. It is worth noting that she is a Cypriot, whereas Tannen's group were from Athens.

In my analysis I wish to concentrate upon the series of epiphanies which happened during her degree course in Community Arts. It was as part of this course that she performed her one woman show described in the Preface.

Map of the Conversation

Others for self	Self for others	Self for self
DC/Discomfort		
	DC/Discomfort	
		Epiphany
	Epiphany	
DC/Discomfort		
	DC/Discomfort	
		Epiphany
AltRM/Influence		
		Epiphany
AltRM/Influence		
AltRM/Influence		
		Epiphany
DC/Discomfort		
	DC/Discomfort	
	DC/Discomfort	
DC/Ambivalence		
		Epiphany
	DC/Discomfort	
AltH/Influence		
	DC/Discomfort	
No role model		
		Epiphany

Her telling is energetic, complex and detailed. By freeing herself from the chronology she makes explicit links with different parts of her experience. Themes are reworked and revisited. Her narrative consists of several layers.

Detailed analysis

The first layer: Beginning with complication

The first layer summarises the whole pattern in three statements to do with her self-image that have a direct movement from outside to inside and an internal resolution, ie

DC/Discomfort

                     DC/Discomfort

                                  Epiphany

                    Epiphany

DC/Discomfort

                     DC/Discomfort

DC/Discomfort

                                    Epiphany

She begins her narrative with a complication, which is a narrative technique used extensively by film-makers. It immediately grabs the audience's attention. This device can be seen earlier in the weddings story, which begins with the potentially shocking statement, 'I hated weddings'. She introduces this first section of her narrative with an account of her desire to be like the 'other' (DC/Discomfort). This is a recurring theme throughout the conversation. In this case it is:

> an Irish friend who lived up the road ... I was really jealous of her ... because she was white. She had blonde hair and she was ever so pale, but like porcelain looking.

This affects how she would like to be for others (DC/Discomfort) and contrasts with her actual appearance

> I think I just loved that sort of image and I thought 'Oh I want to be that' and you can see how it relates. I'm so dark and curly haired ...

This state of affairs lasted a long time:

> I think I carried that all the way through until the end of my degree.

She then moves forward to hint at her epiphany, where there is an anticipation that these discomforts will be resolved. She maintains the narrative interest. Her analytical approach drives her to isolate two causes of the changes. First:

I came out of a long term relationship which was oppressive.

She goes on to explain that this had severely undermined her self-confidence in terms of her heritage. It was also linked to her own experience of teaching. During her school experience as a student, she worked with pupils from similar backgrounds to herself. That experience added another level of insight. It

... suddenly made me realise that you couldn't put people in boxes and deny them who they were. Because with some kids , I'd think, 'I know why you're doing that' and in terms of drama, I know that they've got their sentences mixed up and it sounds awkward and it sounds gawky and that's why the other kids don't want them in their group. And it just clicked and I thought, 'That's me!' or 'That's how I perceive myself' and that's why I can't move forward because I won't let myself move forward ...

All this is linked to the fact that she was in an oppressive relationship at the time (DC/Discomfort). She also realised that some of the criticisms her boyfriend made of her behaviour were culturally inflected. She elaborates:

... he was very middle class, but trying to be ... trying to understand other people, which is positive ultimately ... .my mannerisms, my gestures, what I thought about things he put down to aggression and he told me I was aggressive. Whereas now when I look back and when I started changing I started thinking 'Well actually that's not aggression. It's just me! It's part of my culture. We're like that you know!' (Epiphany)

The second layer: Alternative Role Models

AltRM/Influence

                                               Epiphany

AltRM/Influence

AltRM/Influence

                                               Epiphany

In the second layer, Aliki elaborates further on this transformation and how another person (AltRM/Influence) who took genuine delight in diversity helped her to accommodate those cultural aspects to her identity that she had been trying so hard to bury or deny. Here she weaves in a second theme, which contributes to the resolution of her discomfort

A: It came from another teacher who..er..told me that he thought it was great and I was so lucky to be Greek and so lucky to have such a culture and told me that I ought not to think too much about how I look or how other people see me and really encouraged, you know my family thing and he said, 'I bet you have really nice family meals. And I bet they're really loud and that's really nice' and I said, 'No they're not!'

C: And was he right?

A: Yes, absolutely, because you know, I go home and it doesn't bother me anymore ... I don't resent it (Epiphany). I think a lot of times I resented it I just wanted to leave the room and not be around my family.

Here again she only hints at a resolution. She then returns to her second theme and elaborates on the influence of the other teacher (AltRM/Influence) to analyse the impact of his approval. This is made more forceful by her direct comparison of the two conflicting influences:

to suddenly have someone tell you you were really great for ... .in comparison to someone who says you're aggressive and you ought to be more ladylike and you ought to think about how you speak and you know maybe read a book so that you can articulate and learn more about language ... I couldn't stop myself from accepting that kind of attention because I think that's what I was craving for years and years and years ... it was a release..and ever since then I've phshhheeww... (raises hand to indicate a rapid growth in her self confidence) (Epiphany).

Aliki makes the sudden realisation that the cultural modes of expression she learned at home were an integral part of her identity. At this stage anger replaces embarrassment. In her narrative is criticism of the 'liberal' middle class male who obviously sees his own viewpoint as essentially culture free. It has never excluded him from any public space, so he has no understanding of his own cultural presuppositions. It illustrates the normalising effect of the dominant discourses, which are backed by real social and economic power. It demonstrates the self-confidence that such cultural inflections can bring to the privileged.

The third layer
DC/Discomfort

                                DC/Discomfort

                                DC/Discomfort

      DC/Ambivalence

                                                  Epiphany

                                DC/Discomfort

AltRM/Influence

Once again, Aliki's narrative returns to the theme of alternative role models and how a female tutor's encouragement on the PGCE course bolstered her confidence. This happens before the previously mentioned relationship with the teacher on her school experience. So she builds a picture of her development in thematic layers rather than chronologically.

Together, the teacher and the tutor offer her three things that support alternative ways of behaving:

• approval

• a different interpretation of her own behaviour

• new possibilities of how to live and how to be which are more compatible with her own desires and ways of being

Here we see Bakhtin's theory of loophole. He hypothesised that the individual is alive only 'in the sense of a constant possibility, a constant need to transform my life formally to insert new meaning in my life (the ultimate word of consciousness)' (Bakhtin:1979: 107). It also relates to Bhabha's (1995) theory of the third time space. Both suggest that, within constraints, we can change. Yet as Aliki's story shows, this process becomes easier if we have allies. What Aliki is doing is re-appropriating materials from her own heritage to fashion a new identity. This new sense of identity enables her to reach the next epiphany when:

(I) kept saying to myself, 'I'm not going to be how I was when I did my degree. I'm not going to disappear ... and I'm going to have a voice.

Aliki feels that she was denied an authentic voice while she was on the community arts course. So her narrative now returns by flashback to explore this process from yet another angle. She criticises the course, which she feels was governed by middle class norms which were never explicitly stated. Her flashbacks demonstrate that she was already working through these dilemmas in her creative work, before the alternative role models acted as a catalyst and gave her a new-found confidence. This leads on to the fourth layer of her narrative, where she goes back to enlarge upon and summarise her struggles at college by using a single anecdote. It describes an instance of institutionalised racism, which denied her an authentic voice.

The fourth layer: Reconnecting with the original complication

DC/Discomfort

No role model

Epiphany

By way of introduction she says, 'You're gonna be amazed by this.' She and her non- white friends felt a great deal of discomfort because of her fellow students' lack of understanding and sensitivity (DC/Discomfort). In her narrative she goes on to point out the contradictions:

> And that's really funny because the degree course was in Community Theatre Arts and a lot of it was based around ... erm enabling people from sections of the community that were (...) without a voice, but there were sections of the community that (laughs) had a voice. A very, very strong voice! And there were English people that had very rich fathers and mummies. And I think that was a contradiction ... erm and they used their language skills to crush others.

To compound this she had an ambivalent attitude towards the tutors (DC/ Ambivalence):

> I think I just felt patronised ... they didn't have the skills as educators to do that in a way you believed them.

She then embarks upon a narrative to illustrate her point. She introduces it with the statement, 'You're gonna be amazed by this'. She tells of a time during her second year when the students were left to elect their own groups to devise their own projects. In the second week she discovered that all the white students had formed themselves into groups without really informing the non-white students. The scales fell from her eyes when she discovered that:

> the people who were left was me, my Asian friend Luna, my African friend Zande, my Asian friend, Kaken and my West Indian friend, Cherry. And they were all the black, Greek, Asian people in our year ... and we hadn't even spoken to each other ... [about the project]. And everyone piped up and said, Oh that's great ... you can form a group and do something about (laughs) minority groups..

It was then that her poor self-esteem boiled over into anger. She remembers 'completely freaking out' (DC/Discomfort).

> ... We were all in this room, I said, 'I think it's disgusting. I've not got a chip on my shoulder about being Greek and if I have then, OK fine, but look there's white people over there and there's all us bloody ethnics over here. If we're a Community Theatre Arts Course and we're trying to represent sections of the community that aren't represented in theatre, then why are we all together and you guys are all over there'.

Once more the tutors were ineffectual:

> ... our lecturer came in and said, 'I can't do anything about this ... Maybe you can use the experience as a way of inspiring some sort of theatre'.

She realised there was *no role model* here, in fact this was the pressure which forced her upon her own devices. Her solution was to write a play which represents her Epiphany.

> I wrote a play about a group of sweat shop workers who did not get on. Because I think that was our way of saying, 'Just because we're foreign, it doesn't mean that we must all get on ... or that we all share something, you know that's not the case. It's about people and it's about humanity...'

Here Aliki uses all her experiences to make some sense of her identity and her predicament, just as she does in her one woman play. She is sorting and organising the different strands to make a coherent whole, although it may have less significance when she is actually involved in the creative act. As she remarks later in the interview, when talking about writing plays:

> Even when I do them I don't realise I'm doing them. I mean when I wrote that play, it didn't have as much significance to me as it does now. And it's like when we read plays we don't know why the writer wrote them ... The writers, when they first write them don't really know why. And then they look back and say, 'Oh, yeah. That means that and that's about that.' And you sort of analyse it that way.

So it is a continuous process of writing the self and reflecting upon what has been written. This may account for the fact that towards the end of the conversations with each one of the six there are passages of reflection, even without prompting.

Most of Aliki's conversations have this cumulative narrative which returns to similar themes and elaborates upon them. Her construction of identity is multilayered and complex, yet it is simultaneously coherent in both its narrative style and the values expressed. There is a distinct and culturally formed voice. While Asif's narrative is direct and succinct, Aliki's is layered and analytical. She is aware of this aspect of her style and connects it to her continuing ambitions to follow a career in the legal profession.

Each person had different ways of constructing their narrative of identity. For example, Michael's narrative is philosophical and hortatory. His continual use of the second person has the resonance of a preacher or a skilled orator. Although he tends to be more chronological in his approach he nevertheless explores a theme in a constant layering of argument. In his narratives he returns to the same point and explores matters again and again from different angles. His attractive, almost poetic way of expressing himself lends his speech a particularly persuasive and powerful rhetorical force and resonance.

Michael consciously links his style to his conception of self and self-invention, mythologising the self:

> I'm inventing mythologies ... I believe strongly that at every stage of my life, I've had to invent myself. I've had to reshape myself. This is the thing about the core.. If I didn't reinvent myself throughout, I would have ended up somewhere else.

This reinvention is a complex and layered process, where he is continually moving backwards and forwards to make coherent sense of his experiences and his history. He is constantly mythologising. In recent times, myth has acquired deeply perjorative connotation depicting an earlier more ignorant age. We are keen to dispel myths. But a mythology is actually an attempt to make sense of our experience and to create symbols for things we do not really understand. These are always fashioned out of materials and narratives from the past. The old stories can always be rewritten for other circumstances. Homer's tales are ubiquitous. Elsewhere, I have described the power of the *Odyssey* in terms of the primary curriculum (Kearney:1990.1995). A recent film, *Oh Brother where art thou...?* rewrites the story as a comedy set in the depression, basing it on a film a fictional director in another film (Preston Sturges' *Sullivan's Travels*) failed to make. There are many layers and many possibilities to myth. Perhaps to keep a coherent sense of self, we all engage continuously in this process of myth making. The framework of Bakhtin's triad makes this process visible.

What the framework tells us about identity construction

Certain patterns and understandings can be gained by using the framework to analyse how the self has been constructed in the narratives of the six individuals. The framework helps to isolate and illuminate several patterns in the process of identity construction. In summary these are:

- The framework makes clear the relationships between the internal and external forces as they are produced in the whole dialogue ie:

  - there is a movement from the external to the internal factors

  - there are clear patterns which suggest that epiphanies or authentic understandings of self begin to appear at late adolescence or by the age of 20. Perhaps they are the defining point of adulthood

  - epiphanies are always preceded by periods of discomfort and/or ambivalence

  - the epiphanies of the current group tend to relate to how they can reconcile themselves to their history and heritage. Any which appear at an earlier age usually refer to a resolution of discomfort with the dominant culture

- The framework reveals the complex layering of narratives and the cumulative realisation of identity. The narratives are shaped like geological strata. They may consist of conventional anecdotes, but they are shaped in such a way that they revisit the same themes from different perspectives.

- The framework demonstrates how the development of identity is the constant reworking of memories:

  development rather than adhering strictly to the forward looking arrow of linear time was itself bound up with narrative and thus was thoroughly contingent on the backward gaze of recollection (Freeman: 1993: 224)

- The framework reveals the individual narrative structure by which such moves are expressed.

- The framework reveals the orderly progression of the conversations as a whole.

- The framework gives a clear demonstration of how the different voices and influences are orchestrated, how they are assessed, critically appropriated and fashioned into an individual voice and an integrated understanding of self.

- The framework demonstrates how far reaching powerful individual incidents can be on the sense of self, eg Michael's racist attack and Olgun's experiences as a prisoner of war.

- The framework demonstrates that similar events or dilemmas will have different effects on different people. eg Asif's responses to racism are different from Aliki's in terms of self-esteem.

- The framework reveals self-identity to be a creative and conscious process, which all six individuals engage in profoundly critical and political ways:

  ... the self despite its inability to be a sovereign origin of meaning was significantly more than a merely imaginary artifact of words. The fact is that 'I' am often able to do something new with the words bequeathed me, thereby enlarging the scope of myself and the world. (Freeman:1993:225)

It also reveals how they use all of the narrative resources at their disposal to achieve this.

- The framework reveals that at this stage in their development their emphasis is upon reintegrating into the history and traditions of their heritage culture on their own terms.

Conclusions

Although the description of the development of self in the novel occurs early in Bakhtin's writing it carries the seed of his later thinking on dialogism. As such it embodies aspects of his later extremely complex and sophisticated insights into human consciousness. Therefore the framework allows us to glimpse the relationship between the various outside influences and the orchestration of those influences in every person's inner speech (Vygotsky). At best the framework can provide a kind of X-ray view of this process. X-ray is a suitable metaphor since, although lacking the precision of a photograph, it reveals things which are not readily apparent but exist below the surface. The dynamic process of syncretism becomes apparent as we trace the push and pull of the various forces and examine how they achieved a resolution of these competing forces in their epiphanies.

The second dimension is that the information is deeply contextualised so that we know the time and place such events occurred. Narratives also provide other kinds of contextual information about the emotional and affective dimensions of such interactions. Narratives are not conveyed in neutral and bloodless language. These important factors are absent from most postmodern theory. There is a whole gamut of feelings involved in our interrelationships with others. And our emotional needs go well beyond mere desire. There are also questions of how power is established, negotiated, challenged and changed in the microcosm of family life, with its unspoken attitudes, values codes and etiquettes. The framework reveals how deeply such factors colour our sense of identity.

The third dimension of the framework is that it allows us to note and form hypotheses relating to individual and cultural differences in the narratives in terms of both content and form. This question of form also operates on several levels. The first is at the level of the whole conversation. Like a novel, a conversation has a cumulative impetus with regard to meaning. As the conversation progresses, certain attitudes and basic information established early on is built upon throughout the conversation. It provides its own context. Once embarked upon it acquires a narrative direction. Causal links become established and events are framed in conventional narrative ways to maintain interest and coherence. So as the conversation progresses, the meanings take narrative shape. Futhermore, the audience may not share all of the teller's cultural references and understandings. This is why the majority of conversations are punctuated by rhetorical devices which check understanding ('do you see what I'm saying?; 'you know' etc).

This leads me to another point regarding form. Each speaker has a cohesive and recognisable, but not static or predetermined, narrative style. They often use basic rhetorical devices probably gained from their primary cultural setting; usually their family. Vygotsky's notion is helpful here: words are learned and employed in a wide variety of contexts, so that the meanings themselves have a wide variety of emotional and cognitive associations and saturations. It's not a simple or straightforward process. This notion is linked to Bakhtin's view that the word is only half one's own. Words are soaked with other people's meanings and intentions and we must, therefore, appropriate the word and make it serve our own purposes. I suggest that narrative and rhetorical devices are also learned in this way. Rhetorical devices have both cognitive and emotional dimensions and associations. Indeed this would account for the persistence of culturally distinctive narrative styles and approaches across time and place. It would help to explain what stays the same when we travel. I take this up more fully in the next chapter.

The analysis shows the intimate and continually problematic relationship between memory, identity and narrative. However it is through this process of reworking identity that the individual attains and maintains an individual authentic voice. Each uses the cultural resonances gathered from the past to solve the riddles and dilemmas of the present and try to imagine and attain a more hopeful future. They are working the narratives of others to their own rhythms. They demonstrate what a difficult and complicated endeavour this is, even for people who are socially mobile, economically independent, able and adept. In the next chapter I look more closely at the rhetorical devices that are employed.

What I have tried to demonstrate in this section is how Asif and Aliki rewrite the enigma of self: drawing together and orchestrating the influences, ambivalences and discomforts. Each narrative is intricately layered and complex and draws on preferred styles of expression. All those narrative styles will be influenced by their family storytelling traditions but it is also clear that they have been affected by other forms of discourse. The narratives' styles and conventions also bear the hallmarks of academic discourse. In Aliki's case there are clear narrative influences derived from film. The traditional resonances are revealed more clearly from an examination of the structure and rhetorical conventions of individual anecdotes, as examined in the next chapter.

7

Ghost Values: What persists across the generations?

The fact is that the values and traditions fed to the furnace of American life never disappear altogether – at least not quite. There remains always, in every ethnic tradition, in the generational legacy of every individual family, a certain residue, a kind of ash, what I would call 'ghost values', the tag ends and shreds and echoes of the past calling to us generations after their real force has been spent, tantalising us with idealized visions of a stability or order or certainty of meaning that we seem never to have known, and that we imagine can somehow be restored. Peter Marin: *Towards Something American* (1988)

Introduction

In the city of Chicago
As the evening shadows fall
There are people dreaming
Of the Hills of Donegal
Christy Moore: *Chicago* (1984)

This song not only speaks to the diaspora, it speaks for the diaspora. Christy Moore is something of a legend in Irish music. He is as popular in Ireland as he is in the USA, where he fills stadiums. He is very much in the tradition, but he is not hidebound and has always experimented with the form. The musical tradition almost died out in Ireland in the 1950s. Moore was one of the leading lights in its revival in the late 1960s. Paradoxically, many aspects of the tradition have been kept alive in the United States. Despite its reputation as a destroyer of 'authentic' culture and purveyor of commercial pap, despite the fact that most Irish Americans have been there for a century and a half, that many of the traditional dancers recruited for the highly commercial *Riverdance*, including Jean Butler, were born in the US. Such contradictions and ironies are not confined to the Irish diaspora.

As James Clifford (1997:44) observed, when we travel, a lot stays the same.

> Memory becomes a crucial element in the maintenance of a sense of integrity-memory, which is always constructive ... Oral tradition can be very precise, transmitting a relatively continuous, if rearticulated cultural substance over many generations

The last two chapters showed that cultural change and development of syncretic identities is a slow and often painful process for the individual. It is only ever partial. Moreover, in recent years there has been an upsurge in interest in traditional culture. This has been coupled with the desire of many people to connect with their heritage and their history, but on their own terms. For much of the time it is because we are often 'fixed' by others – through our physical appearance, our accent, our name. Michael and Aliki reveal how powerful such forces are. As Nandine and Asif demonstrate, you can be fixed by your family and community as much as by the dominant culture. In the last chapter we observed how these conflicting strands are orchestrated and partially resolved through narratives and mythologies of self, which we write and rewrite.

Narrating identities

I believe that the narrativisation of self goes still further and affects our language forms at the very marrow. It is well known that the last thing to alter when a person's accent changes is the intonation pattern. This musical element is something we learn first and lose last. Our traditions of rhetoric are learned through listening to countless narratives from which we fashion our own ways of unfolding a tale. Those rhetorical devices and speech rhythms inhabit every curve and cadence of the sentences we speak. My view is that these rhetorical traditions are a major conduit for what remains and resonates across the diaspora.

I have found the most illuminating theoretical writings on this subject to be in the fields of social psychology and literature (explored more fully in Chapter 3). Both areas deal with the way our lives are storied. They foreground the intricate relationship between narrative, memory and history. The early narratives we hear as children *are* our first epistemologies and consequently they hold the greatest resonance for us. As Cortazzi (1993) demonstrates in his exhaustive review of the research on narrative analysis, very few of the literature-based approaches offer useful insights into analysing style and 'voice'. This is because many of the literary researchers are seeking universal patterns. For example, Propp's (1969) analyses of plot or Barthes' (1980) contention that, 'Structurally, narrative shares the characteristics of the sentence without ever being reducible to the sum of its sentences; a narrative is a long sentence..' is an interesting observation but it does not begin to penetrate the mysteries of style or voice. More rewarding are the sociological and ethnographic approaches, which examine cultural inflections of the narrative form.

Cortazzi (1993) makes the point that:

> As a discourse genre narrative is seen as a speech event and 'ways of narrating' involve variations according to components of narrative situation: the participants, setting, purposes of telling, communicating key and cultural norms ...

Certainly, Longacre (1976) and Labov (1972c) and Brooks and Warren (1949) developed frameworks for looking at such elements of narrative structure. It is surprising how close those models are, considering that they were arrived at independently. In figure 2 I have arranged them in parallel to emphasise the similarities. By analysing stories using these frameworks we can make connections between similar emphases in a person's individual style and observe differences between individuals.

Figure 2: A comparison of theories of narrative structure

Longacre	Labov	Brooks and Warren
Aperture	Abstract	
		Exposition
Stage	Orientation	
Episode		
• inciting moment		
• developing conflict	Complication	Complication
• climax		Climax
Denouement	Evaluation	
Conclusion	Result	Resolution
Finis	Coda	

All three frameworks have a similar approach and each elaborates on Aristotle's beginning, middle and end formulation. They have been criticised for their euro-centric approach (see Cortazzi, 1993 and Reissman, 1993), and although it is possible that they could be used in prescriptive ways, most narratives probably contain most of these elements, albeit used in different ways for different purposes and with different values and premises. However, they remain useful frameworks for examining narrative styles.

Analysing narrative style has always been difficult. For many years trans-criptions of narratives were represented in blocks of prose. This is problematic because such a form does not adequately represent, the rhythm and cadence of speech. Kate Millet (1971) stated the problem clearly in her early feminist research on self-narratives of women who had worked as prostitutes:

> What I have tried to capture here is the character of the English I heard spoken by the four women and then recorded on tape. I was struck by the eloquence of what was said, and yet when I transcribed the words on to paper the result was at first, disappointing. Some of the wit of M's black and southern delivery had disappeared, gone with the tang of her voice ... J's difficulty in speaking of things so painful that s h e had repressed them for years required that I speak often on her tapes, hoping to give her support, then later, edit myself out ...

As Reissman (1993) points out, Millet had to find a different way of represent-ing the voices. It was an early signal of the legitimation crisis in autobio-graphical and ethnographic research, examined more fully here in Chapter 3. Millet's solution was to edit herself out of the conversation and present the narra-tives as parallel texts. She saw their voices as 'instruments expressing their diverse experiences.' She attempted therefore to represent them as musicians playing as an ensemble.

Much work has been done recently on the best way to represent research findings (see Denzin, 1997; Tierney and Lincoln, 1997; Ellis, 1997; McWilliam, 1997; Lather, 1997) These writers urge us to experiment using a variety of tech-niques drawn from film documentary, 'new' journalism, poetry and dramatic performance. This is a delicate matter. In the hands of someone skilled and creative the results can be powerful and moving. If mishandled it can end up sounding pompous and precious. In Michael's case I have chosen to represent his speech patterns in a poetical form.

This is not a new technique. It has been used extensively and effectively by Labov (1972,1972a, 1972b, 1972c, 1980), Hymes (1997), Tedlock (1983) and Gee (1989, 1991, 1992). But, it still contentious. Deciding where to start a new line has been a source of fruitful disagreement. Hymes (1997:144) believes it should indicate intonation patterns, breaths and pauses, whereas Gee (1991:22) favours an approach linked more closely to meaning. My own view is that it should represent the speech in such a way as to enable us to get a faithful picture of what we hear on tape. Because space does not allow me to analyse more than one of the six involved in the study, I have chosen to focus on Michael's narrative style. Part of the reason for this is that he has a very distinctive voice, which is highly patterned and therefore relatively straightforward to represent in this way.

In this approach I have used the poetical form creatively, and do not adhere too strictly to the linguistic niceties debated by Hymes and Gee. My aim is that the reader gets a flavour of Michael's distinctive cadences.

Furthermore, I have worked with him on this process to check that it is accurate from his viewpoint. I gave him a copy of his 'story' in the form of lines and stanzas and we agreed to meet a few days later to discuss the approach. I also asked him to think about his own influences in storytelling. He also agreed to allow me to tape our conversation to use in the analysis of the story.

Trying to isolate the cultural dimensions of his narrative style is more difficult. For this I turned to the ethnographic approaches of Hymes (1996:121), which initially seemed promising. The part of Hymes' approach that I find most useful and convincing is his notion that narratives are 'grammars of experience'. He relates his work on Native American myths to a child's acquisition of language. He elaborates:

> Narratives are undoubtedly part of a child's experience of language. These Native American texts turn out to be subtle organisations of lines. The lines are organised in ways that make them formal poetry, and also a rhetoric of action: they embody an implicit schema for the organisation of experience. The patterns may be more finely worked out sometimes in myths, but they are also found in personal narratives. Over and over again, at every level, an implicit organisation of experience into satisfying patterns and may be internalised.

For his analysis of cultural patterning, Hymes draws upon Gee's (1989, 1991, 1992) work on lines and stanzas. He employs this in his examination of Native American myths, particularly the Coyote trickster tales. He seeks to demonstrate that there are narrative patternings of two lines and four lines in the narratives of the Zuni, Native Americans in New Mexico, whereas in Western stories the patterns tend to be two and five. This would certainly hold for Michael's story. After my initial enthusiasm, I found this approach less convincing, since there is degree of arbitrariness in the decision about where to break the lines. In fact for most of the time, he critiques Gee's patterning of narratives and reclassifies them in his own terms. He even adds another subdivision of stanzas, which consists of verses. We can always be tempted to tailor such things to suit our purpose of finding neat patterns and correspondences. In several traditions there are patterns of three: three wishes, three sons, three pigs, three strong women etc. Often this is a mnemonic device for storytellers and is fairly arbitrary. There is no reason that there cannot be two or four or five. I would also argue that this approach is premised on a static notion of culture, even an oversimplification in cultures where traditional stories changed in more gradual ways. In the current research it is not all that useful for examining rhetorical styles of more fluid and syncretic aspects of culture. Moreover, in the poetic forms of most communities there is often variety in line length and line clusters, which would render such a prescriptive view meaningless or at least unhelpful.

As I have indicated, however, there are rhetorical devices for encoding experience and implicit values are embedded in narratives, including the role, status and function of storytelling, which characterise and shape the individual's own narratives. I am convinced that these narrative grammars become the cornerstone for our storied lives and carry certain aspects of this socially learned practice across generations. I believe, moreover, that it affects the way we use a second language. There are distinct flavours to Caribbean English, Indian English or even Irish English, which are recognisable to the ear, both in the accent and the rhetorical devices used. More research is needed to analyse exactly how and why this happens. I have only space here to analyse Michael's story.

Michael' story

The section of Michael's conversation I have chosen is his description of the racist attack. There are several reasons for this. To begin with, it is a clear and self-contained 'story'. Secondly, it illustrates his very distinctive 'voice', which is consistent throughout our conversation. It has many features in common with other extracts quoted in the previous three chapters. Thirdly, in terms of identity, it represents a defining moment in his self-narrative. In what follows I shall analyse his account in some detail, using some of his own observations to draw out some tentative conclusions concerning the genesis of his individual voice. But first let us consider his story:

In prose it is effective enough:

> We were coming back from school and we were crossing the road and ... you know this car was coming down and this fellow went into a bump and because he was ... because he heard, he felt something in the car. He thought we'd done something to the car. We'd touched it. He stopped the car. Didn't ask any questions. He came out and accused us of scratching his car or hitting his car or whatever it was. So we said 'OK' ... . We give him ... We told him we didn't do anything.

> But he felt that we did and he wouldn't let it go. And my friend was much bigger than me. He was also a year older than me, but also very ... No he was two years older than me. He confronted this fellow and told him, 'We didn't do anything but simply we were walking in the road, your car passed and that was that.' And the fellow said, 'OK' you know, he'll be back. So we

started walking. I told my friend, 'Let's run!'. He said, 'Why?' I said, 'It's this fellow, he's not going to let go of this issue.' And he says, 'No', he's not going to run. We were walking down the road (pause) and a few minutes later we saw this gang. Men. Coming down the road and I said, Let's run. But he says that he didn't do anything wrong and he didn't see why we should run. And we passed a bridge, near where I lived, and after we passed the bridge, we were surrounded by these people, grown men. I would have thought these people knew better. You know. Kids. We were kids. You know. We've come from school. Typical. We got books and stuff like that. So they surrounded us and really laid into us. Broke my friend's arm. Broke his jaw. Struck me with a metal bar, across my head. I lost consciousness. Nothing happened with the police. And my parents ... My father was beaten up twice and throughout their life in Britain they had to put up with that. And you come along and you have to put up with it. Then the thing is what my father faced in this country: the verbal abuse, the physical abuse. He had to put up with it, confront it. It did something to him. He became a changed man.

Certain aspects of his style are powerful and immediately recognisable. However, when arranged in lines the poetical force of the language becomes instantly apparent. We can hear the Caribbean cadences of his speech.

Other dimensions also become visible. The stanza form reveals intricate patterning of the narrative that is unnoticeable in the prose version. It is easier to observe the structure of the narrative, which fits in to the patterns suggested as typical by several theorists (1949, Labov, 1972a,b,c; Goodacre, 1976), whose frameworks are detailed in fig 2.

As well as to presenting the story in poetical form I have included an indication of the structure and progression of the narrative in a column on the right, using Labov's framework. The lines and the stanzas are numbered for ease of reference in my analysis.

1.   Orientation

We were coming back from school
and we were crossing the road
and ... you know
this car was coming down
and this fellow went into a bump   5

2.
and because he was ...   Complicating Action
because he heard,
he felt something in the car.

He thought we'd done something to the car.
We'd touched it.   10

3.   Complicating Action
He stopped the car.
Didn't ask any questions.
He came out and accused us of scratching his car
                              or hitting his car
                              or whatever it was.   15

4.   Complicating Action
So we said 'OK'
We told him
we didn't do anything.
But he felt that we did
and he wouldn't let it go.   20

5.   Complicating Action
And my friend was much bigger than me.
He was also a year older than me,
but also very ...
No he was two years older than me.
and much bigger than me.   25

6.   Complicating Action
He confronted this fellow
and told him,
'We didn't do anything
but simply
we were walking in the road,   30
your car passed
and that was that.'
And the fellow said 'OK',
you know,
he'll be back.   35

7.   Complicating Action
So we started walking.
I told my friend,
'Let's run!'
He said,
'Why?'
I said, 'It's this fellow,   40
he's not going to let go of this issue.'

And he says, 'No',
he's not going to run.

8.   Complicating Action
We were walking down the road (pause)
and a few minutes later we saw this gang.   45
Men.
Coming down the road
and I said, 'Let's run!'
But he says that
he didn't do anything wrong   50
and he didn't see why we should run.

9.   Complicating Action
And we passed a bridge,
near where I lived,
and after we passed the bridge,
we were surrounded by these people,   55
grown men.
I would have thought these people knew better. Evaluation
You know.
Kids.
We were kids.   60
You know.
We've come from school.
Typical.
We got books and stuff like that.

10.   Result
So they surrounded us   65
and really laid into us...
Broke my friend's arm.
Broke his jaw.
Struck me with a metal bar,
across my head.   70
I lost consciousness.

Nothing happened with the police.

11.   Coda
And my parents ...
My father was beaten up twice
and throughout their life in Britain   75
they had to put up with that.

12.   Coda
And you come along
and you have to put up with it.
Then the thing is
what my father faced in this country: 80
the verbal abuse,
the physical abuse.
He had to put up with it,
confront it.
It did something to him.   85

He became a changed man.

Representing speech in this way is far more effective. It captures the rhythm and the cadence more forcefully because poetry maintains an unbroken link to an earlier, exclusively oral tradition (See Ong, 1982). It comes from song. (*The Iliad* begins, 'Sing, goddess ...) Both poetry and song depend on the percussive and musical power of language to bolster the affective dimension of meaning. Prose uses different devices to achieve such effects. This is why speech represented as prose has the appearance of being flattened and is rendered lifeless. Putting Michael's narrative in this form enables us to observe his rhetorical devices more clearly. It is fluent, well honed and bears all the instantly recognisable hallmarks of his style: his effective use of repetition, a tendency to cluster qualifying phrases in groups of three and the Biblical resonance in the language of some passages. It also reveals how ordered and balanced his speech is. Very little of this is captured in the prose transcription.

Michael's story is compact and well-rehearsed. Each part fits neatly into the next. It has a cumulative effect, gained by the mirroring of stanzas and occasional mirroring of lines within stanzas. In the last chapter we saw how this effect of layering was also an aspect of his style over the whole conversation. He has a rhythmic and confident voice, which even accommodates his single hesitation (line 7) and his correction of a factual inaccuracy, into his narrative patterning. As the analysis using Labov's framework shows, the story has a very conventional structure, which renders it fluid and accessible. There is predictability about the form which lends power in conveying the ferocity of the attack. The calm narrative contrasts with the violence of the subject matter. A little like Promo Levi's descriptions of his time in Auschwitz, the understated and plain narrative is more effective, since it renders the horrors more believable and more shocking. Much is left unsaid, the threat is merely that 'He'll be back..' Tension is built by two missed opportunities for flight. It is told in a simple style.

What is remarkable about this fluent and almost faultless performance is that it is totally spontaneous. On closer examination, the story unfolds through an intricate patterning, both thematically and in its form. This is because it has the themes which have affected him as an African Caribbean male living in Britain. He realises that these are not unique to him. His own research is involved with examining the mythologies which 'fix' Caribbean boys, coming from the dominant culture through the media in the form of stories and statistics from various sources, educational statistics, police statistics etc. He is also interested in how they respond and the mythologies they create about themselves, which he feels are born out of this social reality. He talks about the daily experience of racism, particularly physical struggle and the grim choices, which he characterises as 'fight or flight'. This is his pivotal story.

My contention is that both the content and the form of the story come out of the Caribbean tradition that has a long history of such oppressions. It is also a tradition that has always put a high premium on verbal performance. This is evident throughout the West African diaspora. From 'playing the dozens' described in Labov's work in Harlem to Shirley Brice Heath's analysis of the 'ways with words' in Tracton in North Carolina. From the sly, salacious and understated lyrics of the blues to the Reggae toasters of the 1970s. From the stories, songs and poems of Calypso and Carnival to the fusion of secular desire, religious fervour and radical politics in the lyrics of Bob Marley. And on and on to the emergence of rap in the late twentieth century, as well as a long line of poets and writers who have transmuted this tradition into novels and volumes of poetry. Powerful, eloquent wordplay and performance has always had high status (see Singh *et al*, 1994, 1996). It reflects the ever changing, yet unbroken, link with West African traditions, even though the relationship between diaspora and 'homeland' is never unproblematic.

Michael's performance, as a detailed analysis will show, draws upon this tradition. The first thing to note about his speech, taken verbatim from tape, is its close resemblance to poetry. All pauses and hesitations are included in the transcript and there are no additions or subtractions. Yet we have a textbook example of narrative structure and closure. Secondly, in turning it into poetical form, I only had to attend closely to the pauses. Thirdly, the narrative itself proceeds at an even pace. Stanzas tend to be of similar length and they have a symmetrical aspect. The complications are layered and progressive. We feel the tension mounting from stanza to stanza.

Note that the abstract is missing from the story. Earlier in the conversation Michael told me that he was once beaten up by racists. He stopped and said, 'You don't want to hear about this'. I then persuaded him to tell me about it, assuring him that we could edit it out if he wished. He replied that this was not the issue but that he thought it would not be relevant to my research. As it turned out, it was the lynchpin to his narrative of identity.

The analysis of the narrative

I begin the analysis by examining how the poem is structured stanza by stanza, to reveal the intricate patterning of the narrative. Some general observations follow. I conclude by comparing Michael's account to one of the fight narratives collected by William Labov in New York in 1972.

The first stanza sets the scene from the point of view of his friend and himself. They are established as young, innocent and defenceless and on their way home from school. The second stanza moves to the driver's vantage point and what appears to be a simple misunderstanding. The third stanza heightens the tension as the driver makes an accusation, 'fixing' the two boys as troublemakers. Michael uses the rhythmic and rhetorical device of listing the driver's complaint in threes. The final 'whatever it was' carries the implication that it was a trivial excuse to confront the boys and that if it had not been that it would have been something else. The implication is that the driver's real reasons lie elsewhere. There is a racial motive. Significantly, the ethnic and cultural identity of all the characters are 'understood'.

In stanza 4 the boys are represented as reasoning with the driver and the driver as persisting unreasonably. The use of 'OK' here is placatory. We are then made to anticipate a tragic outcome by being told 'he wouldn't let it go'. The choice is 'fight or flight', and this leads to the next stanza. His friend is bigger and older and the implication is that it is harder for him to lose face. In terms of style, the first half of the stanza mirrors the second half, even though it incorporates a hesitation. The repetition of 'bigger than me' and 'older than me' are effective emphases. Michael is the smallest and most vulnerable character in his story.

Stanza 6 mirrors many of the features of stanza 4. It reiterates the same argument, but the stakes are higher. It has turned from placation to confrontation. This time the driver says 'OK', but in this context it is a threat. So by using almost identical structures, Michael conveys a very different meaning and heightens the tension. This is economical and powerful storytelling.

In stanza 7, Michael suggests flight, reiterating that 'he won't let go of this issue', by which he is implying the driver's racist agenda. His friend stubbornly refuses. For him it is a question of personal honour. In Stanza 8, the real threat appears. Here Michael builds the picture with two words 'gang' and 'men' – this is all that is necessary to denote the unfairness in terms of size and numbers. He repeats his plea for flight and again the friend refuses, claiming the moral high ground. At this part of his narrative his method seems almost biblical. There is the matter of sacrifice and standing up against impossible odds for what you know is right. Stanza 8 has a similar biblical cadence, particularly the lines 52-54

> And we passed a bridge,
> near where I lived,
> and after we passed the bridge ...

For me this has distinct echoes of sections of the New Testament. The bridge also acts as a symbolic marker in the narrative; it means there is no going back.

The outrageousness of the attack is emphasised, with the repetition of 'men, grown men' and the fact that they should have known better, which gives an inkling of what they were up against. This is echoed in the next part where he contrasts the attackers with themselves

> 'kids ...
> we were kids'

and the detail of

> 'we've come from school,
> typical
> we've got books and stuff like that'

This further emphasises the innocence of the victims and the scale of the attack. The description of the attack is equally succinct and powerful. Again Michael lists three things. This is made more powerful since it echoes the three statements in stanza 3, for which the attack was retribution. This has the effect of making the injustice starker. His passive role is emphasised by the statement 'I lost consciousness', which gives it a wistful conclusion. This is followed by a line that I could not really make into a separate stanza. Though connected to the story, it stands alone, signifying that to seek justice was a useless endeavour.

Stanza 11 widens the context and demonstrates that the attack was a violent but not isolated incident. The use of the word 'confront' again points to maintaining dignity in the face of such abuse. It adds to the powerful conclusion to the narrative. For the coda in stanza 12, Michael adopts a rhetorical device, which again has connotations of religion. He moves into the second person. This hortatory form of narrative is common in sermons and other religious discourses. This stanza echoes stanza 10, especially with the line that stands alone and has the tone of resignation, 'He became a changed man.' In terms of the whole narrative this connects with his first meeting with his father and how he was so different to the stories Michael had heard about him during his childhood in Dominica.

When we examine it in this degree of detail, it is clear what an intricate construction the narrative is. For all the simplicity of vocabulary, it is a beautifully structured poem. It was not intended as such and is unedited. This narrative skill did not emerge by accident or from nowhere; it has been learned and refined.

This is illuminated by the argument put forward by Gee (1992:143), when he makes the link between the cognitive and the social:

> ... in our everyday lives and in much of traditional psychology, what we think of as 'mental' is in fact 'social'. Meaning and memory, believing and knowing, are social practices that vary as they are embedded with different Discourses within a society. Each Discourse apprentices its members and 'disciplines' them so that their mental networks and their folk theories converge towards a 'norm' reflected in the social practices of the Discourse. These ideal norms, which are rarely directly statable, but only discoverable with close ethnographic study are what constitute meaning, memory, believing, knowing and so forth, from the perspective of each Discourse.

The ease and assurance of Michael's elegantly structured, spontaneous oral performance indicates that it emanates from a strong oral tradition. According to Hymes (1996:167):

> When texts come from a culture grounded in an oral tradition and a narrative view of life, it is not surprising to find text after text that shows thorough architecture and rewarding artistry. In a society such as our own, where narrative commonly competes with mass media amidst a perpetual circulation of paper, and personal experience is discounted as anecdote, it would not be surprising to find that architecture and artistry are often less. When texts come from experiences that lack personal identification or circumstances that discourage acquired modes of telling, effective shaping seems even less likely.

> It appears, however, that effective shaping of stories is far more pervasive than one might expect, that the impulse to narrative form is far from paved over or drowned out, even in unfavourable circumstances...

He goes on to analyse three stories told by African American children, which have rhetorical similarities to Michael's story. I should like to make a comparison with one, which has surprising stylistic similarities to his own. It is a fight story collected by William Labov in New York City in the 1960s (Labov, 1972a,b). The young man interviewed by Labov's co-worker is given the pseudonym of 'Norris'. Labov's famous narrative framework, used on Michael's narrative, came out of his analysis of the stories he collected during the research. The framework he devised contained a definition of narrative in terms of a minimum of two temporally ordered sentences and for considering the narrative in terms of the listeners' question, 'So what?' The story has to a have a point or a meaning. Labov calls that element evaluation. I have chosen to compare

Michael's tale to the fight story, because it is a personal narrative, with a very similar theme, from someone in a similar context from a different part of the West African diaspora. The one thing we do not know is whether 'Norris's' family originate in the Caribbean, since there has always been a large African Caribbean community in New York. His story was transcribed by Labov as follows:

> When I was in the fourth grade
> no, it was the third grade
>
> This boy stole my glove
> He took my glove
> and said his father found it
> downtown
> on the ground
>
> [And you fight him?]
>
> I told him
> that it was impossible for him to find downtown
> cause all these people were walking by
> and just his father was the only one
> that found it?
> So he got all (mad)
> So then I fought him
> I knocked him all out in the street
> So he say he give
> And I kept hitting him
> Then he started crying
> and ran home to his father
> And the father told him that he ain't find no glove

In his initial evaluation Labov (1972c:368) makes the point that this is similar to other stories he collected. The point is to make the teller look good in comparison to his opponent. For Labov, the story

> ... follows the characteristic two part-structure of fight narratives in the Black English Vernacular; each part shows a different side of his ideal character. In this account of the verbal exchange Norris is cool, logical, good with his mouth, and strong in insisting on his own right. In the second part, dealing with the action, he appears as the most dangerous kind of fighter, who 'just goes crazy' and 'doesn't know what he did' ... his opponent is shown as dishonest, clumsy in argument, unable to control his temper, a punk, a lame, a coward..

Even when he runs home 'his very own father told him that his story wasn't true'.

Although Michael's is a richer, more accomplished telling, there are marked similarities in the rhetorical devices used. The two-part structure is evident in both. There is the source of contention and the resolution. The stance taken by Michael's friend mirrors the protagonist in Labov's story – both have the moral high ground. They both show physical courage, not backing down. Although Michael urges flight, he refuses to leave his friend to face the consequences alone. The protagonists in both stories keep their cool. The driver in Michael's story becomes so incensed by their resolve to not back down that he goes off to gather a gang. So, although they do not win the physical fight, their courage and dignity remain intact. So the evaluation and the message have similarities. Being older, more experienced and more reflective, Michael locates his story in wider social and political contexts, placing it in the daily routine of 'fight' or 'flight', which is common to many young males of African heritage throughout the cities of the world. It is perhaps unsurprising that their stories should have such equivalence when the social context which gives rise to them is depressingly common. It is part of the mythologising of self that Michael examines in his own research.

There are also some noticeable similarities in the language used. If we look at the opening lines there are distinct resonances. Norris' orienting sequence (A) uses very similar phraseology to Michael's (B) and is common to countless openings I have heard from African Caribbean boys in my eighteen years in inner city classrooms.

(A) When I was in the fourth grade
no, it was the third grade

This boy stole my glove
He took my glove

(B) We were coming back from school
and we were crossing the road
and ... you know
this car was coming down
and this fellow went into a bump

The first two lines set the scene in succinct and very similar ways: lines 3 and 4 in Norris' narrative and lines 4 and 5 in Michael's account are remarkably similar: introduced by the same pronoun and signaling the first complicating action.

There are obvious structural parallels also. The next section of their respective stories casts doubt on their opponents' honesty. A third section brings the conflict to a head with both Norris (in Labov's story) and Michael's friend refusing to back down. This effectively concludes the first part in both stories. The description of the fight is also achieved in short staccato phrases in both accounts. The coda is brief in both cases. The difference is that whereas Norris feels justified that the father vindicated him, Michael reports that the police compounded the injustice. What is remarkable is the structural and rhetorical similarities of the two narratives which are separated in terms of both physical distance and time. The single common thread is the African diaspora. Of course we cannot erect a theory upon such limited evidence. Nevertheless the parallels are interesting and noteworthy.

As well as similarities, there are significant differences. Whereas Norris presents himself as full of bravado in the face of opposition, Michael presents his own character as less reckless. His ethical evaluation of the situation is distinctly different. He is constantly counselling his friend to back off from a confrontational stance. He contextualises the story in broader social and political frameworks. Here he also alludes to his dislike of how young black males are trapped within not only the mythologies the dominant culture constructs for them but also the mythologies of masculinity which they construct for themselves. He is viewing the events from a different vantage point.

Also there is the question of style. Michael's story is a result of his own wide experience of a wide range of literature as both reader and writer; it is a more complex and syncretic piece. Although there is a strong Caribbean element (more obvious in his intonation patterns on tape) there are other influences of European and American writers. Moreover, he belongs to a far wider and more varied set of social networks than Norris. These are aspects I have explored in earlier works concerning children and schooled literacy (Kearney: 1990, 1995).

However, establishing convincing connections between his individual voice and the cultural resources of the Caribbean remains difficult. As I found Hymes' method of counting lines less than convincing, I thought it might be useful to ask Michael directly about his influences. He had already detected the influence of the Dominican storytellers and his father. His style also ties in with many of the observations in the Singh *et al*'s (1994:96) collections dealing with memory, narrative, identity and cultural politics, by examining the work of poets and novelists from a variety of cultural heritages who are wrestling with issues of power and identity. I was particularly struck by the connection to the following observations of the native American novelist, N. Scott Momaday (1996:49) who argues that 'his deepest voice' is 'lyrical and reverent and bears close relationship to the Indian oral tradition ... It proceeds out of an ancient voice. It is anchored in that ancient tradition'.

His earliest memories are laced with voices; as an infant being rocked 'in a little hammock' where he hears:

> the voices of my parents, of my grandmother, of others. Their voices, their words, English and Kiowa – and the silences that lie about them – are already an element in my mind's life. (1969:4)

It also chimes in with Mary Gergen's view that:

> Our cultures provide not only for the contents of what we say but also the forms. We use these forms unwittingly, they create the means by which we interpret our lives. We know ourselves via the mediating forms of our cultures, through telling and through listening. (1992:128)

Michael makes similar claims, explicitly. In our conversation he commented on the transcription of his story into a poetic format. He acknowledged that it reproduced his speech patterns faithfully:

> The instant I saw it I recognised my voice and that is the way I write. It left a resonance in my head when I read it.

When I asked him to clarify where this resemblance was most obvious he replied

> It's in the layout. It's in the rhythm as well, I think ...

I also asked him about his rhetorical device of going into the second person. This hortatory style is common to sermonising. It is a characteristic quality of Michael's speech which has been noted by colleagues. He relates it to his father, who was not a preacher but who loved to talk, tell stories and debate issues:

> My father, when he talks would have a way of talking ... He was extremely articulate and he's very physical sometimes. He would get up and ... almost like acting out what he's saying ...

It is my argument that this influence has penetrated Michael's speech at a profound level and left an indelible mark on his style of discourse, his 'voice'. He acknowledged that they belonged to a community which placed a premium on verbal performance:

> Extremely verbal, always a play with language ... When you meet someone, there are so many ways to greet that person ... always that versatility ... It's bantering ... most societies have an oral tradition ...

The other predominant influence on his language was the storyteller from his Dominican childhood and here he relates it to the music of the language, saying that

> When the storyteller was telling a story he would sing. He would dramatise concretise that story ...

He distinguishes this narrative device from singing songs which were also part of the storyteller's repertoire, and as he points out, also integral to Classical Greek theatre, but adds that

> Those songs, those melodies are intricately linked with memory.

This mention of memory connects with an aspect he raises earlier in the conversation, when he relates it to his own writing, which he sees as a musical experience

> Language isn't solid ... When I'm writing poetry, I try to make the poem sing ... I see the language as song. For me, the words in themselves, they've got music. So if you choose a word instead of another word, you change the rhythm of that poem.

Michael's oral experience is very close to his poetry writing and the two feed off each other. At another point in our conversation he says that certain poems he has written strongly resemble his oral narrative of the racist attack. His voice is obviously constructed from several elements and these three, his father's techniques, and the storyteller ('Whenever I write I see that storyteller') and his own writing, remain a strong foundation for him to move into other forms of discourse.

I would argue that those rhetorical forms also permeate his newer discourses. This is central to his idea of an integrated self and links with his notion of a stable and coherent core to his identity, which was discussed in the last chapter. At one stage he quotes Jung's notion that 'the unconscious mind is filled with relics' to illustrate his view of the process. It is a continuing and complex process of syncretism. He sees not a hybrid discourse, not a graft. Histories and mythologies are being woven, unpicked, examined and rewoven constantly, but there are distinct threads which continue and change and adapt. The stories we hear and learn from and ultimately make our own identities from are fundamental to this process.

Conclusion

Although I have space to examine only one story in sufficient detail, I would argue that similar threads could be found in the stories of the other five. And, just as Michael's style reflects the style of his longer narrative, the same holds true of Aliki, Asif and the others. Aliki's story in particular reveals how clashes with her middle class boy friend centred upon differences in styles of narrative discourse. Both Nandine and Olgun speak explicitly of cultural etiquettes which make certain aspects of the relationships with their English friends problematic. Obviously more detailed research needs to be done, perhaps exploring traditional tales from various heritages. In this way we could observe how different traditions make meanings through narratives.

My contention is that these discourse styles, loaded with implicit values, persist from generation to generation. Family stories are coded in such narratives and although they are retold, they change and adapt to new circumstances slowly, and provide frameworks for dealing with our day-to-day reality. They are also framed within the power relationships we inherit, by being born into particular families with particular histories and particular, culturally inflected styles of discourse.

In turn such understandings could also address the point raised by Sara Michaels in her often quoted article about 'sharing time' (Michaels:1981) where she points out that the teachers she studied were predisposed towards white middle class narrative discourses and could not readily see the point of other styles of narrative. I would go further and assert that teachers need to understand the complex syncretic processes happening before their eyes and attend to them closely. If one of the main aims in developing children's language and literacy is to do so through the development of their authentic voices, we need to be aware of the complexity of that voice. For this, we need to be building children's range not only in terms of genre, but also in different narrative styles. We also need to raise the status of autobiography within the curriculum and not dismiss it as too subjective or too anecdotal. Instead, we need to recognise it as the powerful learning tool it is – for ourselves and the children we teach. The concluding chapter draws out the implications of this research for educational institutions and policy makers.

8

Conclusions
Minds Wide Shut:
identity and policy

What I want is an accounting with all three cultures – white, Mexican, Indian. I want the freedom to carve and chisel my own face, to staunch the bleeding with ashes, to fashion my own gods out of my entrails. And if going home is denied me then I will have to stand and claim my own space, making a new culture – una cultura mestiza – with my own lumber, my own bricks and mortar and my own feminist architecture. Gloria Anzaldua

Introduction

Conducting this research with six people from such varied backgrounds considerably deepened my understanding of identity construction. It confirmed the level of complexity argued by cultural studies theorists. However, it has also highlighted the importance of memory and emotion in the process, which is more evident in the work of the social psychologists. Vygotsky (1986) wrote about the emotional dimensions of language acquisition at the level of the word. I believe this also applies to the acquisition of the rhetorical devices by which we narrativise our lives. This, for me, is the cornerstone of our identity and our basic method of reconstructing and reinscribing our identities. This affective dimension is apparent in the six narratives analysed here and clearly has profound implications for the classroom. Both Michaels (1986) and Gee (1996) have demonstrated that teachers need to examine their own reasons for prefering certain narrative styles above others, but there are wider implications in terms of motivation that are connected with the content of the curriculum which I have examined in detail elsewhere (Kearney (1990a,1990b, 1995, 1996, 1998). As Aliki's testimonies demonstrate, the exclusionary nature of the curriculum has a profound effect on self-esteem and is a considerable obstacle to academic and personal success.

The second important revelation for me concerns the centrality of memory in the construction of identity. This dimension is played down by much post-modern theory. Memory comes not only in the form of our individual reminiscences. Memories are fed by family narratives and other such mnemonics as photographs, songs, personal diaries and journals. Fictional representations are also a part of memory and a resource for analysing collective histories. Here, ironically, at the supposed end of history, we have greater access than ever to documents and artifacts which trace the history of our own families. The very technology which is supposedly destroying our sense of community enables us to restore it. The interest in 'where we are from' is more pronounced than ever. To be truly inclusive, a curriculum must consider ways to incorporate these alternative histories and viewpoints within the compass of schooled learning. Much work has already been done in this area and many teachers work hard even within the constraints of the current curriculum to build on what pupils bring to school. This is a difficult enough process when it receives support from those in charge of education but at present the constraints are galling. My argument is that autobiography and a study of family histories merit a central place within the school curriculum.

Developments over the period in which the research was conducted

Everything changes. Nothing stays the same. As the research ran over quite some time, my own thinking has grown and developed. Also, it needs to be noted that the life stories themselves are framed within the context of public policy on education and immigration in Britain from the end of the Second World War to the present and that context has changed. Britain now has a government which, in rhetoric at least, has exhibited a less shrill advocacy of the crude and narrowly proscribed view of British/English identity that characterised the Thatcher and Major administrations (1979-1997).

Another event which precipitated some change was the public inquiry into the murder of Stephen Lawrence, a black teenager killed in South London by racists. The Macpherson report on the Lawrence Inquiry revealed the endemic nature of institutionalised racism and has had some effect on the policy pronouncements from government sources. However well-meaning these pronouncements have been, the complex issues regarding identity have become sidelined. They have been reconfigured as the apparently less contentious, yet equally problematic, concept of 'citizenship'. Questions of identity scarcely touched the statutory elements of the National Curriculum when it was revised in 2000 and it failed to be more culturally sophisticated.

Despite the rhetoric on equal opportunities and a determination to introduce quota systems in respect of the recruitment of 'ethnic minority' teachers, recent government policy in education appears to be increasingly removed from the reality of many people's lived experience. The present study confirms ethnographic research and recent work in cultural studies demonstrating the rich complexity of the way individuals and groups construct their identities in modern cosmopolitan societies. However, in the sphere of public policy making there has been a trend towards rigidity and homogenisation. This is most noticeable in the content of the National Curriculum and the National Literacy Strategy.

The current notion of 'quality' in education in the marketplace is very much like the Ploughman's Lunch: the reinvention of a tradition that never really existed. Moreover, the concept of equality has been reconfigured as meaning the same treatment for everyone. The government speaks of an 'entitlement curriculum'. I would argue that this is a problematic and disguised form of exclusion. It is important to recognise what and who that curriculum excludes. Successive governments have developed a homogeneous, anglocentric and increasingly rigid curriculum, tested through a narrow set of assessment procedures and policed by an inspection service with an equally narrow definition of 'excellence'. It wholly ignores the complexity of identity construction described and analysed in this book. More importantly it fails to link such complexity to issues of motivation and achievement.

As researchers we are continually being asked to justify our work in terms of relevance to the classroom. I want to question whether current education policy has any relevance to the diverse reality of modern life. How does it deal with awkward issues of culture and power?

Identity and public policy

In this concluding chapter I argue that government policy is premised on crude and obsolete notions of culture and identity and, moreover, confuses the concepts of culture and citizenship. This lack of clarity is constraining educators from developing fully democratic curricula and instead we are becoming embroiled in an unequal and unfair game in which success is only defined by the positions on league tables based on test results. For those of us who are involved in teaching and teacher education and have a commitment to culturally inclusive education, the past few years have been bleak. The first national curriculum for teacher education was a singularly arid framework. Many involved in English teaching were uncertain exactly what children gain when their teachers know what 'morphology' means. It was never clear who decided upon the rather random bag of facts detailed in the circular 4/98 *Higher Status, Higher Standards*, which governed whether new recruits gain Qualified Teacher Status.

Although there is less emphasis on subject knowledge in the revised, slimmed down version which came into effect in September 2002, it is still not clear what is expected of institutions. However, the equally pointless, yet needlessly distressing, QTS subject tests remain in place.

However, the picture is complex. The pronouncements from the TTA and the DFEE are often substantially different. Although there are as yet no substantive developments we can perhaps take comfort in some of the pronouncements that have come out in the wake of the Macpherson report (1999). The report itself put cultural issues back on the educational agenda. The Parekh Report.(2000) *The Future of Multi-Ethnic Britain*, followed a year later. For this the Runnymede Trust had assembled an impressive committee, who drew on a wide body of expertise and statistical research. Many of the people involved are cited throughout this book. Chapters 2 and 3 of the report are impressive in encouraging a radical revisioning of British Identity in complex, realistic and interesting ways. So it is surprising that, in their Checklist of recommendations for educational policy, the content of the curriculum is explicitly referred to only once. Even here, it does not refer to compulsory education. It baldly states:

> **Courses and syllabi in higher education should be reviewed with a view to making them culturally more appropriate and inclusive wherever appropriate (Parekh: 2000: 301)**

Are they making the assumption that the National Curriculum is already culturally appropriate in terms of their vision? Looking at the list of those giving evidence, I would be surprised if such a view had prevailed.

It is worth examining the reasons why the policy of the present government is resistant to any meaningful engagement with the cultural complexity of modern Britain revealed in this research. To do so I consider three pieces, all written immediately prior to the introduction of Curriculum 2000. They reveal clearly the tensions, which lie beneath the calm surface of the Blair government's 'third way':

* *What is education for?* a paper by Nick Tate, then Chief Executive, Qualifications and Curriculum Authority

* *All Our Futures: Creativity, Culture and Education*

* *The review of the national curriculum: The consultation papers*

Nick Tate's paper (Tate: 1999:14) is interesting since he appears willing to return to the most basic question regarding the curriculum: what is education? and to consider the issues of culture and identity. In the paper he highlights the differences between libertarian and liberal viewpoints. He argues that libertarian societies are morally neutral about the choices the citizen makes, whereas 'liberal societies are those where the state is informed in its activities by a shared vision of the kind of civil societies its citizens wish to promote,while respecting individual freedom'. In this he draws on arguments put forward by the UK Chief Rabbi, Jonathan Sacks. He states that 'Sacks's thesis is that for much of the last fifty years both here and in North America, we have inhabited a libertarian rather than a liberal culture. He was one of the first last year to welcome the new government as pointing in a different direction.'

Tate identifies 'three particular roles for education'

1. The need 'to find a way of combining our highly individualist culture, which emphasises autonomy and choice, with a reassertion of the place of community in our lives ... in which there is a clearer sense of limits and shared values'

2. The need 'to find ways of helping ourselves come to terms with a world in which identities are being re-cast under the impact of globalisation'. Here he recognises that in comparison to France ... 'we have even more complex problems of identity to solve' including 'all sorts of legacies from our imperial past'

3. The need for education 'to shape civil society'. He elaborates. 'Talk of a common culture does not mean some stultifying uniformity which fails to respect the different traditions and allegiances which exist and have always existed, in our society'

Whilst it was encouraging to hear such a key figure raising issues about identity in a manner which would have been unimaginable in the Thatcher/Major era, we need to scrutinise this liberal stance a little more closely. Earlier in his article Tate explicitly demonstrates that his view of culture is elitist, when he states:

> Striving to be an educated person ... is of course unashamedly elitist, in the sense of trying to give as many people as possible access to the highest ideals by which people have lived and to what Matthew Arnold called 'the best that has been known and thought.' (1999:9)

'These ideals,' he continues, 'are inherited from our Judeo-Christian and Graeco-Roman roots and in their essentials have remained remarkably constant.' Such statements must temper any optimism over the plight of those whose heritages do not stem from this tradition. The central problem with his argument is his confused view of identity and he makes no real attempt to clarify it. He is rehearsing the same viewpoint as expressed by Matthew Arnold in *Culture and Anarchy* and trying to apply the principles to a different world. Such specious connections are symptomatic of many government policy statements which confuse the notion of citizenship with other, sometimes conflicting, aspects of cultural belonging.

Identity and Citizenship

Moreover, as a nation we have no clear and agreed description of our 'national' identity. There is a fundamental dichotomy between the notion of citizenship and the idea of belonging to various groups in more organic ways. Whereas the notion of citizenship is premised on human rights framed through legislation, the concept of belonging based on friendship, kinship or culture is more complex and much more difficult to legislate for. This is further exacerbated by the global reach of current capitalist economics, which demands standardisation of manufacturing and working practices. We have witnessed the development over the 20th century of fundamental human rights, enshrined in international legislation which transcend the boundaries of local cultures, concurrently with those with previously inscribed 'national identities'. Not that I mean to imply that these rights are universally observed. But they do exist as a point of reference.

As Cesarani and Fulbrook (1996:7) point out:

> The concept of citizenship was always weak in England. Subjecthood was the preferred mode of belonging to a nation ... The creation of the United Kingdom and the British Empire necessitated a flexible category of belonging which was supplied by perpetual allegiance to the crown ... However, the   emergence of the dominions and the entrenchment of racial thinking led to a bifurcation of white and non-white British subjects ... mass immigration from the colonies and New Commonwealth after 1945 strongly accentuated the desire to draw the criteria for national belonging more tightly and to exclude non-white peoples. By the late 1970s, immigration controls and citizenship were overdetermined by considerations of 'race', even if disguised as cultural concerns. The struggle over the definition of an exclusive or inclusive national identity is still not resolved, but the treatment of immigrants and non-white citizens bears the marks of a dominant exclusivist ethos.

I quote this at length for its clarification of the basis of the sets of problems surrounding the issues of culture, identity and curriculum in terms of government policy, particularly as it impacts upon the curriculum. First, it helps to explain why the hegemonic projects undertaken by the Thacherite governments were so successful in putting forward their curiously old fashioned view of English identity, most particularly as it is expressed in the English curriculum. It is a romanticised version of middle class life in the 1950s, despite the fact that Thatcher herself advocated Victorian values. New Labour appear not to want to challenge that particular 'warranting narrative' but merely to give it a modernised gloss. Second, it helps us to understand the ongoing battle between multiculturalism and antiracism, which has been damaging in terms of consolidating any concerted counter hegemonic discourse or struggle.

Finally, the passage helps us to understand why there is a so much excitement and interest in the notion of identity, particularly in exploring it as a many layered, contradictory and complex phenomenon. In many areas of social life, subjecthood is being superseded by networks of contacts and relationships. This is evident in the work of cultural theorists and in the work of film-makers, musicians, novelists, playwrights, poets and artists, who are working on 'border art'. By crossing and re-crossing boundaries, they are creating new forms of expression to describe new types of relationships. First, second and third generation British born settlers are forming new sets of identities. In the process they tend to be critical of traditional cultures from both the home/community and the school.

The people I interviewed for this study have been keen to discuss issues of power and politics which underlie such conceptualisations of culture and identity. The analyses in Chapters 4, 5 and 6 demonstrate how complex the notion of identity is and how intricate and sensitive the processes of identity construction. They are not susceptible to crude policies which are based on mistaken generalisations or the kind of confused thinking epitomised in Tate's paper. However, as I suggest at the end of this chapter, there are ways in which schooling can further the process of identity construction process in constructive ways.

As I've discussed here, the notion of identity is being explored, re-evaluated and reworked in many fields of academic research, particularly ethnography (Geertz 1973, 1983, 1986, 1988, 1995; Clifford 1986, 1988, 1997) cultural studies, (Hall 1980, 1988, 1991, 1997; Gilroy 1992; Mouffe 1995; Bhabha 1995; Ang 1994) media studies (hooks, 1992). This complexity and contradiction has also been explored through studies of literature (see Singh *et al* 1994, 1996) and through film and television. The recent and successful British comedy TV show, *Goodness, Gracious Me*, tapped this vein well, revealing the range and complexity of values and attitudes within the Asian diaspora; exploding myths and preconceptions. By comparison, many aspects of contemporary schooling appear hopelessly dated and irrelevant.

However, the role of the mass media is not simple or clear cut, since it has to balance a range of forces, some of them economic and some ideological. There are the important questions of agency: Who owns the media? Who controls what we see and what we don't? What values are promoted and which are excluded (see Schiller: 1996 and Klein: 2000)? Moreover, the mass media has to render itself accessible to a widely varied population in terms of age, culture and class. As the life stories showed, the media has a powerful and potent influence in how they perceive themselves and their families. The stories illustrate how identities are fixed by the more powerful forces of mass culture working through the media (in terms of fashion especially) and how this in turn guides how they are perceived by others. These forces also affect the ways the media is used by politicians and form the basis of public policy. In the field of education, this is clear in terms of epistemology (What's worth knowing?) and pragmatism (Which approaches work best?). What we have at present is a ploughman's lunch, of the kind served up by people like Nick Tate: that reinvention of middle-class, prep school tradition currently being marketed as education. In terms of policy we cling to a quaint and phony 'Englishness' to redescribe our national identity. All this infects the English curriculum – both the canon and the emphasis on prescriptive and uncritical ways of examining language use. This is far removed from the everyday life of many pupils, especially those who are negotiating the rich and diverse repertoires of their own lives and identities. In short, people not unlike those examined in this study.

Two key aspects of policy have emanated from this old fashioned view. One is the 'consumption of tradition'. Wedded to a market system of funding schools, parental 'choice', a narrow and rigid inspection framework and a published league table of test results, schools now market themselves in curiously old fashioned ways. We have seen the return of school uniforms. An extreme example of this approach was recently criticised by Ofsted, where inspectors discovered that the children were not allowed to speak during the lunch break for reasons of etiquette (*Sunday Telegraph*, 26 July 1999).

The second is the notion of 'entitlement'. With the introduction of the national curriculum in 1988, equality was reconfigured as equality of access. This still appears as the cornerstone of current government policy. In the 1999 review of the National Curriculum, the Secretary of State proposed an introduction to the curriculum which would include the following paragraph:

> The national curriculum secures for all pupils, *irrespective* of culture, social background or gender, an entitlement to a number of areas of learning and to develop the skills, knowledge and understanding necessary for their self-fulfilment and development as active and responsible citizens. (my emphasis)

On the surface this appears to be a more equitable system than equality of opportunity, since it implies inclusion. However, the rhetoric conceals a rather different reality. The question that needs to be asked is: entitlement to what? The narrow curriculum appears to exclude rather than include children from culturally diverse heritages and to privilege white middle class suburban children. There may be exceptions in terms of individual pupils or communities, but any demographic analysis of the current league tables would suggest that middle class privilege is, if anything, more entrenched than ever. More significant is the dramatic increase in the number of black pupils who are being excluded from school. In such circumstances 'entitlement' becomes an ambiguous and mis-leading term.

After the Dearing review of the National Curriculum, I explored issues of policy with reference to multilingualism (Kearney, 1996). I argued that public policy in education was making galling constraints for teachers working with children from diverse cultural backgrounds. The interlocking legislation surrounding the national curriculum was diverting funds away from programmes of support. At that time funding came from the Home Office and had been narrowly targeted on the learning of English language. It was also part of the single regeneration budget, which meant that Local Authorities had to bid for it along with money for other purposes. This meant that distribution was uneven. Following the Dearing review, the curriculum was becoming more narrowly defined, anglo-centric and rigid.

Despite a change of government. there is little evidence in education policy that the emphasis has shifted in any ideological or practical sense. The literacy strategy has become a central plank of the Blair government's policy. Although it was devised by the outgoing Conservative government, it is, if anything, more narrow, prescriptive and rigid than the English curriculum in the Dearing review. The approach of whole class teaching and briskly-paced lessons works against the interests of children at the early stages of learning English. With such a crude view of curriculum entitlement, teachers have to use a great deal of energy and imagination to curb its worst excesses. As with the previous conservative governments there has been almost wilful ignorance of the wealth of educational research that critiques this approach and argues for interactive, holistic, col-laborative approaches, thematically organised and drawing on the children's own experiences (eg Garcia, 1991, Carter and Chatfield, 1989; Lucas, Henze and Donato, 1980; Pease-Alvarez, Garcia and Espinola 1991). Current policy also ignores the rich complexity involved in identity construction explored in this book and, more importantly, the diverse and exciting changes happening in our cultural life in Britain and elsewhere.

'All Our Futures'

The recommendations of the Stephen Lawrence Inquiry report, however, have opened up a few spaces for teachers. In its attempt to deal with complex issues of identity *All Our Futures: Creativity, Culture and Education* (DFEE:1999) is a much more coherent and encouraging document. *All Our Futures* examines in detail the relationship between education, culture, identity and creativity and shows how closely intertwined they are. The authors are explicit in their descriptions and definitions. It is well supported by recent research findings. The committee also take a view which is non-elitist, inclusive and informed. They recognise that the issues are deeply problematic and complex. It is much closer to complex ideas of identity explored here. The passage that follows (DFEE: 1999:47) gives something of its flavour.

> ... diversity is now central to the vitality of our national culture and a distinctive feature of it. There are immense benefits in this and there are deep problems ...

> Culture in the biological sense implies growth and transformation. This is true of social culture. One of the consequences of the dynamics and diversity of social cultures is an irresistible process of change. Some years ago a national newspaper campaigned with the slogan, 'Times change, values don't'. For all the reasons we have suggested, the opposite is true. Many of the values and patterns of behaviour in the closing moments of the twentieth century are wholly different from those of the late nineteenth century; as they were from the preceding century. Contemporary ways of life are not only different from those of the Victorians, they were largely unpredicted by them and were essentially unpredictable. Cultural change is rarely linear and uniform. It results from a vortex of influences and events which is hard enough to understand and impossible to plan in advance.

> ... We have described contemporary cultures as dynamic and diverse. As a matter of urgency, education must help young people to understand these processes and engage with and respect cultural perspectives different from their own.

In the report the Robinson Committee distance themselves from an empty cultural relativism by insisting on two core values:

1. a commitment to the unique value and central importance of the individual

2. the idea of contingency: the view that things might be different from how they seem or are currently believed to be ... It is this that encourages us to

question current perceptions, knowledge and practices and to believe in the virtues of openness in public life rather than closure and censure

The committee identifies four central roles for education in the cultural development of young people:

a) To enable young people to recognise, explore and understand their own cultural assumptions and values

b) To enable young people to embrace and understand cultural diversity by bringing them into contact with the attitudes, values and traditions of other cultures

c) To encourage an historical perspective by relating contemporary values to the processes and events that have shaped them

d) To enable young people to understand the evolutionary nature of culture and the processes and potential for change

It would be difficult to find a better-informed, better-written and wiser document coming out of the education department in recent times. Furthermore, the committee question some of the central assumptions of the National Curriculum in radical ways in terms of both content and assessment, suggesting ways in which it could be truly inclusive. There are significant philosophical differences from Tate's views, since it does not lean towards an elitist and transmission view of learning. What is particularly impressive is that the report contains detailed recommendations for all bodies concerned with implementation of policy.

Although the committee put in a great deal of energy, creativity and commitment it has fallen on stony ground. It was clear that by 2000 none of its recommendations had been taken into account in the curriculum. Although I have concentrated upon the values embedded in the pronouncements from official sources, there have been some very encouraging guidelines issued from various bodies, (eg *QCA: A language in common: Assessing English as an additional language; TTA: Raising Attainment of Minority Ethnic Pupils and the National Literacy Strategy: EMAG Materials: Supporting pupils learning English as an additional language*). However, they still do not tackle the fundamental issues of the curriculum. Their response to Stephen Lawrence Inquiry report is configure the problem in terms of citizenship issues and not the content of the curriculum. In the English section of Curriculum 2000 the equal opportunities issues concentrate on the moral panic about boys and reading. This allows them to leave all those messy issues of culture and identity safely on one side.

Implications for Education

Although cultural content is of great importance, if we are to have a curriculum which is truly relevant and inclusive, then we need to ensure that content is not given precedence over process. We need to ensure space to explore difficult issues and work out creative solutions. We need to ensure that the aim of education is to encourage the development of creative adults with a sense of purpose and a voice, who think critically. We can embrace difference within equality, only if we stop reducing ideas of quality to the memorisation of 'facts'; if we recognise the multiple intelligences (see Howard Gardner:1983) which our pupils have; if we design curricula which allow pupils to build on their own experiences and complex identities and to explore their interests and potential; if we harness the creativity of the majority of teachers instead of burying it under dull, repetitive routines. In short, we need a dialogic curriculum, which prepares pupils for all aspects of their life, not merely for the world of work. The main argument of my own work is that self- narrative should be at the centre of such a curriculum. We need to stop burying our differences and work towards resolving the difficulties and enjoy diversity instead of fearing it.

My research shows how young people are working through the transformations of culture, language and identity. I have attempted to chart the nature of such transformations within the lives of young(ish) people. I am interested in not only what changes but also what persists over time and space and the nature of narrative and voice in this experience. They are creating new and exciting forms of expression, questioning assumptions and values, yet maintaining their critical perspectives and their sense of history and struggle. Education needs to be an integral part of those processes. The prospect is exciting for us all.

As Bakhtin (1986) puts it:

> In the realm of culture, outsidedness is a most powerful factor in understanding. It is only in the eyes of another culture that foreign culture reveals itself fully and profoundly ... A meaning only reveals its depths once it has encountered and come into contact with another, foreign meaning; they engage in a kind of dialogue, which surmounts the closedness and one sidedness of these particular meanings, these cultures. We raise new questions for a foreign culture, ones which it did not raise for itself; we seek answers to our own questions in it; and the foreign culture responds to us by revealing to us its new semantic depths. Without *one's own* questions one cannot creatively understand anything new and foreign (but of course, the questions must be serious and sincere). Such a dialogic encounter does not result in merging or mixing. Each retains its unity and *open* totality, but they are mutually enriched ... We lack only scholarly, investigatory boldness,

and without this we cannot rise to the heights or descend to the depths.

This is clearly a two-way street and policy makers would do well to locate it on their own conceptual maps. Then education may have a part to play in the resolution of the social tensions highlighted by so many reports in the past thirty years. In my view, the complex and highly politicised question of identity is possibly the most important single issue facing us in the modern world. It is about time those who decide upon curriculum policy stopped trying to avoid it.

Ghosts in the wind
That blow through my life
Follow me wherever I go

I'll never be free
From these chains inside
Hidden deep down in my soul
Lucinda Williams: 2001 'Bus to Baton Rouge'

Appendix 1
Examples of grid analysis of part of Asif's narrative

Others for self	Self for others	Self for self
		19. Discomfort: With certain parts of the tradition especially religious aspects
		'being an atheist'
		Disapproves of father's return to faith after heart attack. 'Maybe that's cynical on my part'
	20. Discomfort: Being sent to mosque school • couldn't understand it ie. Arabic • no respect for teacher Only there a short time. Subverted it by teasing the teacher	**21. Discomfort (metanarrative):** formal teaching style goes against current views
	22. Tradition: Was happy to go along with parents wishes No real understanding of the Qur'an	
23. Discomfort: argues with father and uncles about Islam		**23: Epiphany:** Currently has balanced and critical view of religion – would like more knowledge to strengthen arguments **24: Pragmatic view:** **25:** Eschews spiritual aspects. Is candid. Envies people with faith. Has Marxist/sociological perspectives.

Appendix 2
Shape of Conversation with Asif

Others for self	Self for others	Self for self
H/Influence		
H/Influence		
RM/Influence		
		(metanarrative)
Metanarrative/Reflection		
RM/Influence		
		DC/Discomfort
		Epiphany
RM/Influence		
H/Influence		
	H/Influence	
	H/Influence	
RM/Prolepsis		
	H/Influence	
Contradiction metanarrative		
H/Discomfort (metanarrative)		
	H/Influence	
	H/Influence	
	H/Ambivalence	
		Epiphany
	H/Influence	
	HandDC/Discomfort	
H(school)/Discomfort		
		(metanarrative)
	H/Ambivalence	
	H/(school)/Influence	
H/Discomfort		
		Epiphany
		H/Discomfort

Others for self	Self for others	Self for self
H/Discomfort		
H/Discomfort		
		Epiphany
	H/Discomfort	
		Epiphany
		Epiphany
		Epiphany
		H/Ambivalence
		H/Discomfort

Bibliography

Aarons, Victoria (1996) Telling History: Inventing Identity in Jewish American Fiction. In Singh, Amritjit, Skerrit, Joseph T. Jr., and Hogan, Robert. E (eds) *Memory and Cultural Politics: New Approaches to American Ethnic Literatures* Boston: Northeastern University Press

Aboud, Frances E. (1987) The Development of Ethnic Self-Identification in Ethnic Minority Children. In Phinney, Jean S. and Rotheram, Mary Jane (eds) *Children's ethnic socialization, pluralism and development* London: Sage, in cooperation with the Society for Child Development

Abu-Lughod, Lila (1991) *Writing Against Culture In Recapturing Anthropology: Working in the Present* Santa Fe, New Mexico: School of American Research Press

Adorno, Theodor W (1978/1951) *Manima Moralia, Reflections from a Damaged Life* (trans. E F N Jephcot) London: Verso

Alasuutari, Pertti (1995) *Researching Culture: Qualitative Method and Cultural Studies* London: Thousand Oaks. New Delhi: Sage Publications

Andrews, R (ed) (1996) *Interpreting the New National Curriculum* London: Middlesex University Press

Ang, Ien (1994) On not speaking Chinese: Postmodern Ethnicity and the politics of Diaspora *New Formations* No. 24

Appadurai, Arjun (1993) The Heart of Whiteness *Callaloo* 16(4)

Appadurai, Arjun (1996) *Modernity at Large: Cultural Dimensions of Globalisation* Minneapolis: University of Minnesota Press

Aranowitz, S (1995) Reflections on Identity. In Rajchman, J (ed) (1995) *The Identity in Question* London: Routledge

Asch, S (1956) Studies of Independence and Conformity: A minority of one, the unanimous majority *Texas Psychological Monographs*, 10,5

Atkinson, P (1992) *Understanding ethnographic texts* Newbury Park, CA: Sage

Bakhtin, Mikhail (1979) Avtor i geroi v esteticheskoi deiatel'nosti [Author and Hero in Aesthetic Activity] . In The 1979 *Russian Collection M.M.Bakhtin Estetika slovesnogo tvorchestva X* Moscow: Iskusstvo 1979

Bakhtin, Mikhail (1981) *The Dialogic Imagination* Texas: University of Texas Press

Bakhtin, Mikhail (1984) *The Problems of Dostoevsky's Poetics* Manchester: Manchester University Press

Bakhtin, Mikhail (1986) *Speech Genres and Other Late Essays* Texas: University of Texas Press

Bakhtin, Mikhail (1986a) *Rabelais and His World* Indiana: Indiana University Press

Ball, Stephen (1990) *Politics and Policy Making in Education* London: Routledge

Barkan, Elazar and Shelton, Marie Denise (1998) *Borders, Exiles, Diasporas* Stanford, California: Stanford University Press

Barnet, Richard J. and Cavanagh, John (1994) *Global Dreams: The Imperial Corporations and the New World Order* New York: Simon and Shuster

Barthes Roland (1957,1972) *Mythologies* London: Jonathan Cape

Barthes Roland (1977) *Image, Music, Text* London: Jonathan Cape

Barthes, Roland (1980) Introduction to the structural analysis of narrative. In Pugh, A.K, Lee, V.J. and Swann, J. (eds) *Language and Language Use* London: Heinemann

Bartlett, F (1932) *Remembering: a study in experimental and social psychology* Cambridge: Cambridge University Press

Baumann, Gerd (1996) *Contesting Culture: Discourses of Identity in Multi-ethnic* London Cambridge: Cambridge University Press

Beavers, Herman (1996) Tilling the Soil to Find Ourselves: Labor, Memory and Identity in Ernest J Gaines's 'Of Love and Dust'. In Singh *et al. (op.cit.)*

Ben Amos, Dan and Weissberg, Lilian (eds) (1999) *Cultural Memory and the Construction of Identity* Detroit: Wayne State University Press

Berg, Bruce, L (1989) *Qualitative Research Methods for the Social Sciences* Boston: Alleyn and Bacon

Berger, Peter and Luckmann, Thomas (1966) *The Social Construction of Reality* Harmondsworth: Penguin Books

Bhabha, Homi (1994) The Other Question. In Bhabba, Homi *The Location of Culture* London: Routledge pp 66-84

Bhabha, Homi (1995) Freedom's Basis in the Indeterminate. In Rajchman, J (*op. cit.*)

Blumenfeld-Jones, Donald (1995) Fidelity as a criterion for practising and evaluating narrative inquiry In Hatch, J. Amos and Wisniewski, Richard (eds) *Life History and Narrative* Falmer Press: London

Boal, A (1992) *Games for Actors and Non-Actors* London: Routledge

Boelhower, William (1996) Ethnographic Politics: The Uses of Memory in Ethnic Fiction. In Singh *et. al. (op. cit.)*

Bogdan, Robert and Taylor, Steven J., (1992) *Introduction to Qualitative Research Methods: A Phenomenological Approach* New York: John Wiley and Sons

Boggs, Carl (1976) *Gramsci's Marxism* London: Pluto Press

Brah, Avtah (1996) *Cartographies of Diaspora* London: Routledge

Brewer, W.F. (1996) What is Recollective Memory? In D.C. Rubin (ed) *Remembering Our Past: Studies in Autobiographical Memory* Cambridge: Cambridge University Press UK

Brice Heath, Shirley (1982) Ethnography in Education: Defining the Essentials. In Gilmore P and Glathorn, A.A (eds) *Children in and out of school: ethnography and education* Washington DC: Center for Applied Linguistics

Brice Heath, Shirley (1983) *Ways with Words* Cambridge: Cambridge University Press

Bronowski, Jacob (1974) *The Ascent of Man* London: BBC Publications

Brooks, Cleanth and Warren, Robert Penn (1949) *Modern Rhetoric* New York: Harcourt Brace

Browdly de Hernandez, Jennifer (1996) The Plural Self: The Politicisation of Memory and Form in Three American Ethnic Autobiographies. In Singh *et. al. (op. cit.)*

Brown, R and Kulik, J (1977) Flashbulb Memories *Cognition*, 5: 73-79

Bruner, Jerome (1986) *Actual Minds, Possible Worlds* Cambridge Mass: Harvard University Press

Bruner, Jerome (1990) *Acts of Meaning* Cambridge Mass: Harvard University Press

Bruner, Jerome (1987) Life as Narrative *Social Research*, 54. 1-32

Bruner, Jerome (1992) The narrative construction of reality. In H. Beilin and P. Puffal (eds) *Piaget's Theory:Prospects and Possibilities* Hillsdale, N.J.: Lawrence Erlbaum Associates

Bruner, Jerome (1994) The 'remembered self' In U. Neisser and R. Fivush (eds) *The Remembering Self: Construction and accuracy in the self narrative* New York: Cambridge University Press

Bruner, Jerome S and Weisser, S (1991) The Invention of Self: Autobiography and its forms. In D. R. Olson and N. Torrance (eds) *Literacy and Orality* (pp129-148) New York: Cambridge University Press

Buckley, Jerome Hamilton (1984) *The Turning Key: Autobiography and the Subjective Impulse since 1800* Cambridge Mass: Harvard University Press

Burgess, Tony and Rosen, Harold (1980) *The Languages and Dialects of London Schoolchildren* London: Ward Lock

Calvino, Italo (1996) *Six Memos for the Next Millennium* London: Vintage

Cameron, D and Bourne, J (1989) *Grammar, Nation and Citizenship; Kingman in Linguistic and Historical Perspective* London: Department of English and Media Studies, Occasional Paper No.1, Institute of Education, University of London

Carr, David (1986) *Time, Narrative and History* Bloomington/Indianapolis: Indiana University Press

Carter, T.P. and Chatfield M.L. (1989) Effective Bilingual Schools: Implications for Policy and Practice, *American Journal of Education* 95: 200-234

Cesaire, Aime (1983) *Aime Cesaire: Collected Poetry*, translated and edited by Clayton Eschleman and Annette Smith, California: The Regents of the University of California

Cesarini, David and Mary Fulbrook (eds) (1996) *Citizenship, Nationality and Migration in Europe* London: Routledge

Chamberlain, Mary (1998) 'I belong to whoever wants me' *New Formations: Frontlines Backyards* Spring 1998 33:47-58

Chatman , S (1990) *Coming to Terms: The Rhetoric of Narrative in Fiction and Film* Cornell: Cornell University Press

Chen, Kuan-Hsing (1996) Not Yet the Postcolonial Era: The (Super) Nation State and Transnationalism of of Cultural Studies: Response to Ang and Stratton *Cultural Studies* 10.10. 37-70

Christian, D (1994) *Two-Way Bilingual Education: Students Learning through Two Languages* California: National Center for Research on Cultural Diversity and Second Language Learning (NCRCDSLL)

Clandenin, D Jean and Connelly, F Michael (1994) Personal Experience Methods. In N.K. Denzin and Y. Lincoln (eds) *Handbook of Qualitative Research* Thousand Oaks: Sage

Clandenin, D Jean and Connelly, F Michael (2000) *Narrative Enquiry: Experience and Story in Qualitative Research* San Francisco: Jossey-Bass

Clement, B (1995) English as an Additional Language in Wales. Paper given at SCAA conference April 1995

Clifford, James (1988) *The Predicament of Culture: Twentieth-Century Ethnography, Literature, and Art* Cambridge, Massachusetts and London, England : Harvard University Press

Clifford, James (1997) *Routes: Travel and Translation in the Late Twentieth Century* Cambridge, Massachusetts and London, England: Harvard University Press

Clifford, James and Marcus, George E ed. (1986) *Writing Culture: The Poetics and Politics of Ethnography* Berkeley: University of California Press

Cole, Michael (1996) *Cultural Psychology: a once and future discipline* Cambridge Massachusetts and London England: The Belknap Press of Harvard University Press

Conway, M.A. (1990) *Autobiographical Memory, an introduction* Milton Keynes: Open University Press

Cortazzi, Martin (1993) *Narrative Analysis* London: Falmer Press

de Hernandez, Jennifer Browdy (1996) The Plural Self. In Singh *et al* (eds) *op. cit.*

de Saussure, Ferdinand (trans, 1966) *Course in General Linguistics* ed. Charles Bally and Albert Sechehaye, New York: Wade Baskin

Degh, Linda (1995) *Narratives in Society* Helsinki: Academic Scientarum, Fennica

Denzin, Norman K (1991) Representing lived experience in ethnographic texts. *Studies in Symbolic Interaction*, 12, 59-70

Denzin, Norman K (1993) *The Alcoholic Society: Addiction and recovery of self* New Brunswick, NJ: Transaction Publishing

Denzin, Norman K (1997) *Interpretive Ethnography: Ethnographic Practices for the 21st Century* Thousand Oaks: London: New Delhi: Sage

Derrida, Jacques (1978) *Writing and Difference.* Chicago: University of Chicago Press (Original work published in 1967)

Dewey John (1922) *Human Nature and Conduct* New York: Hart, Holt and Co

Dewey John (1929) *The Quest for Certainty: A Study of the Relation of Knowledge and Action* New York: Paragon Books

Dewey John (1934) *Art as Experience Tom's River,* New Jersey: Capricorn Books

Dewey John (1938) *Experience and Education* New York; Collier Books

Dewey John (1916,1961) *Democracy and Education* Old Tappan, New Jersey: Macmillan

Dittmar, Norbert (1976) *Sociolinguistics – A Critical Survey of Theory and Application* London: Arnold

Droysen, Johann Gustav (1960) *Historik: Vorlesungen uber Enzyklopadie und Methodologie der Geschichte* Darmstadt: Wissenschaftliche Buchgesellschaft du Gay, Paul; Evans, Jessica and Redman, Peter (2000) *Identity: a reader* Thousand Oaks: London: New Delhi: Sage/Open University

Dylan, Bob (1974) *Forever Young* (song) from 'Planet Waves' album CBS/Sony

Eade, John (1995) *Routes and Beyond* Roehampton Institute: London: Centre for Bangladeshi Studies

Ellis, Carolyn (1997) Evocative Autoethnography: Writing Emotionally about our lives. In Tierney, William G. and Lincoln, Yvonna S. (eds) (1997) *Representation and the Text: Re- Framing the Narrative Voice* New York: State University of New York Press

Engelmann, Seigfied (1970) Teaching Disadvantaged Children. In Frederick Williams, *Language and Poverty* Chicago: University of Illonois Press

Erikson, J (1968) *Identity, Youth and Crisis* New York: Norton

Everard, Jerry (2000) *Virtual States: The Internet and the Boundaries of the Nation State* London: Routledge

Eysenck, Hans Jurgen (1970) *The Biological Basis of Personality* Springfield:Charles C. Thomas

Ezzy, Douglas (1998) Theorising Narrative Identity: Symbolic Interactionism and Hermeneutics *Sociological Quarterly* 39 239 -52

Fara, Patricia and Patterson, Karalyn (eds) (1998) *Memory* Cambridge : Cambridge University Press

Featherstone, Mike (1996) *Undoing Culture:Globalisation, Postmodernism and Identity* London, Thousand Oaks, New Delhi: Sage

Fentress, J and Wickham, C (1992) *Social Memory* Oxford: Blackwell

Fischer, M (1994) Autobiographical Voices and Mosaic Memory in Ashley *et al* (eds) *Autobiography and Postmodernism* Massachusetts: University of Massachusetts Press

Fitzgerald, Thomas K. (1996) *Media, Ethnicity and Identity in Culture and Power: a media, culture and society reader* Thousand Oaks: London: New Delhi: Sage Publications

Fivush, Robyn and Neisser, Ulrich (1996) *The Remembered Self* New York: Cambridge University Press

Forgacs, David ed. (1988) *A Gramsci Reader, Selected Writings 1916-1935* London: Lawrence and Wishart

Francis, Hazel (1993) Advancing Phenomenography: Questions of Method *Nordisk Pedagogik* 2: 1993, 68-75

Fraser, Ronald 1984) *In Search of a Past:The Manor House, Amnersfield, 1933-1945* London: Verso

Freeman, Mark (1993) *Rewriting the Self: History, Memory, Narrative* London and New York: Routledge

Friere, Paulo (1972) *The Pedagogy of the Oppressed* Harmondsworth: Penguin

Friere, Paulo and Macedo, Donaldo (1987) *Literacy: Reading the Word and the World* London: Routledge and Kegan Paul

Fuentes, Carlos (1988) How I Started to Write. In Simonson, P and Walker, S (eds) *Multi-Cultural Literacy: the Opening of the American Mind* St Paul Minnesota: Greywolf Press

Fukuyama, Francis (1992) *The End of History and the Last Man* London: Hamish Hamilton

Gallagher, S (1992) *Hermeneutics and Education* New York: State University of New York Press

Garcia, E (1991) *The Education of Linguistically and Culturally Diverse Students: Effective Institutional Practices* Santa Cruz: National Centre for Research on Cultural Diversity and Second Language Learning

Garcia, E (1988) *Effective schooling for language minority students* (New Focus No.1) Washington DC: National Clearinghouse for Bilingual Education

Gardner, Howard (1993) *Frames of Mind: the theory of multiple intelligences* London: Fontana

Gee, James Paul (1989) Literacy, Discourse and Linguistics: Essays by James Paul Gee *Journal of Education* 171, 1

Gee, James Paul (1991) A linguistic approach to narrative *Journal of Narrative and Life History 1, 15-40*

Gee, James Paul (1992) *The Social Mind: Language, Ideology and Social Practice* New York: Series in Language and Ideology, Macedo, D (ed) Bergin and Garvey

Gee, James Paul (1996) *Social Linguistics and Literacies: Ideology in Discourses* London and Philadelphia: Routledge/Falmer

Geertz, Clifford (1973) *The Interpretation of Cultures* New York: Basic Books

Geertz, Clifford (1983) *Local Knowledge* New York: Basic Books

Geertz, Clifford (1986) The Uses of Diversity Michigan Quarterly 25,1 Geertz, Clifford (1988) *Works and Lives; The Anthropologist as Author* Cambridge: Polity Press

Geertz, Clifford (1995) *After the Fact, Two Countries, Four Decades, One Anthropologist* Cambridge, Mass: Harvard University Press

Genesee, F (1981) A comparison of early and late second language learning *Canadian Modern Language Review*, 13, 115-128

Genesee, F (1987) *Learning through two languages: Studies of immersion and bilingual education* Cambridge, M.A.: Newberry House

Georges, Robert A and Jones, Michael O, (1980) *People Studying People: The Human Element in Fieldwork* CA: University of California Press

Gergen, Kenneth J (1989) Warranting Voice and the Elaboration of Self. In Shotter, John and Gergen, Kenneth J, ed. *Texts of Identity* London: Sage

Gergen, Kenneth J (1994) *Realities and Relationships* Cambridge Mass: Harvard University Press

Gergen, Mary (1992) Life Stories: Pieces of a Dream. In Rosenwald, George C and Ochberg Richard L (eds) *op. cit.*

Giddens, Anthony (1991) *Modernity and Self-Identity: Self and Society in the Late Modern Age* Cambridge: Polity Press

Gide, Andre (1955) *Si le grain ne meurt* (translated by Suzanne Nalbatian: 1997: 18-19) Paris: Gallimard

Gikandi, Simon (1996) *Maps of Englishness;Writing Identity in the Culture of Colonialism* New York: Columbia University Press

Gill, B (1992) Language, Culture and Identity in the National Curriculum. In Joan Goody (ed) *Multicultural Perspectives in the National Curriculum* London: NATE

Gilroy, P (1987) *There Ain't No Black in the Union Jack* London: Hutchinson

Gilroy, P (1992) Ethnic Absolutism. In Grossman, Nelson and Treichler (eds) *Cultural Studies* New York: Routledge

Ginzburg, Carlo (1980) *The Cheese and the Worms* London: Routledge

Giroux, Henry (1991) *Border Crossings* London: Routledge

Glaser, B and Strauss, A (1967) *The discovery of grounded theory* Chicago: Aldine

Goffman, Erving (1969) *The Presentation of the Self in Everyday Life* Harmondsworth: Penguin

Goffman, Erving (1975) *Frame Analysis: An Essay on the Organisation of Experience* Harmondsworth: Penguin

Goffman, Erving (1981) *Form of Talk* Oxford: Blackwell

Gomez-Pena, Guillermo (1988) Documented/Undocumented. In In Simonson, P and Walker, S (eds) *Multicultural Literacy: the Opening of the American Mind* St Paul: Minn: Greywolf Press

Gomez-Pena, Guillermo (1988) The New World (B)order *Third Text: Third World Perspectives on Contemporary Art and Culture* 21 Winter 1992-93

Goodman, Kenneth (1989) Unpublished lecture given at the Institute of Education, London

Goodson, Ivor F and Ball, Stephen J (1984) *Defining the Curriculum: Histories and Ethnographies* Sussex: Falmer Press

Goodson, Ivor F (1995) The story so far: personal knowledge and the political. In Hatch *et. al. (op. cit.)* London: Falmer Press

Gregory, E (1993 a) What counts as reading in the early years' classroom? *British Journal of Educational Psychology* 63, 214-230

Gregory, E; Lathwell, J; Mace, J and Rashid, N (1993 b) *Literacy at home and at school* Literacy Research Group, Goldsmiths,University of London

Grossman,L, Nelson,C and Treichler, P.A.(1992) *Cultural Studies* New York:Routledge

Halbwachs, Maurice (1925) *Les Cadres Sociaux de la Memoire* Paris: F. Alcan

Halbwachs, Maurice (1992) *Collective Memory* (Trans. L.A. Coser) Chicago: University of Chicago Press

Hall, Kathleen (1995) 'There's a Time to Act English and a Time to Act Indian': The Politics of Identity among British-Sikh Teenagers. In Sharon Stephens (ed) *Children and the Politics of Culture* p243-264 Princeton: Princeton University Press

Hall, Kathleen (1999) Media and the Making of British Sikh Identities Unpublished Paper, University of Pennsylvania

Hall, Stuart *et al.* (1980) *Culture, Media, Language* Birmingham: Hutchinson in association with Centre for Contemporary Cultural Studies: University of Birmingham

Hall, Stuart (1988) *The Hard Road to Renewal: Thatcherism and the Crisis of the Left* London: Routledge

Hall, Stuart (1991) *Old and New Identities* in King, A.D (ed) Culture, Globalisation and the World System New York: Macmillan

Hall, Stuart (1993) 'Culture, Community, Nation' *Cultural Studies* 7(3): 349-63

Hall, Stuart (1996) Response to Saba Mahmood *Cultural Studies* 10(1): 12-15

Hall, Stuart (1996) Introduction: Who needs Identity? in Stuart Hall and Paul du Gay (eds) *Questions of Cultural Identity* London: Sage

Hall, Stuart (1997) Culture and Power *Radical Philosophy*, 86 (Nov/Dec 1997), 24-41

Hall, Stuart (1998) Aspiration and Attitude ... Reflections on Black Britain in the Nineties *New Formations: Frontlines Backyards* Spring 1998 33:38-46

Hannerz, Ulf (1992) Scenarios for Peripheral Cultures. In King, A.D *(op. cit.)*

Hannerz, Ulf (1996) *Transnational Connections: Culture, People, Places* New York: Routledge

Harre, Ron (1989) Language Games and the Texts of Identity. In Shotter *(op. cit.)*

Harvey, David (1990) *The Condition of Postmodernity* London: Blackwell

Hatch, J. Amos and Wisniewski, Richard (1995) *Life History and Narrative* London: Falmer Press

HEFCE (1995) *Special Initiative to Encourage Widening Participation of Students from Ethnic Minorities in Teacher Training* London: HEFCE

Herman, Edward S. and Chomsky, Noam (1988) *Manufacturing Consent: The Political Economy of the Mass Media* London: Pantheon

Herman, Edward S. and Mc Chesney, Robert W. (1997) *The Global Media: The New Missionaries of Global Capitalism* London: Cassell

Hinchman, Lewis D and Hinchman, Sandra K (eds) (1997) *Memory, Identity, Community: The Idea of Narrative in the Social Sciences* New York: State University of New York Press

Hite, K.R (1991) Chile: A Rough Road Home *Report on the Americas* Vol XXIV Number 5 NACLA

HMSO (1985) *Education for All: The Report of the Committee of Inquiry into the Education of Children from Ethnic Minority Groups (Swann Report)* London: HMSO

Holstein, James A and Gubrium Jaber F (2000) *The Self We Live By: Narrative Identity in a Postmodern World* New York.Oxford: Oxford University Press

hooks, b (1996) *Killing Rage, Ending Racism* Harmondsworth: Penguin

hooks, b (1990) Choosing the Margin as a Space for Radical Openness. In bell hooks *Yearning: Race, Gender and Cultural Politics* Boston: South End Press

Hutchins, E (1995) *Cognition in the Wild* Cambridge, Mass.: MIT Press

Hymes, Dell (1996) *Ethnography, Linguistics, Narrative Inequality: Towards an Understanding of Voice* London: Taylor and Francis

Ignatieff, Michael (1992, July 19) The media admires itself in the mirror *The Observer* p 21

James, William (1890) *Principles of Psychology* Vol 1 New York: Henry Holt and Co

Jensen, Arthur (1969) How we can boost IQ and Scholastic Achievement *Harvard Educational Review*, 39

Johnson, Liz and O'Neill, Cecily (1984) *Dorothy Heathcote: Collected Writings on Education and Drama* London: Hutchinson

Kearney, Chris (1990) Living in Translation Unpublished MA dissertation, Institute of Education, University of London

Kearney, Chris (1990) *Open Windows English in Education* Vol 24

Kearney, Chris (1995) Mistaken Identity *English in Education* Vol 29, No. 2

Kearney, Chris (1996) By No Means Marginal. In Andrews, R (ed) *Interpreting the New National Curriculum* London:Middlesex University Press

Kearney, Chris (1998 a) Deep Excavations: an examination of the tangled roots of identity in modern cosmopolitan societies *International Journal of Inclusive Education* Vol 2, No 4 pp 309-26

Kearney, Chris (1998 b) Whose future is it anyway?: the National Curriculum and the next century *Goldsmiths Journal of Education* Vol 1, No 2 pp 2-14

Kearney, Chris (2000) Eyes Wide Shut: Recent Educational Policy in the Light of Changing Notions of English Identity *English in Education* Vol 34 No 3 19-30

Kerby, A.P (1991) *Narrative and the Self* Bloomington, Indiana: Indiana University Press

King, A.D (ed) (1991) *Culture, Globalisation and the World System* New York: Macmillan

King, Nichola (1996) Autobiography as Cultural Memory: Three Case Studies *New Formations: Cultural Memory* Winter 1996-97 30:50-62

Klein, Naomi (2000) *No Logo* London: Flamingo/Harper Collins

Kniep, W (1989) Global Education as School Reform *Educational Leadership*

Kuhn, Thomas S (1970) *The Structure of Scientific Revolutions* Chicago Ill.: University of Chicago Press

Labov, William (1972 a) *Language in the Inner-City: Studies in Black English Vernacular* Oxford: Basil Blackwell

Labov, William (1972 b) *Sociolinguistic Patterns* Philadelphia, PA: University of Pennsylvania

Labov, William (1972 c) The Transformation of Experience in Narrative Syntax. In W. Labov *Language in the Inner-City: Studies in Black English Vernacular* Oxford: Basil Blackwell pp.354-96

Lacan, Jacques (1981) *The Four Fundamental Concepts of Psychoanalysis* New York: W.W.Norton

Laclau, Ernesto (1995) Universalism, Particularism and the Question of Identity. In Rajchman (*op. cit.*)

Langer, Suzanne (1952) *Philosophy in a New Key: a study in the symbolism of reason, rite and art* Cambridge, Massachusetts and London, England: Harvard University Press

Lather, Patti (1993) Fertle obsession: Validity after poststructuralism *Sociological Quarterly*, 34, 673-694

Lather, Patti (1997) Creating a Multilayered Text: Women, Aids and Angels. In Tierney, William G. and Lincoln, Yvonna S. (eds) (1997) *Representation and the Text: Re- Framing the Narrative Voice* New York: State University of New York Press

Lavie, Samdar and Swedenburg Ted (1996a) Between and Among Boundaries of Culture: Bridging text and lived experience in the third time-space *Cultural Studies* 10,1 157-179

Lavie, Samdar and Swedenburg Ted (1996 b) *Displacement, Diaspora and Geographies of Identity* Durham and London: Duke University Press

Lazarus, Neil (1999) Hating Tradition Properly *New Formations: Hating Tradition Properly* 38:9-30

Lee, Laurie (1975) Writing Autobiography. In Laurie Lee *I Can't Stay Long* Harmondsworth: Penguin

Leiris, Michel (1946) *Manhood* London: Jonathan Cape

Lerner, Daniel (1958) *The Passing of Traditional Society* Glencoe, Ill.: Free Press

Lincoln, Y.S and Guba, E.G (1985) *Naturalistic Enquiry* Thousand Oaks: London: New Delhi: Sage

Linde, Charlotte (1993) *Life Stories: The Creation of Coherence* New York: Oxford University Press

Longacre, R (1976) *An Anatomy of Speech Notions* Lisse: Peter de Ridder

Lucas, Henze and Donato (1980) Promoting success of Latino language minority students *Harvard Educational Review*, 60 315-334

Lyotard, Jean-Francois (1984) *The Postmodern Condition: a report on knowledge* Manchester: Manchester University Press

Maalouf, Amin (1998/2000) *On Identity* London: The Harvill Press

Maffesoli, Michel (1996) *The Time of the Tribes: The Decline of Individualism in Mass Society* London.Thousand Oaks.New Delhi: Sage

Mahmood, Saba (1996) Cultural Studies and Ethnic Absolutism: Comments on Stuart Hall's 'Culture, Community Nation' *Cultural Studies* 10(1) 1996:1-11

Majaj, Lisa Suhair (1996) Arab American Literature and the Politics of Memory. In Singh *et al. (op.cit.)*

Malinowski, Bronislaw (1922) *The Argonauts of the Western Pacific* London: Routledge

Malinowski, Bronislaw (1967) *A Diary in the Strict Sense of the Term* New York: Harcourt, Brace and World

Malkki, Lisa H (1995) *Purity and Exile: Violence, Memory and National Cosmology among Hut Refugees in Tanzania* Chicago: University of Chicago Press

Marcus, George E (1998) *Ethnography through Thick and Thin* Princeton New Jersey: Princeton University Press

Marcus, G and Fisher, M (1986) *Anthropology as Cultural Critique* Chicago: University of Chicago Press

Marenbon, J (1987) *English, Our English* London: Centre for Policy Studies

Marin, Peter (1988) Towards Something American *Harper's* July 1988:17-18

McLaughlin, B (1992) *Myths and Misconceptions about Second Language Teaching: What Every Teacher Needs to Unlearn* Santa Cruz: The National Center for Research on Cultural Diversity and Second Language Learning

McWilliam, Erica (1997) Performing between the Posts: Authority, Posture and Contemporary Feminist Scholarship. In Tierney *et. al. (op.cit.)*

Mead, Margaret (1977) *Letters from the Field: 1925-1975* New York: Harper and Row

Meyrowitz, J (1986) *No Sense of Place: The Impact of Electronic Media on Social Behaviour* Oxford University Press: Oxford and New York

Michaels, Sarah (1986) Narrative Presentations: An Oral Preparation for Literacy with First Graders. In Cook-Gumprez, J (ed) *The Social Construction of Literacy* Cambridge (UK): Cambridge University Press

Middleton, D and Edwards, D (eds) *Collective Remembering* London: Sage

Miller, Jane (1983) *Many Voices* London: Routledge

Miller, Jody and Glassner, Barry (1997) The 'Inside' and the 'Outside': Finding Realities in Interviews. In Silverman, David ed. *Qualitative Research: Theory, Practice and Method* London, Thousand Oaks, New Delhi: Sage

Miller, Mark Crispin (1988) *Boxed In: The Culture of TV* Evanston: Northwestern University Press

Millett, Kate (1975) *The Prostitution Papers, A Candid Dialogue* St Albans, Paladin

Mischler, E. G (1986) *Research Interviewing: Context and Narrative* Cambridge Mass: Harvard University Press

Mitchell, W.T.J (ed)(1981) *On Narrative* Chicago: University of Chicago Press

Moi, Toril (1985) *Sexual/Textual Politics-Feminist Literary Theory* London: New Accents/ Routledge

Momaday, N Scott (1969) *The Way to Rainy Mountain* Albuquerque: University of New Mexico Press

Moore, Christy (1984) *Chicago* (song) from the album 'Ride On' WEA Ireland 0407

Moore, Sally F (1987) Explaining the Present: Theoretical Dilemmas in Processual Anthropology *American Ethnologist* 14:727-736

Moore, Sally F (1994) The Ethnography of the Present and the Analysis of the Process In Robert Borofsky (ed) *Assessing Cultural Anthropology* New York: McGraw-Hill

Morson, Gary Saul ed. (1981) *Bahktin: Essays and Dialogues on his Work* Chicago: University of Chicago Press

Morson, Gary Saul (1986) Who Speaks for Bakhtin? In *Bakhtin: Essays and Dialogues on His Work* ed G.S. Morson Chicago: University of Chicago Press

Morson, Gary Saul and Emerson, Caryl (1990) *Mikhail Bakhtin: Creation of a Prosaics* California: Stanford University Press

Moss, Gemma (1989) *Un/popular Fictions* London: Virago

Mouffe, C (1995) Democratic Politics and the Question of Identity. In Rajchman, J (1995) *The Identity in Question* London: Routledge

Nalbantian, Suzanne (1997) *Aesthetic Autobiography: From Life to Art in Marcel Proust, James Joyce, Virginia Woolf and Anais* Nin Basingstoke, Hants:London: Macmillan Press

Neisser, Ulric (1982) *Memory Observed, Remembering in Natural Contexts* San Francisco: Freeman

Nilsson, Harry (1971) *The Point* RCA

Nora, Pierre (1989) Between Memory and History: Les lieux de memoire *Representations* 26 (1989): 7-25

Olney, James (1972) *Metaphors of Self* Princeton: University Press

Ong, Walter J (1982) *Orality and Literacy* London: New Directions

Otis, Laura (1994)   *Organic Memory: History and the Body in the Late Nineteenth and Early Twentieth Centuries* Lincoln and London: University of Nebraska Press

Padilla, A (ed) (1980) *Acculturation: Theory, models and some new findings* Boulder CO: Westview Press

Parker, Ian (1989) Discourse and Power. In Shotter *et. al. (op. cit.)*

Paulston, Christina B. (1971) On the Moral Dilemma of the Sociolinguist *Language Learning* 21

Pease-Alvarez, Garcia, E.E, and Espinosa, P. (1991) Effective Schooling in Preschool settings: a case of LEP students *Early Childhood Research Quarterly*

Phinney, Jean S. and Rotheram, Mary Jane ed. (1987) *Children's ethnic socialization, pluralism and development* London.Thousand Oaks. New Delhi: Sage, in cooperation with the Society for Child Development

Pieterse, Jan Nederveen and Parekh, Bhikhu ed. (1995) *The Decolonisation of the Imagination: Culture, Knowledge and Power* London and New Jersey: Zed Books

Pintasiglio, Maria de Lourdes (1994) Values in a World in Transition In the proceedings from the ATEE Conference *Values and Teacher Education*: Lisbon: September 1993

Polyani, Michael (1958) *Personal Knowledge* Chigago, Ill: University of Chicago Press

Postman, Neil (1985) *Amusing Ourselves to Death* London: Methuen

Propp, Vladimir (1968) *The Morphology of the Folktale* Austin: University of Texas Press

Pryce-Williams, Douglas (1979) Modes of Thought in Cross Cultural Research: An Historical Review. In Marsella, Tharp *et al Perspectives on Cross Cultural Psychology* New York: Academic Press

Polkinhorne, D. E (1990) *Narrative knowing and the Human Sciences* Albany: State University of New York Press

Rabinow (ed.), Paul (1985) *The Foucault Reader* Harmondsworth: Peregrine/ Penguin

Rajchman, J (1995) *The Identity in Question* London: Routledge

Randall, William Lowell (1995) *The Stories We Are: An Essay on Self Creation* Toronto: University of Toronto Press

Rattansi, Ali and Westwood, Sally eds. (1994) *Racism, Modernity, Identity on the Western Front* Cambridge: Polity Press

Rich, Adrienne (1986) *Blood, Bread and Poetry-Selected Prose 1979-1985* London: Virago

Richardson, Lauren (1990) Narrative and Sociology *Journal of Contemporary Ethnography* 19:116-135

Riessman, Catherine Kohler (1993) *Narrative Analysis* Thousand Oaks California: Sage

Ritzer, George (1996) *The McDonaldization of Society: An Investigation into the Changing Character of Contempoaray Social Life* Thousand Oaks: Pine Forge Press

Robertson, Roland (1991) Social Theory, Cultural Relativity and the Problem of Globality. In King, A.D *(op. cit.)*

Rose, Nikolas (1989) Individualising Psychology in Shotter, J and Gergen, K.J. ed. *Texts of Identity* Thousand Oaks: London: New Delhi: Sage

Rosen, Harold (1996) Autobiographical Memory *Changing English* 3(1) 21-34

Rosen, Harold (1998) *Speaking from Memory, the study of autobiographical discourse* Stoke on Trent: Trentham Books

Rosenwald, George C and Ochberg Richard L (eds) (1992) *Storied Lives:The Cultural Politics of Self Understanding* Yale University Press

Rouse, Roger (1995) Questions of Identity: Personhood and Collectivity in Transnational Migration to the United States *Critique of Anthropology* 15(4) 351-381

Rubin, David C (ed) (1986) *Autobiographical Memory* Cambridge: Cambridge University Press

Rubin, David C (1996) *Remembering Our Past: Studies in Autobiographical Memory* Cambridge: Cambridge University Press

Rushdie, Salman (1989) 6 March 1989 *Granta* 28 Harmondsworth: Granta/Penguin

Rutter, Jill (2003) *Supporting Refugee Children in 21st Century Britain* Stoke on Trent: Trentham Books

Said, Edward (1987) *Orientalism* London: Routledge

Said, Edward (1994) *Representations of the Intellectual: The 1993 Reith Lectures* London: Vintage

Salaman, E (1970) *A Collection of Moments: a study of involuntary memories* London: Longman

Sapir, Edward (1949) *Culture, Language and Personality* California: University of California Press

Sarbin, Theodore R (ed) (1986) *Narrative Psychology: The Storied Nature of Human Conduct* New York: Praeger Publishers

Sarbin, Theodore R and Scheibe, Karl E (eds) (1983) *Studies in Social Identity* New York: Praeger Publishers

Sassoon, Anne Showstack (1982) *Approaches to Gramsci* London: Writers and Readers

Scafe, Suzanne (1989) *Teaching Black Literature* London:Virago Education Series

Schafer, R (1992) *Retelling a Life: Narrative and Dialogue in Psychoanalysis* New York: Basic Books

Schank, Roger C and Abelson, Robert P (1977) *Scripts, Plans, Goals, Structures* London: Lawrence Erlbaum

Schank, Roger C (1999) *Dynamic Memory Revisited* London: Lawrence Erlbaum

Schiller, H (1989) *Culture Inc.: The Corporate Takeover of Public Expression* New York: Oxford University Press

Schiller, H (1996) *Information Inequality* London: Routledge

Schon, Donald A (1983) *The Reflective Practitioner: How Professionals Think in Action* New York: Basic Books

Scollon, R and Scollon, S.W. (1981) *Narrative, Literacy and Face in Interethnic Communication* Oxford: Blackwell

Scollon, R and Scollon, S.W. (1995) *Intercultural Communication* Oxford: Blackwell

Segal, M.H., Dasen P.R., Berry J.W. and Portinga Y.H. (1990) *Human Behaviour in a Global Perspective: An Introduction to Cross-Cultural Psychology* New York: Pergamon

Shibutani,T and Kwan, K (1965) *Ethnic Stratification* London: Macmillan

Shotter, John (1993) *Conversational Realities: Constructing life through language.* Thousand Oaks: London: New Delhi: Sage

Shotter, John and Gergen, Kenneth J, ed. (1989) *Texts of Identity* Thousand Oaks: London: New Delhi: Sage

Silverman, David ed. (1997) *Qualitative Research: Theory, Practice and Method* Thousand Oaks: London: New Delhi: Sage

Simon, Brian (1978) *Intelligence, Psychology and Education: A Marxist Critique* London: Lawrence and Wishart

Simpson, John (1992; July 18) The Closing of the American Media *The Spectator*

Singh, Amritjit, Skerrit, Joseph T. Jr., and Hogan, Robert. E (eds) (1994) *Memory,Narrative and Identity: New Essays in Ethnic American Literatures* Boston: Northeastern University Press

Singh, Amritjit, Skerrit, Joseph T. Jr., and Hogan, Robert. E (eds) (1996) *Memory and Cultural Politics: New Approaches to American Ethnic Literatures* Boston: Northeastern University Press

Siraj-Blatchford, I (1993) Social Justice and Teacher Education in the U.K. In Gajendra K. Verma (ed) *Inequality in Teacher Education* London: Falmer Press

Sledd, James (1969) Bi-dialectalism: The linguistics of white supremacy *The English Journal*

Snyder, G (1990) *The Practice of the Wild* San Francisco: Northpoint Press

Spence, D.P (1982) *Narrative Truth and Historical Method* New York: Norton

Spengmann, W.C. (1980) *The Forms of Autobiography: Episodes in the History of a Literary Genre* New Haven, Conn: Yale University Press

Stanley, L (1994) *The Autobiographical I* Manchester: Manchester University Press

Steedman, Carolyn (1986) *Landscape of a Good Woman* London: Virago

Stewart, Susan (1986) Bakhtin's Anti linguistics. In Gary Saul Morson (ed) *Bakhtin: Essays and Dialogues on His Work* Chicago: University of Chicago Press

Stocking, George ed. (1983) *History of Anthropology. Vol 1, Observers Observed: Essays on Ethnographic Fieldwork* Madison: University of Wisconsin

Stubbs, Michael (1983) *Discourse Analysis: The Sociolinguistic Analysis of Natural Language* Oxford: Blackwell

Stubbs, Michael (editor) (1986) *The Other Languages of England, Linguistic Minorities Project* London: Routledge

Sturrock, John (1993) *The Language of Autobiography:Studies in the first person singular* Cambridge: Cambridge University Press

Sue, S and Wagner, N (eds) (1973) *Asian Americans: Psychological Perspectives* Ben Lomond CA: Science and Behaviour Books

Swain and Lapkin (1982) *Evaluating bilingual education: A Canadian case study* Clevedon, England: Multilingual Matters

Swindells, Julia ed. (1995) *The Uses of Autobiography* London/Bristol: Taylor and Francis

Tagore, Rabindranath (1917) *Personality* London: Macmillan

Tate, Nick (1999) What is education for? *English in Education* 33, 2 5-18

Tedlock, Dennis (1983) *The Spoken Word and the Work of Interpretation* Philadelphia, PA: University of Pennsylvania Press

Thompson, Charles; Herrman, Douglas J; Bruce, Darryl; Reid, J. Don: Payne, David G: Toglia, Michael P (eds) (1998) *Autobiographical Memory: Theoretical and Applied Perspectives* Mahwah N.J.: Lawrence Erlbaum Associates

Thompson, Edward P (1963) *The Making of the English Working Class* Harmondsworth: Penguin

Tierney, William G. and Lincoln, Yvonna S. (eds) (1997) *Representation and the Text: Re- Framing the Narrative Voice* New York: State University of New York Press

Tomlinson, S (1997) Diversity, Choice and Ethnicity: the effects of educational markets on ethnic minorities *Oxford Review of Education* 23, 1 63-76

Tonnies Ferdinand (2001) Gemeinschaft und Gesellschaft In Jose Harris (ed) (2001) *Community and Civil Society* Cambridge: Cambridge University Press

Tosi, Arturo (1995) Bilingualism in Schools and the Education of Bilinguals: A European Overview Paper given at SCAA conference April 1995

Turner, V and Bruner, E (eds) (1986) *The anthropology of experience* Urbana: The University of Illonois Press

Usher, R and Edwards, R (1994) *Postmodernism and Education* London and New York: Routledge

Van Maanen, J (1988) *Tales from the Field: On Writing Ethnography* Chicago Ill: University of Chicago Press

Volosinov, V.N.(1976) *Freudianism: A Marxist Critique* London: Academic Press

Volosinov, V.N. (1973) *Marxtsm and the Philosophy of Language* London: Seminar Press

Von Humboldt, William (trans 1971) *Linguistic Variability and Intellectual Development* Coral Gables: University of Miami Press

Vygotsky, Lev (1978) *Mind in Society* Cambridge, Mass: Harvard University Press

Vygotsky, Lev (1986) *Thought and Language* Massachusetts Institute of Technology

Wagley, C and Harris M (1958) *Minorities in the New World: Six Case Studies in New York* New York: Columbia University Press

Wagner, Betty Jane (1976) *Dorothy Heathcote: Drama as a Learning Medium* Washington: Hutchinson

Wallenstein, Immanuel (1991) The National and the Universal: Can there be such a thing in World Culture? In King, A.D *(op. cit.)*

Weintraub, Karl Joachim (1978) *The Value of the Individual: Self and Circumstance in Autobiography* Chicago, Ill: University of Chicago Press

White, Hayden (1981) The Value of Narrativity in the Representation of Reality. In Mitchell, W.T.J *(op. cit.)*

Williams, Raymond (1976, 1983) *Keywords* London: Fontana/ Collins

Williams, Raymond (1977) *Marxism and Literature* Oxford: Oxford University Press

Williams, Raymond (1981) *Culture* London: Fontana

Wolf, Michael J. (1999) *The Entertainment Economy: How Mega-media Forces Are Trandforming Our Lives* New York: Random House

Wundt, William (1921) *Elements of Folk Psychology* London: Allen and Unwin

Yourcernar, Marguerite (1957/1994) *Fires* Chicago:University of Chicago Press

Yourcernar, Marguerite (1974/1997) *Dear Departed: a memoir* London: Virago

Index

A Language in Common 165
All Our Futures: Creativity, Culture and Education 158, 164-165
autobiography (*see also* life histories and self-narrative) 2-3, 61-66

Bakhtin 41, 54, 62, 70, 113-115, 116, 122, 134, 166

citizenship xi, 156, 160-161
Cultural Studies 5, 6, 45, 48, 60-61
culture 4, 5

DFES 158

Economic and Social Research Council xii-xiii
EMAG materials 165
ethnography 43-44, 53, 161

globalisation 7, 44-51, 85

identity 4, 5
  and mass media xi, 13, 105-108, 161-162, 165
  and schooling 3-4, 8
  bounded identities 36, 37-39
  complexity of xii-xiv
  explicit view on 108-110
  postmodern identities 32, 44-51, 61-62, 83
  socially constructed identities 7, 8, 36, 39-44
  storied identities 37, 51-55
  systematic analysis of xiii, 113-136
  theories of identity 35-56

life histories (*see also* autobiography and self-narrative)11-23
  researching life histories 56-76
  analysis of life histories 113-136

Macpherson Report 156
Mass media
memory 42-46, 68-70, 78, 136, 165
multilingualism 24-25

narrative analysis 136-139, 141, 147-150
National Curriculum 47, 156
  Curriculum 2000 156, 165
  Dearing Review of 163
  Review in 1999 162
National Literacy Strategy 157, 163
New Right 46, 48

Parekh Report 158

racism 29
Raising attainment of Minority Ethnic Pupils and the Literacy Strategy 165
relationships of participants
  with dominant culture 98-108
  with families 80-85
  with heritage culture 85-93
  with peers 93-98

self narrative (*see also* autobiography and life history) 78, 136-137
Stephen Lawrence Inquiry 156
syncretism 36, 113-136

TTA 158

validity and reliability 67-70
voice xiv, 135-154